I0886319

Luftwaffe Intruder Operations Over the United Kingdom

Luftwaffe Intruder Operations Over the United Kingdom

Fernnachtjagd Units, 1940 to 1944

Chris Goss

AIR WORLD

First published in Great Britain in 2025 by
Air World
An imprint of Pen & Sword Books Limited
Yorkshire – Philadelphia

Copyright © Chris Goss 2025

ISBN 978 1 03611 115 1

The right of Chris Goss to be identified as
Author of this Work has been asserted by him in accordance
with the Copyright, Designs and Patents Act 1988.

A CIP catalogue record for this book is
available from the British Library.

All rights reserved. No part of this book may be reproduced, transmitted, downloaded, decompiled or reverse engineered in any form or by any means, electronic or mechanical including photocopying, recording or by any information storage and retrieval system, without permission from the Publisher in writing. NO AI TRAINING: Without in any way limiting the Author's and Publisher's exclusive rights under copyright, any use of this publication to "train" generative artificial intelligence (AI) technologies to generate text is expressly prohibited. The Author and Publisher reserve all rights to license uses of this work for generative AI training and development of machine learning language models.

Typeset by Mac Style
Printed in the UK by CPI Group (UK) Ltd, Croydon, CR0 4YY.

MIX
Paper | Supporting responsible forestry
FSC® C013604
FSC www.fsc.org

The Publisher's authorised representative in the EU for product
safety is Authorised Rep Compliance Ltd., Ground Floor,
71 Lower Baggot Street, Dublin D02 P593, Ireland.
www.arccompliance.com

For a complete list of Pen & Sword titles please contact

PEN & SWORD BOOKS LIMITED
47 Church Street, Barnsley, South Yorkshire, S70 2AS, England
E-mail: enquiries@pen-and-sword.co.uk
Website: www.pen-and-sword.co.uk
or
PEN AND SWORD BOOKS
1950 Lawrence Road, Havertown, PA 19083, USA
E-mail: uspen-and-sword@casematepublishers.com
Website: www.penandswordbooks.com

Contents

Introduction vii
Acknowledgements viii
Glossary and Abbreviations ix

Chapter 1 The First Fernnachtjagd 1940–1941 1

Chapter 2 Stopgap Fernnachtjagd, 1940–1941 39

Chapter 3 Interim Measure, 1942 53

Chapter 4 Final Fernnachtjagd 1943–1944 65

Epilogue 135
Appendices 141
Appendix I: Commanders II./NJG 1; I./NJG 2 (July 1940–October 1941) 142
Appendix II: I./NJG 2 Leading Intruder Pilots, October 1940–November 1941 143
Appendix III: Report on Night Fighting over Eastern England, 10–11 May 1941 144
Appendix IV: Report on Night Operations, 28–29 June 1941 146
Appendix V: Report on Night Operations Against England, by Fernnachtjäger, 23–24 July 1941 147
Appendix VI: Report on Night Operations Against England, by Fernnachtjäger, 7–8 August 1941 148
Appendix VII: Report on Night Operations Against England, by Fernnachtjäger, 1–2 September 1941 150
Appendix VIII: Report on Night Operations Against Eastern England, by Fernnachtjäger, 12–13 October 1941 152
Appendix IX: Intruder Claims, July 1940–October 1941 153
Appendix X: II./NJG 1 and 1, 2, 3, 4./NJG 2 Combat Losses/Accidents on Operations, August 1940–October 1941 161
Appendix XI: II./NJG 1 and 2./NJG 2 Dornier Do 17Z-10 Claims, September 1940–May 1941 171
Appendix XII: V./KG 2, I./KG 51 and II./KG 51 Executives, June 1943–August 1944 173

Appendix XIII: Deutsches Kreuz in Gold Winners Who Flew the Me 410 with V./KG2, and I and II./KG 51 176

Appendix XIV: Known Messerschmitt Me 410 Operations Over The UK With V./KG 2 and I and II./KG 51 177

Appendix XV: Messerschmitt Me 410 Claims, N.W. Europe, August 1943–August 1944 188

Appendix XVI: Messerschmitt Me 410 Combat Losses, N.W. Europe, June 1943–August 1944 193

Bibliography 203

Index 204

Introduction

Ever since I bought Simon Parry's ground-breaking *Intruders over Britain* as long ago as 1987, the subject of Luftwaffe twin-engine heavy fighters stalking returning RAF bombers and interfering with RAF trainers carrying out night flying practice in the Second World War has interested me. I have since covered the Ju 88 and Do 17 aspects in two of my books, but I have always wanted to cover, as Simon did, the whole campaign from 1940 to 1941 and 1943 to 1944. In particular, I felt the missions flown by Messerschmitt Me 410s, and prior to that the Me 210, needed greater research, and this is what I hope I have achieved.

I have deliberately not covered Operation *Gisela* on the night of 3–4 March 1945, as, in my opinion, this was a one-off intended as a single-shot knock-out blow by over 142 Ju 88 G-1, G-6 and G-7 night fighters, as opposed to what the Ju 88Cs of I./NJG 2 and Me 410s of V./KG 2 and II./KG 51 aimed to achieve. In any case, Simon has covered Operation *Gisela* very well in his book. I have also not gone into any greater detail in respect of the slaughter of Consolidated B-24s by II./KG 51 on 22 April 1944, as this has been covered by Ian McLachlan in his book *Night of the Intruders*.

Historians may disagree about the value of such Fernnachtjagd (long-range night fighter) missions, but in 1941, they did have an impact. After that, however, the effectiveness of the Me 210 and Me 410 Fernnachtjagd missions had minimal effect, especially compared to the successes of German night fighters over Germany; the Allies' Berlin attack on the night of 19 February 1944, for example, saw seventy-six claims for RAF bombers, far more than what the Me 410 Fernnachtjäger achieved in the whole of their existence, which lasted fourteen months. That said, their operations cost the lives of a number of RAF and USAAF airmen, as well as a considerable number of German lives in what is now, eighty years on, a largely forgotten aspect of the air war of the Second World War.

Chris Goss
Marlow, 2025

Acknowledgements

Yet again I would like to thank the continued help and support from my great friend Bernd Rauchbach. I would also like to thank Matti Salonen in Finland for his patience with my questions.

In no particular order, I would also like to acknowledge the support and help of the following: Martin Mace (UK), Robert Forsyth (UK), Sven Carlsen (Germany), Dr Theo Boiten (Holland), Nick Beale (UK), Simon Schatz (Germany), Roger Gaemperle (Switzerland), Simon Parry (UK), Tim Oliver (UK), the late Chris Ehrengardt (France), Andy Saunders (UK), Ed McManus (UK), Andy Thomas (UK), Andy Wight-Boycott (UK), Mikael Olrogg (Sweden), Ralf Lemser (Germany) and Rene Millert (Germany). If I have forgotten anyone, it is not intentional and I apologise!

I have been doing this research for over forty years, so I would like thank those many veterans and families, both German and Allied, who helped me, and of whom hardly any are still with us.

Glossary and Abbreviations

AA	Anti-aircraft
Ablauflinie	Termination line (pathfinding)
Adj	Adjutant
AI	Airborne Interception
Aufklärungsgruppe	Reconnaissance Wing
Beleuchter	pathfinder
Beobachter (BO or B)	Observer
Bordfunker (BF)	Radio Operator
Bordmechaniker (BM)	Flight Engineer
Bordschütze (BS)	Air Gunner
BG	Bomb Group (US)
BS	Bomb Sqn (US)
Deutsches Kreuz in Gold	German Cross in Gold (DKiG)
DFC	Distinguished Flying Cross (RAF/USAAF)
DFM	Distinguished Flying Medal
Do	Dornier
DSO	Distinguished Service Order (RAF)
E/A	Enemy aircraft
Ehrenpokal (Pokal)	Goblet of Honour – awarded for outstanding achievements in the air war
Eisernes Kreuz (EK)	Iron Cross (came in First and Second Class)
Ergänzungs (Erg)	Training
Erprobungs	Testing and development
Fähnrich (Fhr)	Officer cadet
Feindflug	Operational flight
Feldpostnummer	Field Post number
Feldwebel (Fw)	Flight Sergeant
Fern	Long-range
Fernnachtjagd	Long-range fighter mission
Fernnachtjäger	Long-range fighter
Flak	Anti-aircraft
Flieger (Flg)	Aircraftman
Fliegerführer Atlantik	Air Commander for the Atlantic region
Fliegerschützenschule	Air gunner school
Flugzeugführer (F)	Pilot

Flugzeugführerschule	Pilot's school
Frontflugspange	Mission Clasp – awarded for different numbers of operational flights coming in bronze, silver and gold.
FG	Fighter Group (US)
FS	Fighter Sqn (US)
FuG	Funkgerät-radio equipment
Führer	Leader
GCI	Ground Controlled Interception
Gefreiter (Gefr)	Leading Aircraftman
Generalfeldmarschall	Air Chief Marshal
Geschwader (Gesch)	Group consisting three Gruppen commanded by a Geschwader Kommodore (Gesch Komm)
Gruppe (Gr)	Wing consisting three Staffeln; commanded by a Gruppen Kommandeur (Gr Kdr). Gruppe number denoted by Roman numerals.
Hauptmann (Hptm)	Flight Lieutenant/Captain
HE	High explosive
He	Heinkel
Ia	Operations Officer
IAS	Indicated Air Speed
IB	Incendiary bomb
IFF	Identification Friend or Foe
Jagdgeschwader (JG)	Fighter Group
Ju	Junkers
Kampfgeschwader (KG)	Bomber Group
Kampfgeschwader zur	Normal designation for a special duties unit (KGzbV) besonderen Verwendung
Kette	Three aircraft tactical formation similar to RAF vic
Kommando (Kdo)	Detachment
Küstenfliegergruppe	Coastal flying wing
Lehrgeschwader (LG)	Technical development group
Leutnant (Lt)	Pilot Officer/2nd Lt
Luftflotte	Air Fleet
Luftmine	Air dropped mine
Major (Maj)	Squadron Leader
Me	Messerschmitt
Nachtjäger (NJ)	Night fighter
Nachtjagdgeschwader	Night fighter group (NJG)
Nachrichtenoffizier (NO)	Communications officer
Nav/Rad	Navigator/Radar Operator (RAF)
Oberfeldwebel (Ofw)	Warrant Officer
Obergefreiter (Ogefr)	Senior Aircraftman/Cpl

Oberleutnant (Oblt)	Flying Officer/1st Lt
Oberst	Group Captain/Colonel
Oberstleutnant (Obstlt)	Wing Commander/Lt Col
Pfadfinder	Pathfinder
Raum	Patrol area
Reichsluftfahrtministerium (RLM)	Germany Air Ministry
Reichsmarschall	Marshal of the Air Force
Ritterkreuz (RK)	Knight's Cross
Ritterkreuz mit Eichenlaub	Knight's Cross with Oakleaves (EL)
Rottenflieger	Wingman
SC	Sprengbombe Cylindrisch, a thin cased high explosive bomb
Schlachtgeschwader	Ground attack group
SD	Sprengbombe Dickwandig, a thick walled fragmentation bomb
SKG	Schnellkampfgeschwader, fast bomber group
Sonderstaffel	Special Staffel
Stab	Staff or HQ; formation in which Gr Kdr and Gesch Komm flew.
Stabsfeldwebel (Stfw)	Senior Warrant Officer
Staffel (St)	Squadron (9 aircraft); commanded by a Staffel Kapitän (St Kap). Staffel number denoted by Arabic numerals
Stellvertreter	Deputy
Störangriff	Nuisance attack.
Strassenjagd	Attack on roads/transportation
Tagjagd	Day fighter mission
Technischer Offizier (TO)	Technical Officer
Trialen	German explosive similar to British torpex
Unteroffizier (Uffz)	Sergeant
Verbandsführerschule	Formation leaders school
Werk Nummer (Wk Nr)	Serial Number
WO	Warrant Officer
Zerstörer (Z)	Destroyer/Heavy fighter
Zerstörergeschwader (ZG)	Heavy Fighter Group

Chapter 1

The First Fernnachtjagd 1940–1941

In June 1940, Major Wolfgang Falck, formerly of 2./ZG 76 and latterly Gruppen Kommandeur of I./ZG 1, was tasked to form a night fighter unit for defence of the Third Reich. The preferred night fighter was the Messerschmitt Bf 110 and Junkers Ju 88 C-2, the latter having been operationally tested by Z.St/KG 30 in Norway. In addition there would also be two versions of the Dornier 17 used as night fighters – the Z-7 Kauz I and the Z-10 Kauz II.

On 27 July 1940, II./NJG 1 was formed commanded by Major Karl-Heinrich Heyse. Heyse was an experienced bomber pilot who had flown in Spain with 1.K/88 from April to December 1938, and who, on his return, commanded the Heinkel He 111-equipped 10./KG 157 and then 2./KG 55 from March 1939 to July 1940. Two of the Staffel would operate the Ju 88 C-2; 4 Staffel was commanded by Oberleutnant Herbert Bönsch, formerly of Z.St/KG 30, while 6 Staffel was commanded by Oberleutnant Karl Hülshoff, formerly Staffelkapitän of 7./KG 54 (experienced blind-flying crews from III./KG 54 had formed the nucleus of 6./NJG 1). For its part, 5 Staffel operated the Do 17 Z-7/Z-10 (until converting to the Ju 88 from May 1941 onwards) and was commanded by Hauptmann Rolf Jung.

Generalmajor Josef Kammhuber.

On 17 July 1940, Oberst Josef Kammhuber, former Kommodore of KG 51 and who had recently returned from French captivity having been shot down and taken prisoner on 3 June 1940, was given command of the new 1 Nachtjagddivision. He firmly believed that suitably converted bombers such as the Do 17Z and Ju 88, when flown by experienced crews, would be ideal for Fernnachtjagd, or long-range night fighter, missions over the UK.

Kammhuber had once declared: 'When I want to kill wasps, I smoke out their nest. I don't swat insects in the air one at a time. I go to the nest when they are in!'

Ju 88Cs, formerly of Z.St/KG 30, seen back in Germany after the end of the Norway campaign. Some still carry the markings of KG 30, but it would appear that the nearest is in process of transition to 4./NJG 1. (*Simon Schatz*)

As a result, II./NJG 1, operating from Gilze-Rijen in The Netherlands, began intruder operations over British airfields. The first reported claims came on the night of 23 July 1942, when Feldwebel Otto Wiese and Feldwebel Gustav Schramm of 4./NJG 1 each claimed what they thought were Vickers Wellingtons over the North Sea. That said, the only aircraft reported lost that night was a Bristol Blenheim of 110 Squadron, which, flown by Sergeant Cliff Heyward, crashed off Haamstede. However, crews from Nos. 9 and 149 Squadrons reported being attacked by Bf 110s. Flown by Pilot Officer George Panter, the one from 149 Squadron reported being attacked on its outward journey some sixty miles off the English coast. During the combat, the Observer, Pilot Officer Robert Sterling, was killed. Panter was forced to return to base, landing at 22.55 hours – around the time the German claims were made.

The next claim came on the night of 17 August 1940 when Feldwebel Peter Laufs, formerly of Z.St./KG 30 and now flying with 4./NJG 1, claimed a Hawker Hurricane off Lowestoft at 23.00 hours. The identity of the RAF aircraft has never been confirmed. Some Luftwaffe records state that Laufs was flying a Bf 110 during this combat.

Later that same night, a Ju 88C-2 of 4./NJG 1, that flown by Oberfeldwebel Fritz Zenkel, was reported missing over the North Sea. It has been suggested that he fell victim to Pilot Officer Richard Rhodes of 29 Squadron (who himself would be killed a week later), who claimed shooting down what he thought was a He 111. Rhodes had first intercepted the raider some ten miles south of Chester at 02.28 hours, finally shooting it down at 03.20 hours into the sea east off Spurn Head. Chester's initial interception, though, would have been too far west for a Fernnachtjäger to have been operating, while a Wellington flown by Flying Officer Alban Hough of 37 Squadron reported a combat with what they thought was a Bf 110 forty miles east of Great Yarmouth and claimed to have shot it down in flames.

On 20 August 1940, Luftflotte 2 decreed that all Ju 88s sent on Nachtjagd patrols over England would now carry bombs and that with immediate effect all new Ju 88s delivered to II./NJG 1 had to be equipped with bomb racks – one more way of killing wasps was about to be employed. However, due to the extra armament, this was restricted to no more than ten 50kg bombs.

Feldwebel Hermann Sommer of 2./NJG 2.

There would be one more claim in August 1940, when Oberfeldwebel Merzbach of Stab II./NJG 1 claimed a Hurricane near Grimsby on the night of 27 August 1940. Once again, this is another victim, whether aircraft or pilot, that cannot be substantiated.

On 11 September 1940, II./NJG 1 became I./NJG 2. Another German combat loss occurred five days later when the Ju 88C-2 flown by Feldwebel Werner Palm of 2./NJG 2 failed to return from a mission on 16 September 1940.

In terms of intruders successes that month, there would be one claim flown by recently commissioned Oberleutnant Kurt Herrmann of 4./NJG 1 (presumably flying a Ju 88C-2) on the night of 8 September 1940, an unidentified Blenheim at Waddington, and a second by a Do 17Z-10 flown by Feldwebel Hermann Sommer of 5./NJG 1 on the night of 9 September 1940.

At last, at 21.30 hours on 20 October 1940, the first confirmed victory occurred when Hauptmann Karl Hülshoff of 3./NJG 2 claimed what he thought was a Handley Page Hampden near Dishforth. It would appear that this was the 58 Squadron Whitley flown by Pilot Officer Ernest Brown which crashed at Ingleby, Yorkshire; four crew, including the pilot, would be killed and one severely injured.

Four nights later there would be further success when Oberleutnant Kurt Herrmann claimed two Blenheims near Hemswell, one of which came from 17 Operational Training Unit (OTU); however, both RAF aircraft were only damaged. Feldwebel Hans Hahn of 3./NJG 2 also claimed his first victory of the war that night when he shot down a Whitley of 102 Squadron, this being flown by Pilot Officer Anthony Davies.

Davies had just retracted his undercarriage, having taken off from RAF Linton-on-Ouse tasked to attack Lünen. The following report details what happened:

> On attaining a height of 1,400ft he [Davies] observed tracer to his left and below, and also immediately noticed tracer which he estimated was passing through the starboard wing tanks. At the time he was executing a left hand circuit of the flare path.

Officer aircrew from 102 Squadron. Pilot Officer Tony Davies is fifth left in the centre row, while Pilot Officer Tom Murfitt is on the far right in the middle row. Their Whitley was shot down by Feldwebel Hans Hahn of 3./NJG 2 on 24 October 1940. Davies was injured, while Murfitt was killed.

He throttled back, turned the navigation lights and petrol off, and observed a fire underneath the starboard main plane. Height was lost and an attempt was made to trim the aircraft with the elevator tabs but they did not function. He saw the ground vaguely through the light of the fire, opened the escape hatch. Fire was not intense.

The aircraft struck a tree and flames immediately spread all over the cabin. He hit his head on the roof, but managed to scramble through the hatch and fell backwards to the ground, and then ran a few yards away. He then went back to the aircraft, and attempted to release Sgt Wilson who was caught on a projection in the aircraft by his parachute harness, his hair was on fire but Plt Off Davies put the flames out with his hands. He was unable to release Sgt Wilson but the latter was able to release himself after about 30 seconds.

Leutnant Hahn Hahn, seen here after commissioning and award of the Ritterkreuz.

Plt Off Davies then saw the tail gunner Plt Off Lee, reeling from the tail. He called him and told him to run away from the aircraft and get down beside a nearby railway embankment. The fire was then much too intense to get near the aircraft. One or two bombs exploded also a tank and some pyrotechnics.

Plt Off Davies rallied the two survivors and ran to the railway line, another bomb went off and he

> ordered them to lie flat in a ditch. They eventually crossed the line and lay down beside the far embankment. Three or four bombs went off while they were there, and pyrotechnics fell all around them.

Two of the crew perished in the crash, while Pilot Officer Terry Lee and Sergeant Angus Wilson succumbed to their injuries on 2 November 1940. Only Davies, who was injured, survived.

A little of the tragic aftermath was revealed by newly-arrived Sergeant Douglas Morton:

> Sqn Ldr Beare gave us our first assignment. Six of us were detailed to be the funeral party at two separate funerals. A couple of nights previously, the Sqn had taken part in a bombing raid and one of the planes that was taking off was shot down by a German intruder and as a result four of the crew were killed.

Hahn, formerly of 9./KG 54, would claim another twelve aircraft as an intruder pilot. He was commissioned and awarded the Ritterkreuz in July 1941, before becoming the final I./NJG 2 Fernnachtjagd loss on operations over the UK in a little under a year later.

October 1940 would also see the creation of 4./NJG 2, which was then commanded by former 8./KG 54 pilot Oberleutnant Paul Bohn (Oberleutnant Paul Zimmermann the original Staffelkapitän was killed returning from operations in a Bf 110 on 17 October 1940 prior to converting to the Ju 88). Formed from elements of I./ZG 2, it would remain under the control of I./NJG 2 until the end of February 1942, when it finally joined II./NJG 2.

On 1 November 1940, Unteroffizier Mathias Lang of 3./NJG 2 failed to return from an operational flight, his Ju 88C-4 being the first of that type to be lost. That night I./NJG 2 reported dropping five SC50 bombs on RAF Feltwell.

The next claims by Ju 88s did not occur for almost a month. Luftwaffe records state that during Fernnachtjagd missions on the night of 23 November 1940, Hauptmann Karl Hülshoff of 3./NJG 2 carried out three attacks on a Wellington which crashed in the sea eighty kilometres west of Scheveningen. They also note that Feldwebel Heinz Strüning of 1./NJG 2 claimed another Wellington ten minutes later, this time fifty kilometres west of Scheveningen. The final claim was by Oberleutnant Kurt Herrmann of 1./NJG 2, this being a Hampden north-east of The Wash. Only one aircraft was lost over the North Sea that night, a Wellington of 214 Squadron which was flown by Sergeant Stanley Chester. The intruders also reported dropping ten SC50 bombs on the airfield at Catfoss on the Yorkshire coast, as well as twenty SC50s on Lincoln.

However, losses that night for I./NJG 2 were not good. The first casualty occurred when a 50kg bomb exploded prematurely at Gilze-Rijen, destroying the Ju 88 involved and killing two groundcrew. Then over the North Sea, Ju 88C-4s flown by Gruppen Kommandeur Major Karl-Heinrich Heyse and Feldwebel Kurt Schlicht of 3./NJG 2 failed to return. The possible circumstances of their demise could be explained by a report filed by Sergeant Rupert Oakley who was flying a Hampden of 61 Squadron:

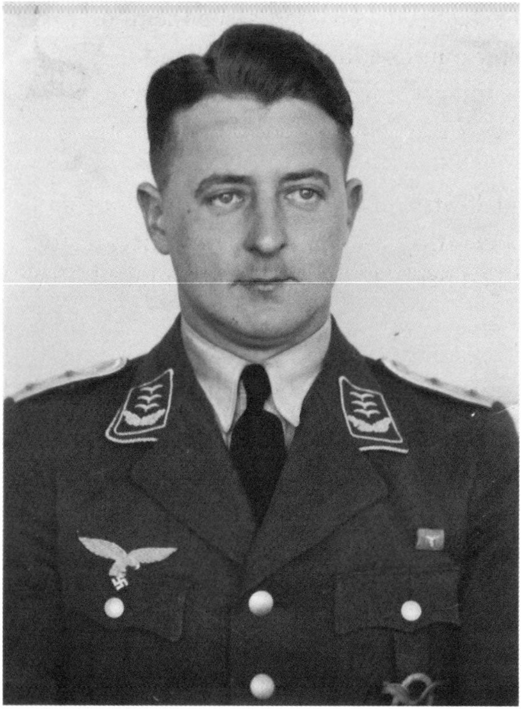

Major Karl-Heinrich Heyse, first Kommandeur of II./NJG 1 and then I./NJG 2, who was killed in action on 23 November 1940.

The new Kommandeur was Hauptmann Karl Hülshoff, formerly Staffelkapitän of 3./NJG 2.

> Sgt Oakley encountered three enemy aircraft when 90 miles off the English coast. They were identified as Ju 88s and were black in colour with no visible markings. Sgt Oakley was forced down from 9,000ft to 2,000ft at which point he jettisoned his bombs in order to add to his manoeuvrability. He and his crew had the satisfaction of dismissing one of the attackers which was seen falling into the sea with its cockpit ablaze and driving off the others.

Kurt Schlicht, like his Gruppen Kommandeur, had flown with 1.K/88 in Spain. Heyse would be replaced by Hauptmann Karl Hülshoff, while command of 3./NJG 2 went to Oberleutnant Ulrich Meyer; Meyer's time in command would last just twenty-seven days.

The next victory for the intruders was not until 17 December 1940, when Feldwebel Wilhelm Beier of 3./NJG 2 claimed a Hurricane over the sea east of Spilsby at 06.36 hours. RAF Scampton was also attacked by two aircraft, with Oberleutnant Paul Bohn of 4./NJG 2 claiming a Hampden over the airfield. Beier, after shooting down the Hurricane, headed for RAF Waddington where he dropped his bombs. The identity of who or what Beier claimed to have shot down has not been established.

Four days later a more concerted series of dawn intruder missions was launched. As part of this assault, I./NJG 2 reported attacking Selby, Lincoln, Gainsborough and Kings Lynn, the airfields of Hemswell, Scampton, West Raynham and Honington, and six ships in The Wash. Unteroffizier Gerhard Blum of 1./NJG 2 claimed a Blenheim off Kings Lynn, though, yet again, this is a victim which cannot be identified.

One Luftwaffe aircraft, that flown by Oberleutnant Ulrich Meyer, the recently appointed Staffelkapitän of 3./NJG 2, failed to return. RAF records reported the following:

> This aircraft flew over RAF Manby at about 175ft and was engaged by machine gun fire. It is understood that the aircraft was operating in company with others in the vicinity. There was evidence that the cabin had been set on fire and pilot killed. The aircraft was blown to bits on impact.

Meyer's Ju 88C-2 crashed near Louth, two miles from the airfield, killing all on board crew. Command of 3./NJG 2 now passed to Oberleutnant Paul Semrau, another former Z.St./KG 30 pilot. A second Ju 88C-2, that flown by Gefreiter Kurt Ludescher of 1./NJG 2, crashed on landing at Gilze-Rijen that morning. All three crew members lost their lives.

The intruders were back again that same night, as well as the night after that. During the latter, a Do 17Z-10 from 2./NJG 2 claimed a Blenheim which, yet again, has not been identified.

This was it as far as intruder claims and losses for 1940 but 1941 would see an increase in intruder missions, such missions continuing for just another nine months.

Hauptmann Paul Semrau (left) of 3./NJG 2.

It would not be long before the first claims of 1941 came. Just one intruder was active on 1 January 1941, this being flown by Leutnant Rudolf Stradner of 1./NJG 2, another former member of III./KG 54. He targeted York, Hull and Grantham, before claiming a Wellington east of Lowestoft at 18.40 hours. Two Wellingtons were lost that night, both were from 301 Squadron. The aircraft flown by Squadron Leader Stefan Floryanowicz crashed on land near RAF Digby at 22.25 hours, while the other, which was flown by Flying Officer Boleslaw Murawski, crashed at Wellingore, south of Lincoln. It would appear that Stradner's Ju 88 returned having been damaged in the combat. This would be Stradner's only victory, as he was killed during operations on 9 July 1941.

The claims for the next two nights were more positive for 3./NJG 2. On 2 January, four intruders attacked Scampton, York and Ripon. Unteroffizier Helmut Arnold of 1./NJG 2 claimed a Wellington fifty kilometres east of Happisburgh (no Wellingtons were lost), while Feldwebel Hans Hahn of 3./NJG 2 got his second 102 Squadron Whitley, this one being flown by Flying Officer Desmond Coutts.

Then, on 3 January, six intruders attacked Lincoln and Lowestoft. During these sorties, Leutnant Gerhard Böhme of 3./NJG 2 claimed a Whitley thirty kilometres east of Flamborough Head. This appears to be the aircraft flown by Pilot Officer Gerald Williams of 10 Squadron who recorded the following:

> On the way out at 1752hrs at 2,000ft, a multi-red Verey cartridge light was observed ahead followed by a burst of tracer bullets and this coincides with the position of an enemy aircraft reported near RAF Catterick. No damage or casualties were sustained.

The time of the attack coincides with the time of Böhme's dubious claim.

Only two more incidents of note occurred in January 1941, albeit a pilot from 2./NJG 2, possibly flying a Do 17Z-10, did make two claims in the early hours of 16 January. The Ju 88C-2 flown by Unteroffizier Otto Krähler of 3./NJG 2 failed to return from a mission on the night of 9 January 1941, while two Ju 88s from 1./NJG 2 apparently claimed seven barrage balloons over London on 29 January 1941.

February 1941 would be a more successful month for the intruders. From a Ju 88C perspective, just one aircraft was lost returning from operations, but they claimed ten aircraft over England. The most successful night was 10 February 1941, which also saw conventional German bombers attacking a number of airfields. In addition to two aircraft claimed by Hauptmann Rolf Jung and Oberleutnant Albert Schulz of 2./NJG2, Oberleutnant Paul Semrau of 3./NJG 2 claimed two Blenheims near RAF Feltwell, both were probably from 21 Squadron, being flown by Squadron Leader John Sabine and Sergeant Bert Chattaway respectively. Chattaway and one of his crew were killed, the remainder survived.

The other successful pilot was Oberleutnant Kurt Herrmann of 1./NJG 2, who claimed two Hampdens over Waddington. These were from Nos. 49 and 144 Squadrons. The former, flown by Sergeant John Butterworth, was shot down (Butterworth and one crew member were killed), while the latter, which was flown by Sergeant Bill McVie, was badly damaged.

There would be another six claims in February 1941. The first came at 07.30 hours on 15 February 1941, when Feldwebel Heinz Strüning of 1./NJG 2 claimed a Hudson seventy-five kilometres east of Great Yarmouth.

At 08.25 hours, almost exactly the same UK time as the German time, a Hudson of 206 Squadron, which was flown by Squadron Leader Oliver Dias DFC, on patrol off Great Yarmouth, encountered a Ju 88. The Hudson's gunner got in a good burst of 250 rounds before the Ju 88 'dived into cloud streaming smoke'. It would appear that the gunner had possibly been successful, as a Ju 88C-2 of I./NJG 2 later landed back at Gilze-Rijen with 20 per cent combat damage.

Oberleutnant Herbert Bönsch, Staffelkapitän of 1./NJG 2.

That same night, the Fernnachtjäger were back and together with bombers attacked a series of airfields between 21.00 hours and 05.05 hours. Claims by Strüning (a Wellington sixty-five kilometres off Southend) and Oberleutnant Herbert Bönsch of 1./NJG 2 were seemingly optimistic, though two 44 Squadron Hampdens reported being damaged over Lincoln and Waddington, but at times later than the German claim; the crews landed safely. An Airspeed Oxford of 2 Service Flying Training School (SFTS) also force-landed at Fulbeck east of Waddington at 00.15 hours, this presumably being the 'Blenheim' claimed by Bönsch at Waddington.

Ten days later, Feldwebel Ernst Ziebarth of 1./NJG 2 shot down a Wellington of 218 Squadron that was being flown by Sergeant Ron Hoos. Four crew were injured when the Wellington force-landed near Swaffham.

The following night, in another series of attacks on bomber airfields in eastern England, the last two claims of the month were made by 1./NJG 2. Herbert Bönsch's Blenheim near RAF Scampton cannot be confirmed, while Oberleutnant Kurt Herrmann's Blenheim, again near RAF Waddington, was another Oxford, this time from 2 Central Flying School (CFS) which was based at RAF Cranwell. The Oxford crashed at Fulbeck, killing Flight Lieutenant Desmond Trench. This would be Herrmann's ninth and final claim; just eleven days later he would be taken prisoner.

March 1941 started quietly for I./NJG 2. On the first night of the month, its aircraft attacked Boston, Hill, Norwich, Bircham Newton, Lincoln and Scampton. During the night Herbert Bönsch claimed to have intercepted a Blenheim over RAF Scampton at 02.55 hours – he reported that he hit it in the fuselage and that it then caught fire. Despite

Formation flying practice for I./NJG 2.

the description, no RAF losses can be matched to this claim. Meanwhile, a Ju 88C-4 was hit by anti-aircraft fire over Norwich at 01.15 hours; having lost an engine, it crash-landed back at Gilze-Rijen.

Very little occurred for the next eight days, a quiet run which ran until 23.50 hours on 10 March 1941, when a Ju 88C-4 of 1./NJG 2 slithered to a halt at Terrington St Clement in Norfolk. Oberleutnant Kurt Herrmann had suffered double engine failure which was caused by the con-rod on the starboard engine shearing and going through the crank case and the port engine overheating due to failure of the oil system. All three crew were captured. Only the Bordfunker was injured when the aircraft tipped onto its starboard wing, trapping him. For that reason, the crew did not set fire to the fighter.

Oberleutnant Kurt Herrmann of 1./NJG 2 was emerging as I./NJG 2's top scorers before he was taken prisoner in March 1941.

At long last the RAF had a relatively undamaged example and at last knew what they were up against. One subsequent report stated the following:

> Armament: One MG151 belt fed below three MG17 all fixed and firing forward out of a nose which was covered. These guns were fitted around the bomb aimer's position and were fired by one press button on the pilot's control column.
>
> Armoured bulkhead 11mm thick was fitted in the nose immediately in front of the ammunition containers and in front of the pilot's seat which is slotted to allow the guns to pass through. Bullet proof glass was also fitted in front of the gun sight. One MG17 in lower gunner's position with no armour protection. All the forward guns were belt fed on a lengthy and complicated belting system.

A Ju 88C-2 or C-4 of I./NJG 2 showing the Englandblitz badge.

> The feed for the MG17s was taken from two containers fitted between the pilot's legs with the rudder pedals either side and one container on the aft starboard side of the cabin. No external bomb racks were fitted but internal racks were provided for eight 50kg bombs in the rear bomb compartment.

Although another nine Ju 88C-4s from I./NJG 2 would crash on mainland Britain over the next seven months, none revealed as much as this aircraft did.

Born in December 1913, Herrmann had joined the Luftwaffe in 1934. He had first flown with Jagdgeschwader 134 'Horst Wessel' in 1936, before then becoming an instructor at Jagdlehrgang Lippstadt, following which he joined II./Lehrgeschwader Greifswald at Barth. Herrmann was posted to 2.(Z)/Lehrgeschwader 1 in April 1938, the unit flying Bf 110s until October 1939; he claimed to have shot down two aircraft over Poland on 2 and 8 September 1939.

Promoted to Oberfeldwebel, Herrmann was then posted to Luftkriegsschule Fürstenfeldbruck from November 1939 to March 1940 after which he joined Z.St./KG 30 before moving to 1./NJG 2 in September 1940 (having been commissioned as an Oberleutnant at the start of August 1940). At the time of his capture, at which point he was Gruppe Technischer Offizier and Staffelführer of 1./NJG 2, he was the top scoring Fernnachtjagd pilot, with a total of nine victories. He confirmed to his captors that he had flown fifty-nine war flights, of which twenty-five were over the UK, fourteen over Poland and twenty over Norway.

Being the top scorer on I./NJG 2, in February 1941, Herrmann had been recommended for the award of the Ritterkreuz, but his capture put paid to this. Consequently, he had to wait until October 1942 to eventually receive the Deutsches Kreuz in Gold. He was promoted to Hauptmann in January 1943.

A heavily camouflaged Ju 88C-2 or C-4 of I./NJG 2, minus the Englandblitz badge.

The remainder of the month would see Feldwebel Hans Hahn of 3./NJG 2 taking his score to four. This included a Blenheim in the early hours of 13 March, which was possibly the aircraft from 21 Squadron that was flown by Squadron Leader Arthur Allen who reported encountering fighters on his return. During the attack his gunner was wounded.

Wellington W5612 of 103 Squadron after crash-landing near RAF Newton on 31 March 1941. Squadron Leader Mellor was on final approach when he was attacked by a Ju 88 intruder of NJG 2. (*Tim Oliver*)

Squadron Leader Ken Mellor with Flight Lieutenant Jimmy Havers, of 103 Squadron, in the winter of 1941. (*Tim Oliver*)

Hahn also claimed an Avro Manchester the same evening (from 207 Sqn flown by Fg Off Hugh Matthews).

The remaining two claims, both by 1./NJG 2, came at dawn on 18 March 1941, when Feldwebel Peter Laufs claimed a Wellington for his seventh victory; a 221 Squadron Wellington reported being attacked by what the crew took to be a Bf 110 off the coast at 06.40 hours, causing very minor damage. Meanwhile, Leutnant Rudolf Pfeiffer targeted a Wellington of 149 Squadron that was flown by Sergeant Ron Warren, who had been trying to land at RAF Mildenhall at the time.

Of greater concern to I./NJG 2 was that on 14 March 1941, a Ju 88C-4 of 4./NJG 2, that flown by Gefreiter Hans Körner, was the first of the year to be confirmed shot down by a British night fighter. A Beaufighter of 29 Squadron, which was being piloted by Wing Commander Charles Widdows, had closed in unseen by the Ju 88 crew:

> The Beaufighter was directed southwards towards a raid flying south-east. When approaching Boston at about 0326hrs the Beaufighter was directed to Raid 478 which was flying north and was plotted as one aircraft at 6,000ft.
>
> About 0326hrs the pilot of the Beaufighter sighted an aircraft right ahead of him which he identified as a He 111 or Ju 88 (subsequently it proved to be a Ju 88). The Beaufighter closed to about 300yds and opened fire from dead astern giving one short burst which could be seen entering the fuselage of the Ju 88.
>
> The pilot of the Ju 88 appeared to have been killed outright as the aircraft went straight into a dive from which it never recovered. There was no return fire from the

> Ju 88. The Ju 88 crashed near Withcall village and was badly wrecked. Three bodies were found and it appears the crew had apparently attempted to bail out.

The smashed remains of the Ju 88, which were spread over two miles, revealed very little. The RAF, meanwhile, had acquired an almost complete example of a Ju 88C-4 four days previously.

A second aircraft was lost by 4./NJG 2 on the night of 30 March 1941, when three aircraft were active. The intruders reported attacking RAF Driffield, and at 01.35 hours a Blenheim at RAF Finningley, though no claim was made despite it being attacked three times.

At some stage during the night, Gefreiter Otto Kröger's Ju 88C-4 disappeared. It is assumed to have crashed in the North Sea due to engine failure.

Two RAF aircraft reported intruders. The first was a Wellington from 150 Squadron, which, flown by Sergeant Victor Coleman, suffered a punctured starboard wheel and fuel tank following an attack while landing at RAF Newton at 00.25 hours.

Squadron Leader Ken Mellor, of 103 Squadron, was also about to land at Newton. While circling with his navigation lights on, an attack was made by what his crew believed was a single-engine aircraft, but which subsequently was thought to be a Ju 88. The rear gunner had already left his turret in preparation for landing, so they were fortunate that only minor damage was done. Mellor elected to force-land away from the airfield, hitting a telegraph pole in the process. He suffered slight cuts to the legs. His Wellington, however, was damaged beyond repair.

Victor Coleman was commissioned in 1942 and, as a Squadron Leader, was the only survivor when his 582 Squadron Lancaster exploded near Pforzheim on 29 July 1944. Ken Mellor would end the war as a Group Captain having been awarded the DSO and DFC.

With twenty-five claims over the UK, for I./NJG 2 April 1941 would prove to be the most successful month to date. The most successful pilot was Leutnant Heinz Völker of 3./NJG 2, who would claim five, taking his score to seven. Three of them occurred on the night of 24 April, when he claimed three Blenheims at RAF Lindholme, while his Bordfunker, Feldwebel Herbert Biehne, got another (his other crew member was Bordmechaniker Feldwebel Hermann Gärtner). The German crew reported the following:

> During a night fighter mission over East England, one of the aircraft (crew: Lt Völker, Fw Biehne and Fw Gärtner) shot down four enemy Bristol Blenheim aircraft over Lindholme airfield.
>
> 0030hrs, one Bristol-Blenheim was attacked at 300m altitude, the plane crashed burning, on impact a very heavy explosion was observed.
>
> 0037hrs, the second kill followed at 100m altitude. After firing, the enemy aircraft lost single parts and flick rolled to the left.
>
> 0044hrs, the third enemy aircraft was attacked at 150m altitude, tipped over the left wing and crashed on fire.

0050hrs, the Bordfunker, Fw Biehne, shot down the fourth opponent at 150m altitude. The enemy aircraft crashed vertically, the crew watched the burning plane on the ground when flying over it.

Then, at 0100hrs five SC50 and five SD50 were dropped on Lindholme airfield without observed effect.

Flight Lieutenant Guy Gibson in front of the 29 Squadron Beaufighter he was flying when attacked by Feldwebel Hans Hahn on 8 April 1941. (*Edward McManus*)

Three Blenheims from 54 OTU were attacked that night. Two of the aircraft were damaged. One was flown by future ace Sergeant Arthur Spurgin, the other by Sergeant George Attenborough; former Battle of Britain pilot Flight Lieutenant Richard Denison was forced to bail out. The success of Völker's crew was reported in Berlin, but strangely did not result in any major award for him or his crew.

Feldwebel Hans Hahn of 1./NJG 1 took his score to eight in April. One of his claims was a notable one. It was at 23.45 hours on 8 April 1941, when he attacked what he reported was a Wellington at Wellingore. In fact, this was a Beaufighter flown by none other than Flight Lieutenant Guy Gibson, who would later rise to fame as the leader of 617 Squadron, the Dambusters, Operation *Chastise* in May 1943 – a role for which he would be awarded the Victoria Cross.

At the time of Hahn's attack, Gibson was flying with 29 Squadron. Returning from a patrol, Gibson was in the process of landing at Wellingore at 23.48 hours when he reported being attacked by a 'bandit':

> Flt Lt Gibson with Sgt Bell took off from WC.1 on patrol. The flight proved uneventful till they were about to land at WC.1 at 2348hrs when an enemy aircraft suddenly opened fire upon them from above and from the rear. The Beaufighter was unable to return fire and in fact the pilot never saw the enemy aircraft. The Beaufighter fortunately was not seriously damaged although its brakes were put out of order and upon landing ran through a hedge into a nearby field.

Sergeant Ralph Bell, who was on loan from 219 Squadron for a week, was wounded in the leg. Gibson gave his own account of the incident in his book *Enemy Coast Ahead*:

> Many times our night fighter aerodromes would get bombed. Often lonely Ju 88s would sit above our flare-path at night, waiting for us to land, and would try to shoot us down. I myself had an affair of this kind with a Ju 88; we had been returning from Manchester where we had seen 'sweet nothing' except a lot of inaccurate flak and were circling WC.1. looking forward to bacon and eggs and coffee.
>
> I called up the control and asked them if there were enemy aircraft about. No, there were no enemy aircraft, they said. This was fine. So I turned on my navigation lights and began the approach. Down went the wheels and flaps according to plan.
>
> Meanwhile, down on the ground watching events, but unable to do anything as there were no RT facilities, stood [Wing Commander] Charles Widdows. He had been looking at a suspicious aeroplane which had been floating around for some time. Now he saw it get into position behind my tail.
>
> When about 50ft off the ground the Ju 88 let me have it. But he too was a bad shot and all we did was to crash through some trees on the far side of the 'drome, although one cannon shell went into the radio operator's leg and wounded him.

Oberfeldwebel Hermann Sommer, with his crew of Feldwebel Otto Glas and Oberfeldwebel Heinz Reinagel, of 2./NJG 2 (this Staffel now appearing to be in the process of starting to convert from the Do 17Z-10 to the Ju 88C-4) claimed three Blenheims and a Beaufort between 00.15 hours and 01.30 hours on 30 April 1941, at airfields in the Tollerton, Hucknall and Bircham Newton area. This took his score to five. Strangely, the only casualty that can be matched is a 2 CFS Oxford at Tollerton. While it has been suggested Sommer was responsible for shooting down a Wellington of 99 Squadron, that flown by Sergeant Frank Hewitson, the last radio transmission from this aircraft was made much later, at 03.14 hours, as it was homing in on another airfield, so almost three hours after Sommer's last claim.

It is possible that these are events that Guy Gibson also wrote about in *Enemy Coast Ahead*:

> One night, one lone Ju 88 spent about two hours over Lincolnshire, prowling up and down between Hemswell and Cranwell, sometimes having a bang at a bomber, now and then getting amongst the 'Oxfords' at that very famous flying school. Each time his route took him over a certain fighter station. There, the Station commander stood on top of one of his hangars and watched, swearing loudly each time he came over. He was a last war pilot and had won both the DSO and DFC flying Camels in France [this was probably the Station Commander at RAF Digby, one Group Captain Gilbert Murlis-Green DSO and Bar, MC and two Bars].
>
> The sight of this Ju flying unmolested over his 'drome on this bright moonlight night irked him considerably. At last he could stand it no longer. He ordered a Hurricane to be started up. In its cockpit he sat, waiting patiently for the reappearance of the Hun. At last it came along, flying north at 2,000ft. He took off.
>
> Almost immediately he intercepted and got into a position astern for the kill. With memories of the sky above Amiens in 1917, he pressed the button.

Nothing happened. Again. No cannon even clicked. He swore down the RT, but this wasn't working.

Suddenly the Hun turned out to sea and he followed it for some 20 minutes, all the time trying to get his guns to fire, but, needless to say, in vain.

Regretfully he turned around for home, breathing dire threats to those on the ground. Some say at this station that you could hear him shouting when he was coming in to land. Others say he put every armourer on the Station under arrest. Whatever happened, he was very annoyed until the Squadron Commander turned up. 'Did you turn the ring, sir?' he asked politely.

'What ring?'

'Why, the safety ring on the gun button, sir. The guns won't fire unless you turn it anti-clockwise, like this – then press, like this.' Four cannons roared healthily into the night.

The two I./NJG 2's losses this month were from 4 Staffel, albeit on 18 April 1941 a 3./NJG 2 aircraft crashed at Dongen north of Gilze-Rijen killing all of its crew. On 9 April, Gefreiter Franz Brotz was shot down by Sergeant Stanley Bennett of 25 Squadron, his aircraft crashing near Oakham in Rutland.

The German pilot was killed and his aircraft totally destroyed, but the two remaining crew were captured. Their interrogations revealed more on the Gruppe and its personnel. For example, it was discovered that the Bordfunker had flown previously with Oberfeldwebel Martin Jeschke, formerly of the Legion Condor and Z.St./KG 30, and had flown in Poland and Norway and had completed sixty-three operational flights. He also stated that I./NJG 2 had so far shot down thirty-eight aircraft.

A second loss on 17 April 1941, remained a bit of a mystery for many years. It involved an aircraft that dived into the ground vertically and burnt out near Thorney in Cambridgeshire at 21.23 hours. In 1978, the crash site was excavated, at which point it was discovered from evidence in the wreckage to have been the Ju 88C-4 flown by Obergefreiter Wilhelm Beetz. The remains of Beetz and his two crew members were found in the wreckage and subsequently buried at the German Military Cemetery at Cannock Chase in Staffordshire.

Obergefreiter Wilhelm Beetz, who was killed in action on 17 April 1941. (*Andy Saunders*)

No bombs were found, nor was there any evidence of bullet or cannon strikes. It has been suggested that this aircraft was shot down by another intruder, but no claims were submitted that night by either the Luftwaffe or the RAF. How and why it crashed will probably never be known.

No doubt with an improvement in weather and an increase in the intensity of Bomber Command's attacks, I./NJG 2 would claim thirteen 'kills' during May 1941. Of these, four were in fact only damaged, while a further five cannot be linked to any RAF losses. There were no Ju 88s lost in combat that month.

Recently promoted, Oberfeldwebel Hans Hahn was particularly successful. He claimed attacking what he thought was a Fairey Fulmar at RAF Coltishall on 4 May 1941, and a Blenheim on 5 May 1941. The 'Fulmar' was in fact a Spitfire of 222 Squadron being flown by Pilot Officer Bernard Klee. What happened was recorded in the squadron's unofficial diary:

> That night seven 50kg bombs were dropped in a field in front of the Officers' Mess by a Ju 88; no damage resulted. Later two Spitfires flown by Plt Off Klee and Sgt Burgess took off to patrol base. Soon the Controller warned both pilots who were patrolling independently that an e/a was orbiting with them and we on the ground could plainly see the e/a manoeuvring to get on their tails. The Junkers was continually weaving, making steep turns and otherwise evading our aircraft.
>
> Sgt Burgess managed to get e/a in his sights and was about to open fire when e/a fired a two star cartridge (two reds) which dazzled him and caused him to loose e/a. He next saw two bursts of tracer flash past his aircraft without doing any damage.
>
> At 0330hrs observers on the ground saw a Spitfire (now known to be Plt Off Klee) fly straight across the aerodrome from north to south followed by e/a who fired a burst of cannon shells at the Spitfire which crashed in flames to the south-east of the aerodrome and was burnt out.

Aged twenty, Klee was killed when his Spitfire was shot down by Hahn, together with his crew of Unteroffizier Ernst-Wilhelm Meissler and Unteroffizier Helmut Scheidt, at a height of 200 metres at 00.42 hours. His squadron's diary concluded by adding that, 'The exhausts from the Spitfires showed up very plainly whereas the e/as exhaust was not visible. The speed and manoeuvrability of the e/a was truly remarkable'. That night I./NJG 2 reported attacking airfields at Feltwell, Watton, Bridlington, Grantham and Leconfield. Hahn also stated that he had a forty-minute running combat with the 'Fulmar'.

The following night no Blenheims were recorded as being attacked, but a Hurricane being flown by Sergeant Reg Parrott from 257 Squadron was shot down while attempting to land at RAF Duxford:

> Sgt Parrott took off on a night weather test at midnight and was ordered to land at Duxford as an enemy aircraft was in the vicinity of RAF Coltishall. He proceeded to Duxford, put on his navigation lights and whilst circling preparatory to landing was shot down in flames four miles north east of the aerodrome by an unidentified

> and unplotted enemy aircraft and killed instantly. Coltishall was bombed by the e/a which prevented Parrott from landing.

The same diary that detailed Hahn's victory the night before, also noted the following for this night:

> Just after midnight raider dropped a stick of bombs between the Officers Mess and No 5 Barrack Block. One airman was killed and five others injured. They were standing in and about the doorway of the Block where some windows were blown in otherwise no damage.

Again, I./NJG 2 was active attacking Great Yarmouth, Digby, Lincoln, Waddington, Newmarket and Leconfield. Hahn's claim for a Blenheim at RAF Feltwell, north-east of Duxford, was at 01.13 hours, while Parrott is reported to have crashed at 01.15 hours. The Luftwaffe recorded that this was Hahn's tenth victory over eastern England. It was followed by promotion to Leutnant and the award of the Ritterkreuz on 9 July 1941, his success in air combat and the sinking of a freighter off Dunkirk in May 1940, when still with 9./KG 54, being the justification.

Hahn's next victory would not be until 16 August 1941. Just under two months later he and his regular crew of Meissler and Scheidt, neither of whom received any major award, would be dead.

June 1941 would see another twenty-one German claims, of which four were damaged, not destroyed. Eleven cannot be positively linked to any RAF losses.

Ju 88C-4 of I./NJG 2 seen at Gilze-Rijen, in the spring or summer of 1941. Note the victory bars on the tail.

One of the aircraft damaged, on the night of 17 June 1941, came from 142 Squadron. It was being flown by Flight Lieutenant Alexander Gosman, who subsequently recalled what happened:

> We were about an hour out on our way to Duisburg when Sgt Doug Maclean told me there was somebody following us. We were fairly high approaching our operational height and at that time of year it is fairly light.
>
> I turned south towards the dark and our follower turned with us and opened fire. Simultaneously fire also came at us from ahead i.e. from the south. There was no sound from the rear turret and something told me instinctively that Maclean was dead.
>
> Durham, the navigator, jettisoned our load as we headed down, fast, and turned for home with undercarriage hanging loose and all hydraulics gone.
>
> We could see one of our attackers following us but as we were almost at wave-top height, he apparently gave up and disappeared.
>
> We managed the rest of the journey fairly easily and belly flopped in the dark on the edge of the airfield at Binbrook away from the flare path.

No other Wellingtons other than Gosman's were lost that night. It was Oberleutnant Herbert Bönsch who claimed his sixth aircraft, a Wellington, at 00.08 hours that night, the location given as some 115 kilometres east of Cromer. Bönsch would claim his seventh victory on 23 June 1941.

Another unattributed success occurred at RAF Feltwell at 01.53 hours on the night of 13 June 1941. On this occasion a Manchester of 61 Squadron was damaged by bomb splinters.

Leutnant Johannes Feuerbaum's Ju 88C-4 from 2./NJG 2 after it had flown into a hillside near Whitby on 4 June 1941. (*Andy Saunders*)

Flight Lieutenant Alexander Gosman's Wellington from 142 Squadron, after its encounter with Oberleutnant Herbert Bönsch of 1./NJG 2 on 18 June 1941.

It is interesting to note that this month saw the RAF formally acknowledging these intruder operations. Due to the fact that an effective RAF night fighter force was still evolving, it published tactics on what to do. Simply put, this advice boiled down to little more than if intruders were reported in the vicinity, RAF aircraft were to divert immediately to an airfield further north and west where intruders had not been reported. For some RAF bomber crews, the prospect of diverting, especially after having returned from a raid and with a damaged aircraft or dead and wounded crew, was not always that easy or welcome.

In addition to Oberleutnant Herbert Bönsch, the other successful pilots in June 1941 included Oberfeldwebel Hermann Sommer of 2./NJG 2, who took his score to nine on 27 June. Meanwhile, Oberfeldwebel Wilhelm Beier of 3./NJG 2 took his score to six on 13 June and Oberleutnant Paul Semrau of 3./NJG 2 raised his tally to five on 13 June. Only Semrau's claim, a Halifax at RAF Finningley, can be positively linked to a loss – in this case a Wellington of 25 OTU being flown by Sergeant Walter Collyer. It was in the circuit when it was shot down, the crew all being killed.

For the German side, losses amounted to the worst month so far in the campaign. First to be lost was Leutnant Josef Feuerbaum of 2./NJG 2. No doubt hoping to increase his score of three victories so far, just after midnight on 4 June 1941, his Ju 88 flew into a hillside near Whitby in bad visibility. Eight unexploded 50kg bombs were found in the wreckage, proof that he had not yet begun attacking airfields that night.

The next two to be lost both came from 4./NJG 2. These occurred in the early hours of 14 June 1941. The first, flown by Unteroffizier Richard Hoffmann, was intercepted by Squadron Leader Harold 'Flash' Pleasance of 25 Squadron:

> Sgt Bent then gave the pilot the necessary corrections and speed was slightly reduced and after following the e/a which turned south a visual developed at 500yds practically straight ahead.

Squadron Leader Harold 'Flash' Pleasance of 25 Squadron. (*Andy Thomas*)

Feldwebel Heinz Schulz, Unteroffizier Helmut Bähner, and Unteroffizier Jakob Ried of 4./NJG 2, shot down by 25 Squadron on 14 June 1941. (*Andy Saunders*)

Sqn Ldr Pleasance closed on the enemy which was flying at about 200mph and noticed that it had a single fin and was not burning resin lights. Sqn Ldr Pleasance immediately attacked from dead astern and slightly below and fired short burst at a range of 100yds of which no result was observed.

He then fired a second burst at 75yds range expending the contents from the four magazines which caused a vivid flash to come from the port engine of the e/a which went into a glide followed by a stream of white smoke.

After descending to 9,000ft the e/a began to climb slowly doing S turns at about 130mph followed by the Beaufighter in wider turns but when the e/a had regained height to 10,000ft fires began to spread over the e/a which then went down vertically in flames and exploded on the ground near Swaffham.

Hoffmann's crew bailed out after the first attack. As the combat report states, his aircraft crashed near Swaffham, at the village of Narford, five of its bomb load exploding on impact. Hoffmann and one of his crew survived, but could reveal little to their interrogators as they had only joined 4./NJG 2 in April 1941 and this was only their fourth flight.

Plt Off Thompson put down flaps and throttled back and started to follow the e/a which disappeared from view but Plt Off Britain maintained AI contact and a second

> visual was obtained a minute or two later only to be lost again, however, minimum range was again reached on the AI and Plt Off Britain got a third visual of the e/a which was about 350yds away on the port side of the Beaufighter.
>
> Plt Off Thompson crossed over to get a silhouette to starboard against the northern light and identified the e/a as a He 111 which was still flying west and gradually climbing.
>
> At 0105hrs, Plt Off Thompson closed right in and fired a short burst from the port quarter at about 100ft range which immediately caused the e/a's starboard engine to burst into flames, the e/a then dived to the ground and exploded near Terrington.
>
> At the same time as this combat Sqn Ldr Pleasance and Sgt Bent saw an e/e descend in flames and explode and shortly afterwards the Observer Corps reported the location of the burning wreckage near Terrington.

Unteroffizier Helmut Bähner and his crew were killed. Although their aircraft had broken up on impact, eight 50kg bombs were discovered, proof that they too had only just arrived over the UK that night. Of interest, one victory stripe was noted on the tail with the date 9 April 1941. That night the Ju 88 is believed to have been flown by Unteroffizier Hans Berschwinger, this 4./NJG 2 pilot shooting down a Wellington of 211 Squadron being flown by Pilot Officer Peter Brown.

Brown had just taken off from RAF Bircham Newton's satellite airfield at the time he was attacked:

> Aircraft R1049 on local night flying programme at Langham satellite aerodrome was intercepted by an enemy aircraft believed to be a Ju 88. Both aircraft opened fire simultaneously. Our aircraft was set on fire in the air and crashed out of control at Burnham Westgate. The crew were all killed, this being the Squadron's first casualty.

This is believed to be the Ju 88C-4 flown by the Bähner crew which crashed near King's Lynn, 14 June 1941. (*Andy Saunders*)

Berschwinger, who would later be awarded the Ehrenpokal and Deutsches Kreuz in Gold, the latter posthumously, was killed on 16 February 1944. Having shot down eleven aircraft, he was still with 4./NJG 2 at the time.

To make matters worse for 4./NJG 2 that night, while circling a dinghy with survivors from a ditched He 111 from 8./KG 4, the wingtip of Unteroffizier Vitus Alt's Ju 88C-2 hit the water. The aircraft cartwheeled into the North Sea killing all of the crew.

For I./NJG2, its losses in June 1941 did not end there. At 01.20 hours on the 22nd, the Ju 88C-4 flown by Oberfeldwebel Otto Wiese was intercepted by Flying Officer Michael Herrick of 25 Squadron in what the German records referred to as the Raum B patrol area:

Michael Herrick of 25 Squadron. (*Edward McManus*)

> After a chase on the AI lasting about four minutes, Fg Off Herrick got a visual of an aircraft 2–300ft below and straight ahead flying south at 9,000ft. Fg Off Herrick at once turned to port, lost height and approached aircraft from below, the aircraft was flying at 180mph.
>
> Closing to about 100yds Fg Off Herrick saw that the e/a which was not burning resin lights had two engines showing four exhaust flames and had a single fin and he identified the e/a as a He 111, not being fully satisfied and unable to manoeuvre so as to get the e/a against the northern light he drew level alongside it at 100yds and confirmed in his opinion that the aircraft was hostile.
>
> Fg Off Herrick then spoke to the Controller to confirm that the e/a was definitely hostile and dropping back to dead astern he opened fire from slightly below at 100yds range just as the e/a which had by now seen the Beaufighter, did a diving turn to starboard.

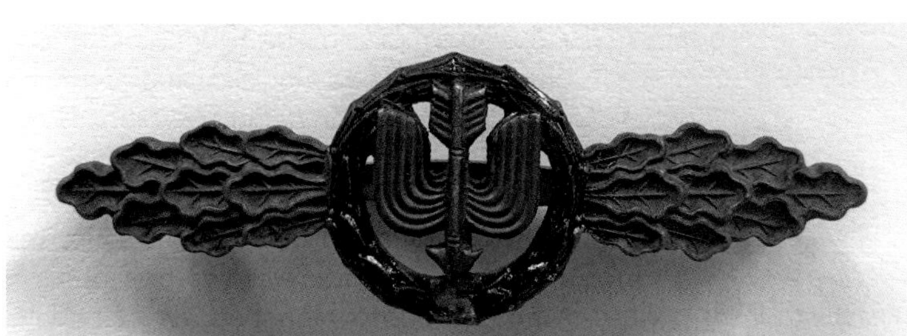

The Frontflugspange in Bronze which was awarded to intruder aircrew.

> Fg Off Herrick followed and being unable to use his reflector sight while keeping pace with the e/a and maintaining the visual continued to fire using his guns in the manner of a hosepipe. Strikes were observed upon the e/a which burst into flames and partially exploded, the e/a continued to descend and appeared to circle at about 7,000ft whereupon our pilot got into position to put in another burst but there was another explosion inside the e/a from which one member of the crew was seen to bail out and the e/a then spiralled to the ground in flames and exploded where it was seen to be burning furiously by the crew of the Beaufighter which by then was at 5,000ft.
>
> The German who had bailed out was the only survivor and he was captured immediately unhurt. Another German who bailed out was unfortunate in that his parachute caught fire.

The only survivor of what was later confirmed to be a Ju 88, not an He 111, was the Bordfunker, Unteroffizier Heinrich Beul. Beul provided the following account:

> Our aircraft was hit from behind. Our starboard wing, with two 400ltr fuel tanks in it, caught fire. Otto went into a steep dive in an attempt to extinguish the flames but to no avail in fact the flames got bigger.
>
> Otto gave the order to bail out and Gefr Hermann Mandel tried to open the bottom gondola but couldn't, the handle having been damaged by a cannon shell. We had to jettison the cockpit hood.

The tail of Oberleutnant Paul Bohn's Ju 88C-2 of 4./NJG 2 after it crashed in Italy. Note the five victory bars on the tail. (*Simon Parry*)

> I stepped onto my seat and rolled out. I was lucky to get out first and immediately tried to pull my parachute release. I was spinning over and over. I reached the handle and pulled. There was a tremendous jerk and I swung like a pendulum.

The stricken German fighter crashed at a shallow angle at Deeping St James in Lincolnshire. Once again, it was discovered that the German crew had not dropped all of their deadly cargo of eight 50kg bombs, as five of these were found in the wreckage.

There would be one more 4 Staffel casualty in June 1941. Just after midnight on 26 June 1941, Staffelkapitän Oberleutnant Paul Bohn was closing in on his fifth victim when he was killed by return fire. Bordmechaniker Unteroffizier Walter Lindner pulled his pilot's body out of its seat and turned the fighter for home.

As they flew over the Continent, a static line was attached to Bohn's parachute and he was pushed out. The rest of Bohn's crew followed his body out, eventually landing near Charleville in France. Bohn's body was found twelve days later near Eclaibes, to the south of Maubeuge on the French-Belgian border. As for the Ju 88, it continued southwards. Finally, its fuel having run out, it crashed near Milan.

Although Bohn was credited with a Whitley at 00.15 hours, none were lost. Oberfeldwebel Hermann Jung, another 4./NJG 2 pilot, also claimed a Whitley in the same location twenty minutes later.

The only other unaccounted RAF loss was a Wellington of 99 Squadron, which, being flown by Sergeant John Hancock, is believed to have crashed in the North Sea.

Flying Officer William Villers of 49 Squadron reported an encounter with a night fighter. He only missed being rammed by pushing his Hampden's nose down, causing the German aircraft to pass overhead.

Sergeant Peter Griffin, in a Whitley of 51 Squadron, described being attacked seventy-five miles north-west of Texel by what he took to be a Bf 110. The latter inflicted only slight damage, and having jettisoned his bombs Griffin landed safely at 02.10 hours. This was Griffin's first operational flight; he was destined to be shot down and killed by Oberleutnant Helmut Lent of 4./NJG 1 on 15 August 1941.

Command of 4 Staffel now passed to Oberleutnant Hans-Georg Schütze formerly of 2 Staffel.

Of note is that the Gruppe's 100th victory went to Oberfeldwebel Hermann Sommer of 2./NJG 2 on 27 June 1941. This was his ninth kill, though the identity of the aircraft he claimed to have shot down has not been established.

Oberleutnant Hans-Georg Schütze of 2./NJG 2.

The first of the intruders' claims for July 1941 went to Oberfeldwebel Peter Laufs of 1./NJG 1. In this instance, he stated that he had attacked a Fairey Battle near Wells next to the Sea at 01.00 hours on 5 July. The Spitfire-equipped 452 Squadron explains what had actually transpired: '0108hrs. Sgt A.G. Costello killed at Fen Lane Farm near North Somercotes after being attacked preparing to land at aerodrome, his Spitfire being complete destroyed.' Twenty-three-years-old Andrew Costello, an Australian, was Peter Laufs' ninth victory of the war.

Between 5 and 30 July 1941, I./NJG 2 would claim a total of nineteen aircraft, of which two were only damaged and eight unidentified. In addition to Oberfeldwebel Peter Laufs, the top scorers that month were now Oberfeldwebel Wilhelm Beier of 3./NJG 2, who took his score to eleven on 18 July, while, on the same night, Oberleutnant Paul Semrau increased his tally to eight.

Another pilot who had eight victories at this stage was Leutnant Heinz Völker of 3./NJG 2. He would have one further claim when, at 01.30 hours on 22 July 1941, he collided with a Wellington of 11 OTU. Being flown by Flight Sergeant Walter Hannah and Australian Sergeant Bruce Thompson, the Wellington had been preparing to land at RAF Bassingbourn when the collision occurred. Both aircraft crashed at Ashwell in Hertfordshire, resulting in the deaths of the three German and eight RAF airmen. The wreckage of the Ju 88 revealed very little, apart from the fact that Völker had not dropped his bombs as they were found in the burnt out remains.

There was one unusual claim on the night of 15 July 1941. Just two Ju 88s from I./NJG 2 were operating over the UK, one in Raum C, the other in Raum B. The aircraft operating in Raum C reported attacking what he thought was a Fairey Swordfish over Upwood at 300m altitude at 02.25 hours, but observing no results did not claim.

This was in fact a Tiger Moth from 22 EFTS using the airfield at Caxton Gibbett. Another pilot from 22 EFTS airborne that night wrote the following:

What one intruder pilot thought was a Fairy Swordfish was in fact a Tiger Moth of 22 EFTS which, although he did not claim, was shot down over RAF Upwood on 16 July 1941.

> My friend (the one who had excellent night vision) and I were ordered to do some night flying in the Tiger Moth. We both took off to do some circuits and landings but every time that I came into land, I was given a flashing red Aldis by Air Traffic Control.
>
> This happened time and time again and I wondered what on earth could be wrong. I decided to go and circle a beacon station near St Neots.
>
> I returned to base a little later and this time was given a green light to land. When I taxied in, I was told that an intruder had been in the circuit and that he had shot my pal down. Luckily, he escaped without being too badly hurt.

The Tiger Moth's tail was apparently severely damaged by cannon fire and the pilot, LAC Stanley Hassall, managed to bail out successfully. However, as mentioned by his colleague, Hassall was injured.

Again there would be a number of losses in addition to Völker's. Leutnant Rudolf Stradner of 1./NJG 2 crashed off the Dutch Coast on 9 July, having declared an emergency at 03.18 hours. There were no survivors.

Then, on 24 July, the Ju 88C-4 of Obergefreiter Heinz Ladiges of 4./NJG 2 crashed at Bondy in Lincolnshire. He had dropped his 50kg bombs on RAF Elsham Wolds, but twenty minutes later his aircraft was seen to burst into flames, dive into the ground and explode making a crater 40ft in diameter and scattering wreckage over a wide area. It was initially assumed they had been shot down by an RAF night fighter (no claims), then another intruder (no claims), so it can be assumed that Ladiges' Ju 88 had been hit when engaged by light and heavy anti-aircraft guns.

The final loss was Leutnant Dr Lothar Bisang of 2./NJG 2. His Ju 88C-4 dived vertically into the ground at Wivenhoe in Essex at 04.20 hours on 28 July 1941. Bisang had just shot down his first aircraft, an Oxford of 2 SFTS, which was flying circuits at Akeman Street landing ground north-east of Minster Lovell in Oxfordshire. LAC Ralph Smith was killed.

Though Bisang's Bordfunker had reported the successful combat, nothing else was heard from the aircraft. It has been suggested that Bisang may have panicked on seeing an RAF night fighter. In fact, Pilot Officer Fred Burnard and Sergeant Reeves of 85 Squadron, who were airborne in a Douglas Havoc at 03.40 hours, reported, after landing at 04.35 hours, 'seeing an e/a crashing near Colchester for no particular reason that could be observed'. At thirty, Bisang was older than many of his fellow pilots, having been promoted to Leutnant from Feldwebel in March 1941.

What would have been of concern to the RAF was the fact that Bisang's claim was the furthest west so far in the Fernnachtjäger campaign. Until then, I./NJG 2 operated in three patrol areas known as Raum. Raum A was East Anglia, Raum B Lincolnshire and Yorkshire, while Raum C went up to the Scottish borders. While inspecting the wreckage of Obergefreiter Heinz Ladiges' aircraft four days earlier, the RAF intelligence personnel had found fragments of a map on which was marked a patrol area that included Leicester, Woburn, Reading, Salisbury, Trowbridge and Gloucester – an area where many training units, such as 2 SFTS at RAF Brize Norton, and their airfields were located. It is believed this was designated Raum F. Strangely, Bisang reported his success in Raum C, which is nowhere near where the Oxford was attacked or where his Ju 88 subsequently crashed.

In reality, the discovery of the map, and the information it contained, made little difference, as in just over two months later, intruder sorties ceased.

The last two full months of Fernnachtjagd operations by I./NJG 2 resulted in fourteen claims in August and four in September 1941. Again, a number of these cannot be matched with any Allied losses, especially the three claimed by Oberfeldwebel Wilhelm Beier of 3./NJG 2 on 8 August 1941, 'kills' which took his score to fourteen and resulted in the award of the Ritterkreuz in October 1941. No record of any RAF bombers being shot down by intruders that night can be found (see Appendix 6 which analyses missions on that night).

Other Experten also did well in this period. Peter Laufs of 1./NJG 2, for example, increased his score to ten, Leutnant Hans Hahn of 3./NJG 2 to eleven, Oberfeldwebel Heinz Strüning of 1./NJG 2 to eight, Feldwebel Hans Köster of 3./NJG 2 to ten, and Oberleutnant Paul Semrau of 3./NJG 2 to nine.

Losses in combat were three. Leutnant Rudolf Pfeiffer of 4./NJG 2 failed to return on 17 August 1941, while Feldwebel Walter Kleine of 4./NJG 2 did likewise on 2 September 1941. One of the men in Kleine's crew was Feldwebel Hans Engmann, who had previously survived when Oberleutnant Paul Bohn was killed on 26 June 1941. This time Engmann was not so lucky; his was the only body to be washed ashore in The Netherlands.

The last intruder to be shot down over the UK in the first Fernnachtjagd campaign fell on 15 September 1941. The victim on this occasion was Oberfeldwebel Erwin Viel of 1./NJG 2. Viel had only joined his Staffel at the end of June 1941, having flown operationally with 4./KG 51 in the Battle of France, Battle of Britain, Blitz, the Yugoslavian Campaign and the first week of Operation *Barbarossa*, the attack on the Soviet Union. He claimed to have flown over sixty missions as a bomber pilot and then twenty as an intruder before his luck ran out.

Squadron Leader Harbourne Stephen of 234 Squadron on the wing, who accounted for the Ju 88C-2 flown by Major Karl Hülshoff on 12 August 1941. Squadron Leader Mungo Park, killed 27 June 1941, is in the cockpit.

Coming in over the English coast at Southwold in Suffolk, and having encountered no RAF aircraft, Viel and his crew made for what they believed was RAF Stradishall, dropped their 50kg bombs and headed for Clacton, before turning for home. It was there that they were intercepted by a Havoc of 85 Squadron, which was flown by former bomber pilot Squadron Leader Gordon Raphael.

The Ju 88C-4 flown by Major Karl Hülshoff, (*John Foreman*)

After a fifteen-minute chase, and despite Viel's frantic efforts to throw off his pursuer, a short burst hit the German fighter in the starboard wing, which then caught fire. The crew immediately bailed out and the Ju 88 crashed in the sea at 21.25 hours; two of those onboard swam to shore, while the third was rescued by boat.

Squadron Leader Gordon Raphael of 85 Squadron, who shot down the Ju 88C-2 flown by Oberfeldwebel Erwin Viel of 1./NJG 2 on 16 September 1941. (*Andy Brooks*)

There was one more loss which could have been more serious for I./NJG 2. On 12 August 1941, a force of fifty-four Blenheims carried out a daring daylight attack on the power stations at Knapsack and Quadrath near Köln. There was a massive RAF fighter presence, both to protect the bombers and divert German fighters. The German response resulted in the destruction of twelve Blenheims (with more returning damaged) and six Spitfires.

The crews of I./NJG 2 were ordered to carry out patrols along the coast. Feldwebel Vincenz Giessübel of 2./NJG 2 reported taking off on such a mission at 13.02 hours and landing again without incident at 14.47 hours, while Oberleutnant Heinz-Horst Hissbach of 1./NJG 2 carried out a similar task with nothing to report.

Another pilot involved was the recently promoted Gruppen Kommandeur of I./NJG 2, Major Karl Hülshoff. What happened next is best related by former Battle of Britain pilot Squadron Leader Harborne Stephen, who was leading 234 Squadron on an offensive sweep to cover to the Blenheim bombers on their way home:

> We were approaching the coast near Veere when a twin-engined aircraft I had been watching decided to come and visit us. On approaching he fired two series of four star cartridges in all. The cartridges broke up into four red stars after firing.
>
> I had identified him as an e/a for some time back and was waiting until I had reassembled my squadron. At this point an Me 109 made a beam attack developing into a quarter astern attack on me but this I evaded, gave him a quick burst but did not worry more about him. As I resumed my course, the Ju 88 nightfighter, who was painted entirely black, gave me a quick burst with his front guns but as he was on the beam, was not accurate. I turned onto the tail of the Ju 88 and opened fire from about 150yds and immediately observed hits on the port wing, engine and fuselage.
>
> The fuselage finally began to tear open but I transferred my fire to the port engine and gave it a three second burst. The pilot then took immediate evasive action by shutting both throttles causing me to close my range too fast while I was concentrating on my firing, and making me break away to starboard. I had the satisfaction of knowing that before I broke to starboard the port engine of this aircraft was well alight and the e/a dived into cloud.
>
> I saw him once more but could not close the range although we were at 1,500ft. At this moment about 1222hrs.

With a badly damaged Ju 88C-4, Hülshoff force-landed at Steenbergen, due east of Veere, while en route to Gilze-Rijen. Although Hülshoff was unscathed, both Oberfeldwebel Willi Mayer (Bordfunker) and Oberfeldwebel Paul Licht (Bordmechaniker) were wounded.

It is interesting to note that intruders were having an effect in August 1941, as noted by RAF Driffield in eastern Yorkshire:

> Enemy activity in the neighbourhood showed a considerable increase over that experienced in July and warning were received practically every night. No attacks, however, were made on the station, the decoy lighting at Skerne being successful in attracting to itself the bombs of at least two hostile raiders.

October 1941 would be the last month of operations over Britain for I./NJG 2 as the Gruppe was informed on 12 October that it would be moving to Sicily to conduct operations over the Mediterranean. The reason for stopping intruder missions was simple – Hitler wanted to see RAF bombers burning on the ground in Germany, where the German public could see them, rather than over the UK where they could not.

As a result there would be just three claims over England that month, but one very serious loss.

The first claim, on 3 October 1941, was for a Short Stirling of 7 Squadron flown by Squadron Leader Don McLeod. Feldwebel Alfons Köster of 3./NJG 2 struck while the bomber was on its approach to land at RAF Oakington. A ten-minute dogfight ensued, with the Ju 88 making six attacks at a height of fifty metres, with another Stirling flown by Sergeant Sidney Matkin joining in, but to no avail. By now, McLeod's Stirling was on fire and two crew successfully bailed out; the aircraft itself crashed at Caxton Gibbet, killing the pilot and five crew. This was Köster's 11th victory.

A second victory came on the very night that I./NJG 2 was informed that it would be ceasing operations over England. This involved Oberfeldwebel Heinz Strüning of 1./NJG 2, who achieved his ninth victory when he shot down a Blenheim of 51 OTU. The latter crashed at Sherrington, north-east of Milton Keynes in Buckinghamshire, killing Sergeant Francis Filmer, the only one on board.

There would be one more victory which was pyrrhic. At 21.30 hours on 11 October 1941, a Ju 88 collided with an Oxford of 12 SFTS over Grantham in Lincolnshire. Both aircraft crashed at Barrowby, killing the crew of the Oxford, Sergeant Tom Graham and Corporal Sam Edwards, and the three unidentified Germans in the Ju 88.

Identification of the German aircraft was difficult, a situation that was exacerbated by the fact that two bombs in the wreckage exploded soon afterwards. Clues that were found in the wreckage included the collar patch of a Leutnant and a crew list for 3./NJG 2. Thirteen dates of victories were found on a section of wreckage, these starting on 17 December 1940 and ending with three on 8 August 1941. These victories match those claimed by Oberfeldwebel Wilhelm Beier of 3./NJG 2, who claimed victories twelve through to fourteen on 8 August 1941. However, Beier, who had received the Ritterkreuz on 10 October 1941, was in fact very much still alive and would survive the war.

That night, the Ju 88C-4s of I./NJG 2 were active from 21.12 hours until 03.05 hours, dropping bombs on RAF Honington, RAF Cranwell, RAF Driffield, RAF Feltwell and two unidentified airfields, as well as non-airfield targets in Southwold and Ipswich. No claims were made for air combat victories, but one aircraft was reported missing – this being one flown by Leutnant Hans Hahn on 3./NJG 2.

This is believed to be Leutnant Hans Hahn's Ju 88C-4 after an accident at Deelen, 4 September 1941.

Oberfeldwebel Wilhelm Beier of 3./NJG 2 was awarded the Ritterkreuz on 10 October 1941. He is seen here (centre) with Generalmajor Josef Kammhuber (left) and Major Wolfgang Falck, the Kommodore of NJG 1. (*Andy Saunders*)

One of the last photographs of Leutnant Hans Hahn taken before his death on 11 October 1941.

Since being commissioned and receiving the Ritterkreuz, Hahn had little luck. He and Unteroffizier Helmut Scheidt were injured in a take-off accident on 31 July 1941, and then suffered another accident on landing on 4 September 1941.

On 17 August 1941, he had taken his score to eleven when he shot down a Wellington of 104 Squadron near Scunthorpe, killing Sergeant Bill Stephenson and his crew. The collision with the Oxford over Grantham would be his twelfth and final victory. He and his two crew, Unteroffizier Ernst-Wilhelm Meissler and Unteroffizier Helmut Scheidt, were buried at Grantham, but now lie at Cannock Chase.

It would appear that 12 October 1941, the penultimate night of operations, saw a final flurry of attacks on airfields which included Newmarket, Newton, Church Fenton, Kirton in Lindsey and Leconfield, with thirteen separate

The original wooden crosses on the graves of Leutnant Hahn and his crew at Grantham. (*Andy Saunders*)

In 1942, I./NJG 2 returned to north-west Europe and left its Ju 88C-4 and C-6s with 10./ZG 76. (*Wolf Seidemann*)

At the end of 1941, I./NJG 2 moved to the Mediterranean.

attacks being recorded between 22.50 hours and 03.14 hours (but there is no mention in official German reports of the shooting down of the 51 OTU Oxford – this was incorrectly recorded by the Luftwaffe for the following night).

Then on the night of 13 October 1941, just two intruders were active dropping bombs on what was believed to be RAF Feltwell, RAF Hemswell, Norwich and RAF Manby. By then, 2./NJG 2, which until the end of the year was still flying some Do 17Z-10s, was only using the Ju 88C-4 on operations.

I./NJG 2's time over Britain now came to an end and it headed off to pastures new in the Mediterranean. The unit had claimed to have shot down 146 RAF aircraft. Of these, fifty-three can be positively matched with RAF losses. As we shall see, intruders, in the form of Me 410s of V./KG 2, did not return in force until August 1943. By then, however, the air war over the UK was not going in favour of the Luftwaffe.

A view of one of I./NJG 2's Ju 88s after the move to the Mediterranean.

Groundcrew and armourers about to load bombs on to one of I./NJG 2's Ju 88s while in the Mediterranean theatre.

One of I./NJG 2's Ju 88s running up its engines, possibly while preparing to take-off for a flight or sortie, from an airfield in the Mediterranean.

Another of I./NJG 2's Ju 88s at the unit's Mediterranean airfield.

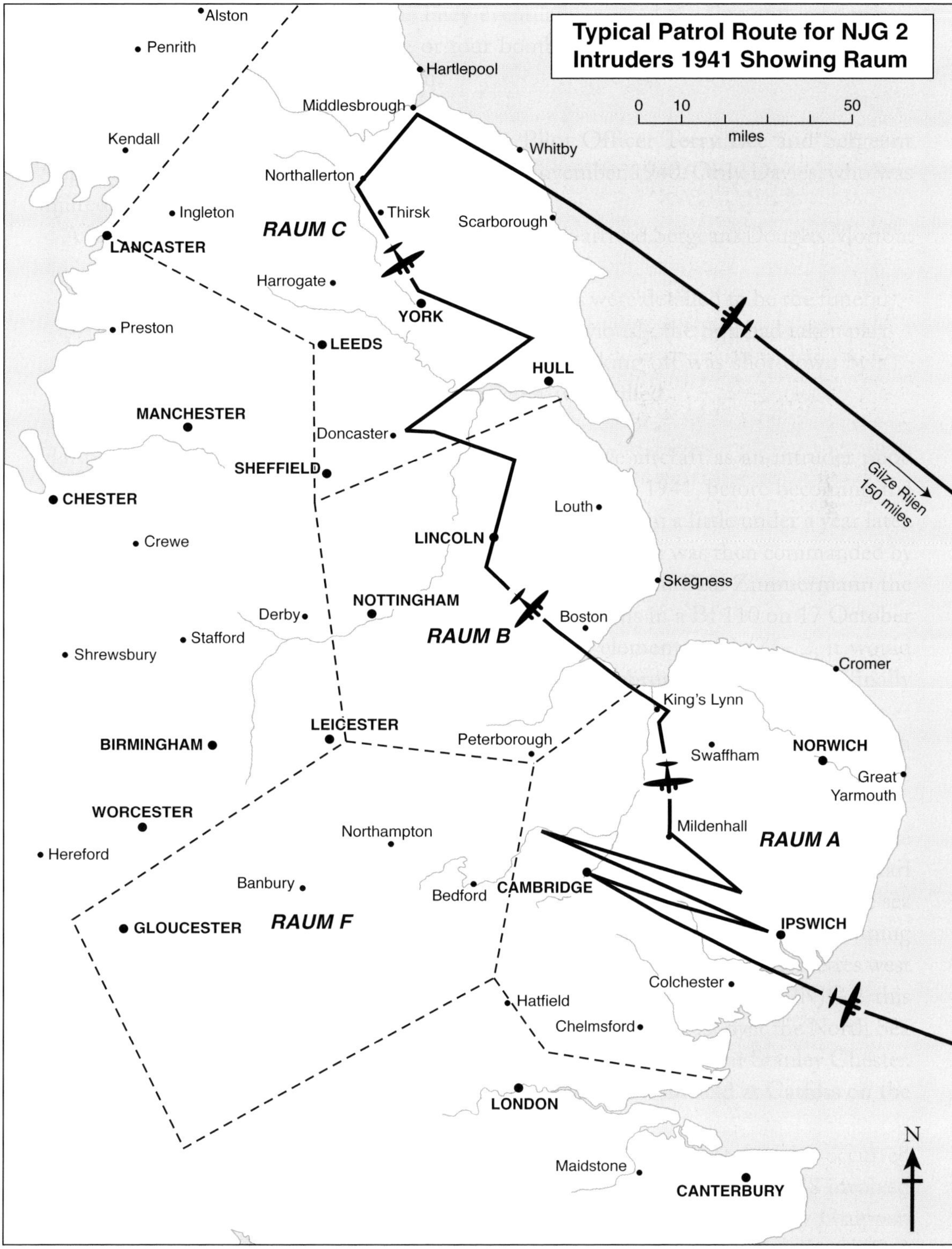

A typical patrol route for NJG 2 intruders in 1941, showing Raum.

[illegible]naby	- Preston	294	420	7/2
Leeming	-Scruton	273	562	[illegible]
Dishforth	[illegible]	[illegible]	[illegible]	[illegible]
Linton	- Youlton	[illegible]	145	1/2
[illegible]field	- Arram	320	635	4/3
[illegible]holme	- Westend	660	180	[illegible]
Finningley	- Rossington	[illegible]	710	9/2
Hemswell	- Corring[illegible]	[illegible]	190	1/2
Scampton	- Broxholme	286	170	1/2
Waddington	- Hykeham	320	630	8/6
W-Raynham	- [illegible]wich	[illegible]	780	9/5
Marham	- Fincham	348	360	5/3
Feltwell	- Methwold	532	[illegible]	[illegible]
Mildenhall	- [illegible]	330	460	7/4
Honington	- Ixw[illegible]	[illegible]	530	5/4
Wyton	- Upwood	720	420	[illegible]
Stradishall	- Kirtling	120	450	7/4
[illegible]	- Gr[illegible]	[illegible]	630	6/4
Caxt[illegible]	- Drayton	720	[illegible]	[illegible]
[illegible]ourn	- Litlington	462	730	[illegible]

Found in a navigation bag when the Thorney Ju 88 was excavated in 1978 was a document, the last three pages of which were three letter codes used to transmit information back to Gilze-Rijen. However, the first page is intriguing as the first column lists airfields and the second column villages near to the airfield. The next three columns are a series of numbers. The airfields are listed from north (Thornaby) to south (Bassingbourn). It is assumed that this was, therefore, a patrol line which began in Raum A and ended in Raum B. It is then assumed that the villages alongside each airfield were an initial aiming point from which they attacked the target after which they aimed for the next initial point to attack the next airfield. For example Scruton is north of Leeming, after which they headed for Norton le Clay to the east of Dishforth, then aiming for Youlton, north of Linton on Ouse – all were Bomber Command airfields. The numbers are a mystery, as was where the Ju 88 was headed and why it crashed.

Chapter 2

Stopgap Fernnachtjagd, 1940–1941

In addition to the Ju 88C-2/C-4 being used by II./NJG 1 (which then became I./NJG 2), there would also be two versions of the Do 17 used as night fighters – the Z-7 Kauz I and the Z-10 Kauz II, Kauz meaning 'Screech Owl'.

In these, the glazed nose was removed from a Do 17 Z-2 and replaced by the nose from a Ju 88C-2/C-4. The armament was three 7.9mm machine-guns and one MG151 cannon, the aircraft designated the Do 17 Z-7. This was soon found to be unsatisfactory and an entirely new nose designed. This increased the armament to four machine-guns and one MG151 cannon. In the tip of the nose was an infra-red spotlight called Spanner-Anlage, which was later apparently replaced by first-generation FuG 202 Lichtenstein radar. This was now designated the Do 17 Z-10.

It would appear that pilots for the Kauz were taken from various units such as I./KG 2, II and III./KG 76 (both Do 17 units), as well as Kampfgruppe zur besonderen Verwendung (KGrzbV) 11 and KGrzbV 105, the latter two both being recently disbanded transport units. Such pilots must have had high levels of blind flying competency necessary to fly a bomber as a night fighter.

Precise numbers of Do 17 Z-7s and Z-10s are hard to define, but it is thought that in the region of five Z-7s were produced. The survivors of these were later converted to be Z-10s, of which around fourteen were produced.

The Z-7 first entered service with Hauptmann Günther Radusch's I./NJG 1 on or about 22 June 1940. The first recorded combat probably came in the early hours of 29 June 1940, when a Whitley of 58 Squadron, being flown by Pilot Officer Bill Espley (who had only joined the Squadron five days before), reported damaging a night fighter near Eindhoven. However, the 58 Squadron Operations Record Book (ORB) made scant mention: 'Aircraft was attacked over Eindhoven by a Me 110 at 8,000ft. Fired five bursts from the rear turret at the enemy which was hit and broke off the engagement.'

A Do 17 Z-7 of 1./NJG 1, that coded G9+GK and flown by Unteroffizier Hugo Schwarz, was damaged in combat and later crash-landed near München-Gladbach (it is possible he was flying a Bf 110 as records appear contradictory). Schwarz, formerly of Stab II./KG 76, and his Bordfunker, Feldwebel Gerhard Palm, were both injured, whilst the Bordmechaniker, Feldwebel Ludwig Born, later died of his wounds.

In August 1940, the Do 17 Z-7s and Z-10s now became part of II./NJG 1 commanded by Major Karl-Heinrich Heyse. Two of Heyse's Staffel (4 and 6./NJG 1) operated the Ju 88 C-2/C-4, but 5 Staffel appears to have been the one that operated the Do 17 Z-7/Z-10. It

Major Wolfgang Falck, who was tasked with forming a nightfighter and intruder force.

Major Rolf Jung seen greeting Hermann Göring at Catania in January 1942. Staffelkapitän of 2./NJG 2, Jung took command of the Gruppe in November 1941.

was commanded by Hauptmann Rolf Jung; very little is known about his previous career, apart from he is believed to have flown in Spain. When Major Heyse was reported missing in action over the North Sea on 23 November 1940, he was replaced by Oberleutnant Karl Hülshoff.

It is difficult to attribute the vast majority of kills to the Kauz II as it was only used in very small numbers, the type flown was not recorded and it was soon replaced by the Ju 88 C. For example, during the period June to October 1940, Do 17 Z-7s and Z-10s were only used on nineteen nights, flying a total of twenty-two sorties. Unteroffizier Vincenz Giessübel, formerly of 2./KG 2, and who had been shot down and taken prisoner over France on 15 May 1940 but then joined the new night fighter unit after his release, flew his first intruder mission in a Do 17 Z-10 on the night of 15–16 November 1940. He would only undertake a further three before the end of 1940.

The first confirmed and recorded success by a Do 17 Z-10 came on the night of 9 September 1940. It was the first success of the war for Feldwebel Hermann Sommer of 5./NJG 1 (formerly from 5./KG 76), albeit the claim was optimistic. Sommer had taken off from Gilze-Rijen in a Do 17, that coded G9+DN, at 21.05 hours. He claimed to have shot down a Blenheim in the circuit at RAF Waddington in Lincolnshire at 23.15 hours. Although not mentioned in any detail in the 15 Squadron records, it is believed that Sommer attacked the Blenheim flown by Pilot Officer James Kee, who was the pilot of

Groundcrew are pictured working on a Dornier Do 17Z-10 of 2./NJG 2. Note the Spanner Anlage fitted in the nose and the scope in the cockpit.

one of ten aircraft briefed to attack Ostende. All that it said is that he was attacked by an enemy aircraft and managed to land the damaged aircraft at RAF Wyton.

The first confirmed kill by a Do 17 Z-10 came at 21.25 hours on 16 October 1940. It was credited to Leutnant Ludwig Becker of 4./NJG 1 (formerly of 3./ZG 26), this Staffel was still operating the Do 17 Z-10 before converting to the Bf 110 shortly afterwards. Becker recorded the following:

> I was well positioned at the correct altitude of 3300m and directed onto enemy by a series of continual corrections. Suddenly I saw an aircraft in the moonlight about 100m above and to the left. On moving closer I made it out to be a Vickers Wellington. Slowly I closed in behind and aimed a burst of five to six seconds duration at the fuselage. The starboard engine caught fire immediately and I pulled my aircraft up. For a while the Englishman flew on, losing height rapidly. The fire died away but I then saw him spin towards the ground and burst into flames on crashing.

The Wellington was from 311 Squadron, which had been tasked with an attack on Kiel. Pilot Officer Bohumil Landa and three crew were killed when the bomber crashed at Oosterwolde in The Netherlands, and two more crew were captured. Unteroffizier Werner Fick, also of 4./NJG 1, claimed to have damaged an unidentified Wellington over the Ijsselmeer at 00.30 hours.

The first confirmed intruder success that was almost certainly made by a Do 17 Z-10 was a Hampden shot down by Leutnant Heinz Völker, near Scampton in Lincolnshire, at 00.30 hours on 28 October 1940. The 49 Squadron ORB states what happened:

> One aircraft was attacked by an enemy aircraft whilst circling the Q site on return. The aircraft suffered slight damage including three burst tyres and shot accumulator. Hampden X3027 landed in the sea half a mile off Skegness. It is believed that they had been shot up by an enemy aircraft whilst over this aerodrome [Scampton].

The damaged Hampden, serial X3001 and coded EA-H, was flown by Pilot Officer John Green, who landed without incident at 01.40 hours. Green, flying the same Hampden, was shot down by a Bf 110 flown by Leutnant Leopold Fellerer of 5./NJG 1 on 11 February 1941; he and two of his crew were captured, one killed. There were no survivors from Pilot Officer John Bufton's aircraft, X3027.

Völker then claimed a Blenheim over the North Sea on the night of 22 December 1940, though some records state the claim was near RAF Cranwell in Lincolnshire. He was again probably flying a Do 17 Z-10, but this claim cannot be matched with any RAF losses.

In 1941, Völker would convert to the Ju 88C-2/C-4 and fly with 3./NJG 2 claiming another five RAF aircraft on intruder missions, becoming one of the most successful intruder pilots to date.

There would be one more claim for him when, at 01.30 hours on 22 July 1941, he collided with a Wellington of 11 OTU flown by Flight Sergeant Walter Hannah and Australian Sergeant Bruce Thompson which was preparing to land at RAF Bassingbourn. Both aircraft then crashing at Ashwell in Hertfordshire with the deaths of the three German and eight RAF aircrew.

Flying Officer Hugh Wyrill with his Nav/Rad, Flight Sergeant Jock Willins. On 16 January 1941, Wyrill, then with 54 OTU, was attacked by Oberleutnant Albert Schulz of 2./NJG 2. (*Tim Oliver*)

There were only three other nights where Luftwaffe records specifically mention Do 17 Z-10s shooting down RAF aircraft. The first was the night of 10–11 February 1941, when four aircraft, three of them flown by Hauptmann Rolf Jung, Oberleutnant Albert Schulz and Leutnant Johannes Feuerbaum, were involved.

The first claim was made by Oberleutnant Schulz who reported:

> Take-off 2350hrs, landing 0351hrs, over target area 0100–0300hrs. Shot down a Bristol Blenheim near airfield 10242 [West Raynham] at 0110hrs. Attack took place at 200m altitude from 100m distance. After the first shots, the left engine broke off. The plane spun vertically over the right wing. A crash could not be observed because Defiant or Spitfire nightfighters attacked the Do 17. Own aircraft was shot at by nightfighters four times without success. Dropped 120 incendiary bombs from 800m altitude on airfield 10841 [Weybourne] at 0205hrs. Several persistent fires observed in barracks and airfield installations.

Schulz's claim was optimistic and no losses can be attributed to his attack. Furthermore, he actually attacked RAF Coltishall, where Spitfires of 222 Squadron and Hurricanes of 255 Squadron were carrying out night flying practice. The ORB for 222 Squadron notes the following:

> While night flying was in progress at about midnight, one enemy aircraft was seen by Sgt [Rainford] Marland to be making the circuit behind the aircraft flown by Sgt [Norman] Ramsay who was then fired upon. Sgt Marland made five separate

A Do 17Z-7 of 2./NJG 2 showing the Englandblitz badge and with white-tipped spinners.

attacks on this e/a which was identified as an Me 110. Shortly afterwards incendiary bombs were dropped and two hangars sustained slight damage. A second stick was dropped and it is believed that e/a was then intercepted by a Hurricane [Sgt Leslie Barnes of 257 Sqn] and chased out to sea.

Hauptmann Jung, with his crew of Unteroffizier Theo Schürks and Unteroffizier Herbert Thomas, was the next to claim. He duly reported:

> Take-off at 2345hrs, landing at 0346hrs, over target area 0100–0130hrs. Observed four landing aircraft near illuminated airfield 10280 [Coltishall]. Own plane was detected too early. The lights of the airfield were switched off.
>
> Dropped 120 incendiary bombs on accommodation and hangars from 0100–0145hrs in three attacks from 500m altitude. Observed numerous persistent fires. Fired at fire brigade crews in six low-level attacks. Observed six landing aircraft at airfield 10242 at 0220hrs.
>
> Attacked an aircraft at 100m altitude, the navigation lights were immediately switched off, further pursuit was without any result. Shot down a Wellington near 10242 in 200m altitude at 0230hrs.
>
> After two bursts of fire, the right engine burned and the plane exploded in the air. Despite the air combat there was well-aimed light anti-aircraft fire, six hits in own machine.
>
> Attacked a Bristol Blenheim with three bursts near Great Yarmouth at 800m altitude at 0300hrs. The Blenheim was shooting recognition signals (red-yellow). Hits and fire effect recognized perfectly. Further observation of the aircraft was not possible. Subsequent loss of the aircraft can be expected.

The only loss than can be attributed to this account was a Wellington from 115 Squadron that, captained by Sergeant Harry Rogers, was returning from an attack on Hannover. Rogers pilot managed to crash-land at Narborough near Swaffham in Norfolk with just the rear gunner suffering injuries.

On the night of 7–8 April 1941, Leutnant Hans Feuerbaum almost got another victim whilst flying a Do 17 Z-10 when he claimed a Hudson near Wells. The latter was flown by Pilot Officer Charles Alexander DFM of 206 Squadron. The ORB states what happened:

> Plt Off Alexander was giving night flying instruction from Langham when at 800 feet was attacked simultaneously by a Ju 88 and a Do 17. Plt Off Alexander took control and took avoiding action first to port then to starboard, down to 200ft, then shaking off both enemy aircraft. Rear Gunner fired a burst of 25 rounds when then disappeared. Estimated that enemy aircraft between them fired 500 rounds including some cannon shells, one of which hit the tail. Hudson then climbed to 3,000ft and tried to locate enemy aircraft but returned and landed safely at 0115hrs.

The nose of a Do 17Z-10 showing the armament and Spanner Anlage.

A similar view of a Do 17Z-10 showing the armament and Spanner Anlage, this time with an inspection cover open.

A Do 17Z-10 Wk Nr 2867 PF+DH (2./NJG 2 in Sep 41; later 2./NJS 1 and 2./NJG 101) showing the armament and Spanner Anlage.

On the way home Feuerbaum then claimed what he thought was a Hereford, but was probably the Whitley of 51 Squadron flown by Pilot Officer Gordon Mattey. Mattey reported being attacked by a German aircraft sixty miles east of Flamborough Head, he himself being slightly wounded in the action.

Feuerbaum would claim just one more RAF aircraft on the early morning of 3 May 1941, but by then he was possibly flying a Ju 88C. Even the crew of his intended victim, a Whitley of 77 Squadron flown by Sergeant Ken Mills, failed to establish what their assailant was flying:

> Whilst circling over the beacon at base, the aircraft was attacked by an enemy aircraft, the type of which could not be ascertained. The attack was made from the rear of the Whitley and the enemy aircraft opened fire at 400yds range severely damaging the controls of the Whitley. The engagement lasted for only a short time, the enemy aircraft breaking away when the rear gunner returned fire. The damage to the aircraft controls made landing very difficult and a crash landing was unavoidable. None of the crew was injured however.

Feuerbaum would last for one month and one day more, before he and his crew were killed on 4 June 1941. That night their Ju 88C-2 flew into the ground in bad weather near Whitby in Yorkshire.

The final kill that can be positively attributed to a Do 17 Z-10 intruder was made by the recently promoted Feldwebel Vincenz Giessübel, who shot down an 11 OTU

The nose section of a Do 17Z-7 of 2./NJG 2. (*Mikael Olrogg*)

A Dornier Do 17Z of I./NJG 2 Do 17Z seen at Gilze-Rijen during the winter of 1940–1941.

A Do 17Z-10 of 2./NJG 2. The Do 17s of 2./NJG 2 appeared to have white tips to their spinners.

Wellington captained by Sergeant Phillip Nicholls over RAF Bassingbourn at 00.50 hours on 24 April 1941. The Wellington then crashed into and destroyed a second Wellington. Nicholls was badly injured, and two crew killed. It had been Giessübel's thirty-seventh operational flight of the war. He would continue to fly the Do 17 Z-10 infrequently with 2./NJG 2 for another thirty-three operational flights, though he failed to increase his score. His last operational flight with the Do 17 occurred on 13 October 1941, after which he only flew the Ju 88C-4.

Do 17 Z-10 losses were understandably light due to the small numbers involved. That said, on 13 October 1940, Do 17 Z-10, Wk Nr 2851 and coded R4+DK, crashed on landing at Gilze-Rijen, injuring Unteroffizier Erich Götz (who had flown previously with 4./KG 76) and two of his crew.

Then on 9 November 1940, Oberfeldwebel Herbert Schmid's Wk Nr 2817, coded R4+HK, was damaged by anti-aircraft fire on an intruder sortie and crash-landed at Gilze-Rijen. Interestingly, Schmid, formerly of 1./KG 53, had flown in Spain and on 9 May 1943, now flying with 10./NJG 3, he and his crew defected. The Ju 88R-1 they were flying is in the collection of the RAF Museum.

Finally, on 5 February 1941, Oberleutnant Otto Häuser's Wk Nr 2859, which was coded R4+BK, went missing on an intruder sortie. Häuser had previously been a transport pilot with 4./KGrzbV 105.

The second, and, as it would turn out, last Z-10 combat loss, which was also the last Do 17 to crash on British soil during the Second World War, came on 8 May 1941. On this occasion Feldwebel Wilhelm Lettenmeier's Wk Nr 2843, coded R4+GK, was intercepted

Do 17Z-7 of 2./NJG 2 which was damaged by Flak on an intruder sortie and crash-landed at Gilze-Rijen, 9 Nov 40.

An air-to-air picture of a Do 17Z-7, that coded R4+FK, of 2./NJG 2. (*Mikael Olrogg*)

by a Beaufighter of 25 Squadron flown by Pilot Officer David Thompson, who was flying with radar operator Pilot Officer Leslie Britain.

The RAF crew had difficulty getting behind the German aircraft due to its low speed:

> I throttled back which caused exhaust flames to appear from our aircraft which was up moon of the Dornier which apparently sighted the Beaufighter and immediately

> made a steep turn to port in an attempt to evade and did evade the first burst of one second which I fired attacking on the starboard beam at a range of 100yds.
>
> I followed the Dornier which continued on a straight course after making the steep turn to port giving me the impression that the pilot of the Dornier thought he had succeeded in evading me.
>
> I followed him and fired two further one second bursts at about 100 yds range from below and to starboard and I saw hits from the first burst and after the second burst the port motor of the Dornier caught on fire.

Bordmechaniker Unteroffizier Herbert Thomas recalls what happened next:

> There was an awful crash and grinding noise and the port engine began to burn brightly. The noise was terrific. My first reaction was to get the canopy clear, close the fuel tap, cut the ignition, cut everything. I went to help Lettenmeier but our Dornier simply went down.
>
> The fire closed on the cockpit and together we gave the command to get out. Tracers went under me and the Bola but I could not find the switch for the bail out buzzer so with a great effort I forced open the hatch against the air stream. I climbed onto the Bordfunker's position and to my surprise found that Georg [Unteroffizier Herden] was still at his post. I screamed at him to jump and together we got out.

Both survived but the pilot was killed. David Thompson would be killed in a flying accident on 8 July 1941.

A Do 17Z-10 which appears to have no Spanner Anlange.

The Do 17 as a night fighter could have been replaced by the Do 215B-5 for intruding, but by then the decision had been taken to cease intruder operations.

The Do 17 crashed at West Fen, Medlam Drain, Carrington in Lincolnshire. It struck the ground at high speed, exploding on impact and causing a deep crater. The body of Wilhelm Lettenmeier, who had previously flown with the transport unit 2./KGrzbV 11, was found 100 yards away with an unopened parachute.

Despite being the first Z-10 to crash on land, all that the RAF could find of note was a plate stating the aircraft had been made by Dornier at Friedrichshafen. Fragments of machine-guns were located in the wreckage, as well as a single 15mm round. It was noted that the Z-10 had been carrying 1kg incendiaries.

Although the Do 17 Z-10 soldiered on, meeting with little success but no further losses, it was soon replaced by more adept night fighters, namely the Bf 110, Ju 88C-4 and even the Do 215B-5 (Kauz III); the latter was not used as a Fernnachtjäger.

Despite this, surviving Luftwaffe records reveal the occasional intruder mission still being flown by Do 17s. For example, on the night of 9 July 1941, five Ju 88s and a single Do 17 were active over eastern England. The Do 17 was patrolling Raum F when its crew spotted a Wellington at 00.15 hours at an altitude of 3000m but failed to attack.

Then on the night of 2 August 1941, three Ju 88s and a single Do 17 carried out what was termed a 'Twilight Sortie' over the sea with no success. On the night of 5 August 1941, a single Do 17 was one of sixteen aircraft carrying out intruder missions in Raum B, C and F, attacking RAF Stradishall at 00.35 hours. It dropped seventy-five incendiaries on the airfield, the crew subsequently reported seeing two fires.

The last recorded incident involving a Do 17 Z-10 came on 19 September 1941, when Wk Nr 2867 of 2./NJG 2 suffered an undercarriage collapse at Gilze-Rijen.

The Kauz I and II were no longer operational and the last record of a Do 17 being used on intruder operations came on the night of 28 September 1941, when a single Do 17 patrolled Raum C, seeing nothing and not dropping any of its bombs.

This one year, one month-long intruding campaign had been met with some success, helped mainly by the RAF night fighters only starting to have an effect from the spring of 1941. Some, therefore, might say that the decision to withdraw I./NJG 2 was a mistake and to continue it would have met with more successes and more RAF assets being tied up countering the intruders.

As it was, with the departure of the Ju 88s of I./NJG 2 at the end of 1941, Fernnachtjagd missions ceased. That said, in the middle of 1942, a new potential menace emerged, albeit that the trials unit and aircraft in question flew just in daylight in very small numbers. These sorties, however, were the precursor of what could been considered a second Fernnachtjagd campaign a year afterwards.

Chapter 3

Interim Measure, 1942

At the end of April 1942, Erprobungsstaffel Me 210, the Messerschmitt Me 210 test and development unit, was formed at Lechfeld in Germany. It would be commanded by 25-year-old Oberleutnant Walter Maurer, an experienced former Bf 110 pilot. After officer and pilot training, Maurer was posted to 3./JG 137 at Bernburg in 1938, after which he flew with 1./Jagdgruppe 88 in Spain (where he shot down one aircraft on 13 June 1938).

On his return, 3./JG 137 then became 3./JG 231 and on the outbreak of war, it became 3./Jagdgruppe 102. Maurer scored his second kill over Poland on 11 September 1939. His unit then withdrew to Germany and began converting to the Bf 110, the unit then becoming I./Zerstörergeschwader 2 (I./ZG 2) and commanded by Major Johannes Gentzen.

By the start of the French campaign on 10 May 1940, Maurer was flying with 3./ZG 2, which was commanded by Oberleutnant Hans Röderer and was operating out

An Me 210 being evaluated at the Erprobungsstaffel Me 210 at Rechlin.

Me 210A-1 Wk Nr 057 and coded NT+CA. This particular aircraft would eventually become 2N+DT with 9./ZG 1, and was damaged in combat off Tobruk on 18 November 1942. The Bordfunker, Unteroffizier Hans Ziesch, was wounded. It would be damaged again on 2 December 1942, and further damaged in a bombing raid on Bizerta three days later.

of Darmstadt-Griesheim. Maurer managed to get two more kills before, just twenty-four hours after the start of the campaign, he and his Bordfunker, Unteroffizier Stefan Makera, were shot down by Hawker Hurricanes of 1 Squadron during an escort mission for Heinkel He 111s attacking railway targets at Sainte-Menehould. The RAF fighters were flown by Flight Lieutenant Peter Hanks, Pilot Officer Peter Mould and Flying Officer Leslie Clisby. Maurer crash-landed near Vendresse at 15.15 hours, both he and Makera being taken prisoner.

A view of the thirteenth Me 210 prototype.

Oberleutnant Walter Maurer.

Following the French surrender on 22 June, Maurer was released from captivity and rejoined his old Staffel in time to participate in the Battle of Britain. Due to heavy losses, ZG 2 was then disbanded and in October 1940, he was posted to the Zerstörer Ergänzungsgruppe (Bf 110 training unit) at Værløse in Norway. Maurer then joined III./ZG 76 which became II./SKG 210 and where, as a member of the Stab, he took part in ground attack and escort missions over the Soviet Union during which time he shot down another three aircraft.

In October 1941, he and his Bordfunker, Feldwebel Rudolf Jansen, were selected to be part of the Me 210 development team at Rechlin, replacing Ritterkreuz holder Oberleutnant Heinz Forgatsch who had been killed in an accident testing Me 210A-1 Wk Nr 0117 at Rechlin on 23 September 1941. Maurer was then selected to lead the operational development, reporting personally to Major Walter Storp at the Luftwaffe Führungsstab. Storp was the former commander of Schnellkampfgeschwader 210, the unit that was originally to be equipped with the Me 210 and which had experienced considerable problems training on the type late 1941/early 1942.

It is not known how many crews were posted to the unit, but it would appear that the majority came from the Zerstörerschule at Wunstorf and generally did not have combat experience. One such pilot was Feldwebel Hermann Bolten who had finished his training at the start of March 1942 and first flew an Me 210 at Landsberg on 29 April 1942. He had flown a total of eighty-seven flights on the Me 210 by 7 July 1942, when the decision

A view of an Erprobungsstaffel Me 210 showing off the new type in 1942.

was made for the Me 210 to undertake tactical tests under operational conditions. The unit flew to Évreux in France on 18 July 1942, but very little flying was carried out. Then, on 29 July 1942, Erprobungsstaffel Me 210 moved to Soesterberg in Holland. It was there that it began operations in earnest.

So far the unit had suffered just one accident. This occurred on 31 May 1942, when Me 210A-1 Wk Nr 2343 suffered 45 per cent damage at Stade as a result of an undercarriage problem. However, on 31 July 1942, Feldwebel Hermann Bolten and his Bordfunker, Feldwebel Wilhelm Lohf, were injured when, as a result of engine failure, they had to force-land Wk Nr 0063, which carried the factory code NT+CG, near Neer-Andel to the east of Dordrecht in Holland; their injuries meant that they did not rejoin their unit again until October 1942. This might have been fortunate for them as ten days later the first of a series of operational losses occurred.

It is believed that around this time reconnaissance flights and anti-invasion patrols were carried out over the North Sea, and up to the East Coast of England, the aircraft involved flying at low-level and maintaining strict radio silence. On 3 August 1942, two aircraft, one of which was flown by Oberleutnant Maurer, and each carrying a bomb, took

A three-quarters type view of the same Erprobungsstaffel Me 210.

Two of Erprobungsstaffel's Me 210s pictured while airborne circa 1942.

off from Soesterberg to attack a convoy at sea off the Yorkshire coast. Flying at sea-level, the pair climbed to 1,200ft into a bank of mist, after which they dived to 600ft, released their bombs and headed for home, not knowing if their bombs had been successful.

So far, the Me 210 had just experienced Flak, but sooner or later it would meet the RAF. At 19.25 hours on 9 August 1942, Rhodesians Pilot Officer Norman Lucas and Pilot Officer Ian Munro of 266 Squadron, took off from RAF Matlask in Norfolk to undertake a patrol over the North Sea. After about thirty minutes they spotted an aircraft about a mile away approaching from their two o'clock and flying at zero feet. Being at 50ft, the aircraft passed beneath both Typhoons, but they identified it as German and believed it to be a Junkers Ju 88. Their combat report reads as follows:

> P/O Munro (Red 1) turned to port and P/O Lucas (Red 2) to starboard and chased it … E/a opened inaccurate green tracer fire and then started to weave to port but this brought him dead ahead of Red 2, he returned to his original course and presumably decided to rely on speed as he used his emergency boost. Red Section was overtaking fast. Red 1 gave a momentary burst and saw strikes low on water.
>
> Throttling to plus 2 boost, range was rapidly closed to 200yds and a three second burst given. E/a was flying straight and level. Red 2 also opened fire from port quarter a very short burst at 600yds and then 400yds and a longer burst at 200 yds.
>
> Immediately after opening fire on the last burst, flames appeared inboard of both engines. A hood came off and one of the crew started to climb out but as fire was continued, he slumped back. E/a attempted a belly landing but bounced, dropped a wing and went in nose first.

No Ju 88s were reported lost over the North Sea that night. However, Oberleutnant Ernst Haberland and Unteroffizier Heinz Danigel, flying Me 210 A-1 Wk Nr 2322 and coded GF+CB, were reported missing from an operational flight.

An Me 210A-1, with tactical markings of Erprobungsstaffel/Eprobungskommando Me 210, pictured over the North Sea in the summer of 1942.

This Me 210A-1 of Erprobungsstaffel/Eprobungskommando Me 210, coded 2H+DA, was also photographed in the summer of 1942.

Four days later, 266 Squadron struck again, but still failed to correctly identify what they had shot down. At about 18.30 hours on 13 August 1942, Me 210 A-1 Wk Nr 0184, now carrying the new unit tactical code 2H+VA, took off from Soesterberg on an anti-invasion reconnaissance up to the English eastern coast. Flying the aircraft was Leutnant Heinz Menger, with Unteroffizier Erich Rudolph as Bordfunker.

Thirty minutes later, four Typhoons of 266 Squadron, led by Flight Lieutenant Tony Johnston, got airborne from RAF Duxford in Cambridgeshire in the hope of catching a Ju 88 of the reconnaissance unit 3.(F)/122. The Typhoons' intention was to fly to just south of Southwold on the Suffolk coast, then fly some twenty-five to thirty miles out to sea, before heading north for fifty miles and then return south for a further fifty miles.

Forty minutes into the sortie, an aircraft was spotted flying west at zero feet. The Typhoons, flying line astern, turned port to intercept; the aircraft, which also turned to port, was thought to be a Ju 88. It was Tony Johnston, flying as Blue 1, who got closest first:

> Blue 1 got astern of the e/a which at once opened fire using tracer and self-destroying ammunition, some of which came close. Using full boost, range was closed but Blue 1 feared that the e/a might reach the cover of the rain storm so he gave a short burst at 1,000yds and saw strikes on the water below e/a. For the same reason he gave another short burst at 600yds, again short. Closing to 400yds he saw one strike on starboard engine.
>
> Closing from 300 to 30yds firing a series of short bursts he saw the port engine smoking and the starboard engine and under part of the fuselage catch fire. Up to this point, e/a had flown straight and level but when well on fire it climbed to 600ft,

The remains of Me 210 Wk Nr 1073, which was coded 2H+CA, on 6 September 1942.

> a hood cover came off and one man bailed out; e/a dropped a wing and went into the sea and sank.

Erich Rudolph subsequently recalled that when the Me 210s were off Great Yarmouth and flying at sea-level they had been attacked by four Typhoons flying in line astern at 19.36 hours. He had tried his best to return fire with the blister guns, but found it hard to bring them to bear. His pilot climbed to 600ft and with the port engine and fuselage on fire, he transmitted an SOS, jettisoned the cockpit canopy and bailed out. The aircraft then crashed into the sea and sank, taking its pilot with it. Rudolf was picked up six days later 'somewhat the worse for wear' and in no fit state to be interrogated.

On 19 August 1942, Eprobungskommando Me 210 as it was referred to in German records, was well and truly blooded when it became involved in actions around the Allies' Combined Operations raid on Dieppe. At 08.20 hours on that day, an Me 210 reported the presence of a convoy 25km north of Dieppe together with a number of torpedo boats.

At 10.00 hours, five Me 210s, together with three Do 217s, then attacked shipping off Dieppe. They reported two near misses with two of the three SC500 bombs dropped.

Six Me 210s operating from Évreux were back in action again at 11.30 hours. Their crews reported two near misses against warships off Dieppe.

Then, at 13.10 hours, five Me 210s with fighter escort attacked a transporter mid-Channel, dropping four SD250 and three SC500 bombs. One of the aircraft returned early with a technical problem.

A further attack probably took place at 16.35hours, but the exact circumstances of this is not known.

On 1 September 1942, Erprobungsstaffel/Eprobungskommando Me 210 became 16./KG 6. Coincidentally, a few days later, Major Walter Storp took command of the newly formed KG 6. Also at the start of the month, Walter Maurer carried out a night probing flight over East Anglia, this being made at heights between 0ft and 10,000ft. He was fortunate to hear British night fighter transmissions, which allowed him to turn and dive away.

Shortly after this, on 3 September 1942, he had a discussion with Major Storp, after which, on 5 September, it was decreed that the Me 210 could carry out its first bombing attack on mainland Britain.

Between 15.00 hours and 16.00 hours on 5 September 1942, two Me 210s, those flown by Oberleutnant Maurer and Feldwebel Max Blättler, took off from Soesterberg and flew towards the Thames Estuary at 26,000ft. With the probable target of Chatham, they were, however, intercepted off Southend by two Spitfires of 610 (County of Chester) Squadron. The latter were flown by two Australians, Flight Sergeant 'South' Creagh and Sergeant Rupert Gregory. Creagh attacked first. His target, correctly identified as an Me 210, had dived from 20,000ft to 15,000ft, at which Rupert Gregory took over:

> I closed in astern and fired a short burst closing from 400yds. I saw no results so I closed in to 100yds and fired a two second burst. The port engine began to burn

behind the nacelle. I noticed that the starboard propeller had stopped and the aircraft turned slowly to starboard and dived into the sea.

Both Blättler and Unteroffizier Reinhold Graf were killed when their Me 210A-1, Wk Nr 2348 and coded 2H+LA, crashed into the sea. Maurer, meanwhile, dropped his bomb near Southend and streaked back to Soesterberg. Less than twenty-four hours later, Maurer would not be as lucky.

Mid-morning on 6 September 1942, two Me 210s flown by Walter Maurer and Feldwebel Heinrich Mösges headed towards Middleborough, their route taking them initially towards Texel, and then west to a point ten miles off Hartlepool. From there, the pair turned west-south-west and headed towards the mouth of the River Tees.

However, at 11.16 hours, two Typhoons of 1 Squadron, flown by Pilot Officer Des Perrin and Pilot Officer Tom Bridges respectively, lifted off from RAF Acklington in Northumberland. They were ordered to fly towards the Farne Islands and then south to Blyth, climbing to 30,000ft. It was when they were off Redcar at 28,500ft that they spotted two aircraft which they identified as either Me 210s or Ju 88s. The raiders, they noted, were at the same height and headed north-west while weaving gently.

When these unidentified aircraft turned west, the Typhoons gave chase. After about four minutes, they spotted one of the aircraft jettisoning its bombs before turning steeply

Me 210A-1s were moved to the Mediterranean, where they flew with 10./ZG 26 and III./ZG 1.

A trio of Me 210A-1s photographed after their arrival in the Mediterranean area.

away from the coast. Perrin then went after the port aircraft, Me 210A-1, Wk Nr 0173, 2H+CA which was flown by Mösges, while Bridges concentrated on the starboard aircraft, which was flown by Maurer.

The RAF combat reports make quite exciting reading. Regarding Perrin, the following was written:

> Plt Off Perrin turned steeply to port, diving and following the port aircraft … Closing to approximately 250yds, he fired a two second cannon burst from astern and slightly to port. Pilot saw strikes and saw pieces fly off the port engine. He then crossed over and fired another two second burst from astern and slightly to starboard and saw strikes and pieces fly off starboard engine. Typhoon then began to overtake e/a and fired a third burst of one to two seconds from 100 to 50yds from dead astern and saw e/a's rudder on fire and partly shot away. E/a then turned on its back and dived vertically.

Perrin tried to follow, but he blacked out with his air speed indicator reading 520 mph. When he recovered, the starboard cockpit door had come loose and was hammering in the slipstream. So, having had a cursory look for his victim, he then returned to base.

What he did not witness is the tail of the German aircraft break off at 3,000ft, following which the rest of the stricken aircraft then fluttered down to crash on its back at New Buildings Farm, New Marske, near Redcar. The Bordfunker, Austrian Obergefreiter Eduard Czerny, whose 23rd birthday was that very day, had managed to get out, but his

A pair of Me 210A-1s flying low over a typical Mediterranean countryside.

parachute failed to open. Mösges also managed to get away from the aircraft just before it crashed, but he had left it too late and his body fell into a pool alongside a reservoir.

Meanwhile, Tom Bridges was busy attacking Walter Maurer's aircraft, Me 210A-1 Wk Nr 2321, which was coded 2H+HA:

> Pilot fired a short deflection burst from port quarter at long range to test cannons … . e/a continued turning to port and began diving in a south-east direction. Typhoon closed rapidly and fired two or three bursts at approximately 200yds from port quarter astern and saw strikes between port engine and fuselage and on top of the fuselage and cockpit cover. He saw pieces fly off and white smoke from port engine.
>
> E/a then began weaving violently but stopped turning to port. He then fired a final burst from 100 to 50yds from dead astern and slightly to port . He saw port engine catch fire and more pieces fly off. E/a then slowed down and dived steeply to port.

Like Perrin, Tom Bridges also blacked out in his dive. He recovered over Whitby, where he saw a launch headed for a patch of something in the sea. This turned out to be Maurer, who had bailed out and, none the worse for wear, landed in Robin Hood's Bay. He was picked up by the motor boat *Florence*. Also unwounded, Rudolf Jansen landed on land, coming down close to the village of Sledgate where he was taken prisoner by a holidaymaker. The pair's aircraft fell to earth at Sunnyside Farm, Thorpe, seven minutes after the other Me 210 had crashed.

Within twenty-four hours of the Me 210 being cleared for operations over Britain, three aircraft, including one flown by the Staffelkapitän, had been lost. Of those, two came down on land. Furthermore, the RAF had captured three crew and, as a result, managed to produce a very comprehensive intelligence report on both the aircraft and unit. In fact, the wreckage of Mösges' aircraft was recovered for analysis by the Royal Aircraft Establishment at Farnborough; Maurer's aircraft had not only disintegrated, but also caught fire, so would reveal little, if any, of its secrets.

It is believed that Leutnant Walter Lardy now took temporary command of 16./KG 6, but it is not known whether it flew any more missions over the UK. What is known, however, is that it moved from Soesterberg to Beauvais in France.

It suffered one more accident on 16 September 1942, when Me 210A-1 Wk Nr 2335 was all but written off as a result of an engine failure, crashing at Beauvais.

When Oberfeldwebel Hermann Bolten arrived back in October 1942, his aircraft now carried tactical codes 3E and the final letter Q. Then on 28 October 1942, he picked up a new Me 210 from the Messerschmitt factory at Augsburg and flew to the Mediterranean where the Me 210s would fly missions while subordinate to 10./ZG 26.

Bolten would fly just seventeen operational flights from Crete, Italy, Tunisia and Sicily, before, in January 1943, he would start flying the Ju 88C-6 with 10./ZG 26. From there he was sent back to Lechfeld in February 1943 to join a new unit-Erprobungsstaffel Me 410.

The Me 410 was an improvement on the Me 210, and when cleared for operations with V./KG 2 (formerly II./KG 40) it started to appear over the UK from July 1943 onwards. The next Fernnachtjagd phase was about to begin.

Most Me 210s did not last long in the Mediterranean. This is possibly Me 210A-1, Wk Nr 110205, and coded 2N+LT, of 9./ZG 1, which suffered engine failure on take-off at Gerbini on 4 March 1943.

Chapter 4

Final Fernnachtjagd 1943–1944

Following the failure of the Me 210 as a credible replacement for the Messerschmitt Bf 110, the Luftwaffe pushed ahead with the development and introduction of the Me 410. This was essentially the same as the 210, but with Daimler Benz DB 603A engines, which increased the aircraft's length by eight inches. It also had other minor modifications such as leading edge slots.

The initial version was the Me 410A-1. This was designed as a light bomber with fixed forward firing machine-guns and cannon, two rearward firing remotely controlled cannon and an internal bomb load of two 250 kg bombs. The A-1/U1 was an armed photo-recce version, the A-1/U2 a heavy fighter, and the A-1/U4 a bomber destroyer with a 5cm cannon. These were further improved with the A-2 (destroyer), A-3 (reconnaissance), B-1 (bomber), B-2 (destroyer) and B-3 (reconnaissance). It was the Me 410A-1 that was now used for Fernnachtjagd missions over Britain from late June 1943.

The Luftwaffe had decided that II./KG 40 (just 4 and 5 Staffel), which had been carrying out bombing attacks against British targets with the Do 217, would now operate

The Me 410 differed very little in appearance to its predecessor.

Most of these Me 410s seen here at the Messerschmitt factory at Augsburg were converted from Me 210s. The Me 410A-1 coded SI+ID was Wk Nr 2100110238, while SI+IF was Wk Nr 2100110240. Both were formerly Me 210A-1s.

the Me 410A-1. It would also be re-designated V./KG 2 from 1 June 1943, and would be commanded by Hauptmann Friedrich-Wilhelm Methner.

Methner, who had recently taken over from Major Martin Kästner, formerly Kommandeur of II./KG 40, was an experienced pilot who began his operational career as a transport pilot with 2./KGrzbV 1. He had 122 operational flights to his credit and had been awarded the Frontflugspange in Gold as early as 7 May 1941, and the Deutsches Kreuz in Gold in November 1942 having commanded 4./KG 40.

The distinctive canopy of an Me 410.

The rear firing MG131s seen on a captured Me 410, 1945.

The forward firing armament and bomb bay are visible on this Me 410A-1.

Me 410A-1 U5+NX of 13./KG 2, 1943.

Methner had recently gone training at the Verbandsführerschule KG 101 and at the end of June 1943 was recommended for command of the new unit. Commanded by Oberleutnant Günter Näder, 5./KG 2 had also begun receiving a number of Me 410s around the same time and would go to form 16./KG 2. Training of aircrew was undertaken by Oberleutnant Eugen Limberg's 13./KG 2.

Although designated as pathfinders, V./KG 2 would operate at night, dropping bombs predominantly on airfields, as well as attacking RAF bombers taking off or returning

Mechanics working on the rear-facing armament of an Me 410.

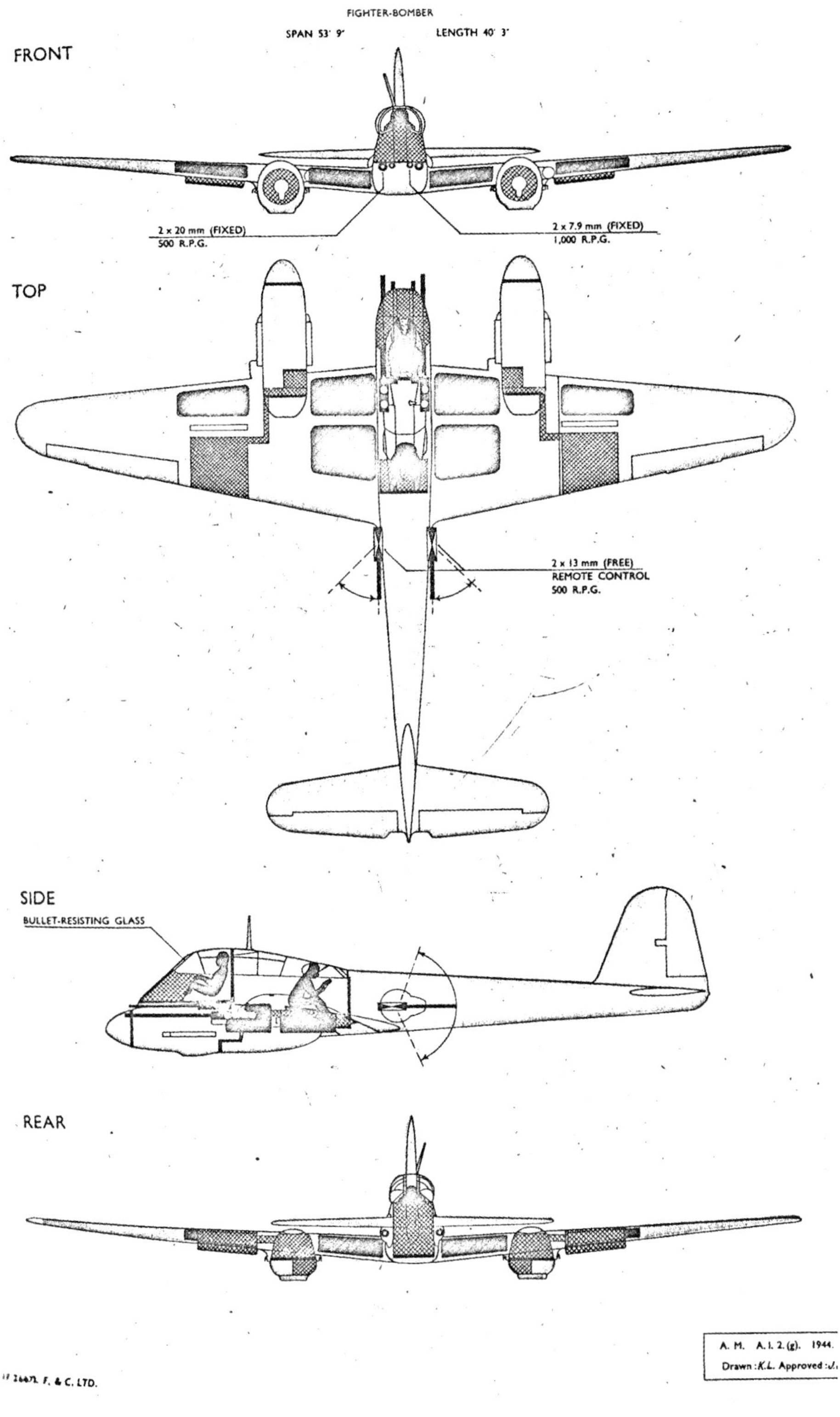

An RAF Aircraft identification sheet dated 1944 for the Me 410.

from missions over Europe if the opportunity arose. The logbook of Unteroffizier Albert Wolk, a Bordfunker with 4./KG 40, shows that he started converting at Memmingen, together with his pilot, Unteroffizier Heinz Holzmann, on 5 June 1943, before moving to Lille-Vendeville. It was from the latter that they flew their first operational flight with a Me 410 of 14./KG 2, an intruder mission in the Cambridge area, during the early hours of 23 August 1943.

The first recorded Me 410 loss on operations was an A-1. Crewed by Feldwebel Peter Hoff and Feldwebel Walter Hillebrand of 16./KG 2, it crashed at Avord on 27 June 1943, having been damaged in combat, presumably by Flak. Both crew were killed.

The first loss attributable to an Allied night fighter came at 00.10 hours on 14 July 1943. On this occasion, Feldwebel Franz Zwissler and Oberfeldwebel Leo Raida were shot down off Felixstowe by Flight Lieutenant Nigel Bunting and his Nav/Rad, Pilot Officer Fred French, of 85 Squadron.

This being the first Me 410 to have been shot down, the RAF pilot described the combat in some detail:

> It was crossing from starboard to port and Operator brought pilot in behind at 10,000ft range. When the range closed to 7,000ft a visual was obtained on the exhausts but the e/a appeared to have gained height. Climbing at full boost and revs, pilot very gradually reduced the range but when radiator flaps were opened on account of over-heating, the e/a gained very slightly. When radiator flaps were closed however, the Mosquito decreased range.
>
> The chase was continued in this manner for about 15 minutes at 220mph IAS during which the e/a took no evasive action. Eventually a visual was obtained against the light northern sky at a range of 1,800ft, the height being 25,000ft.
>
> No resins were showing nor was there any response to the interrogator. The type was definitely not British and the pilot believed it to be an Me 410. He closed to

This Me 410A-1, Wk Nr 10042 and coded GH+YG, was damaged while serving with I./KG 51 at Hörsching on 6 October 1943.

A view of the Me 410A-1 coded U5+CX of 13./KG 2, 1943.

Another shot of Me 410A-1 coded U5+CX of 13./KG 2 with its engines running, 1943.

Me 410A-1 U5+CX of 13./KG 2, about to take-off in 1943.

Another Me 410A-1 of 13./KG 2, this time U5+BX, pictured in the summer of 1943. It is possible that this was Wk Nr 10298, which crashed at Montigny during a training flight on 15 December 1943. The pilot, Feldwebel Ernst Kagelmacher, was killed, while Gefreiter Karl Osterwind was injured.

Mechanics working on the DB603A engines of a V./KG 2 Me 410A-1.

Hauptmann Friedrich-Wilhelm Methner, the first Kommandeur of V./KG 2, who was reported missing in action on 16 July 1943.

Oberfeldwebel Leo Raida of 16./KG 2 was the Bordfunker of the Me 410 shot down by Nigel Bunting on 14 July 1943. (*via Simon Parry*)

Aircrew from 85 Squadron in 1942. The first pilot to shoot down an Me 410 was Flight Lieutenant Nigel Bunting on 14 July 1943. He can be seen in the back row, fourth from left.

Hauptmann Methner was shot down by Flight Lieutenant Bernard Thwaites of 85 Squadron, who is seated far left. Squadron Leader Bill Maguire, seated second from the right, and Lieutenant Johan Rad, seated far right, also accounted for Me 410s.

> 200yds to attack but his aim was spoiled by getting into the slipstream of the e/a. He dived below and closed in again firing two short bursts of 1½ and one seconds at the fuselage which burst into flames immediately.
>
> The e/a seemed to get out of control and went down on its back with the fuselage burning furiously, its dive becoming vertical. Pilot watched it until it nearly hit the sea and just after he lost his visual there was a very bright red flash.

Bunting also described what he had seen that night:

> The e/a was recognised from astern as an Me 210 or Me 410 by the low wing position, high fin and distinctive position of the tail plane in relation to the wing. The four exhausts were bright blue and easily distinguishable from those of a Mosquito. When it was on fire the shape of the fin was clearly seen as was the shape of the cockpit, both conforming to those on an Me 210. The wings on which the black crosses were visible also seemed to be those of Me 210. As the Me 410 is known to be on the Western Front now but the Me 210 is not, pilot claims a Me 410 destroyed.

The next Me 410 loss, two nights later, was a serious one. This involved Hauptmann Friedrich-Wilhelm Methner, who was shot down off Dunkirk, probably a victim of Flight Lieutenant Bernard Thwaites and Flying Officer Bill Clemo, again of 85 Squadron:

> Pilot put his nose down slightly and range closed fairly fast to about 6,000ft when a visual of e/a silhouette was obtained against the light northern sky. E/a climbed, silhouette being momentarily lost against a darker layer of high cloud. Operator

Oberleutnant Hermann Walther, right, was one of the first pilots to claim an RAF bomber on 11 August 1943, though the identity of his victim cannot be confirmed.

> ordered a gentle left turn and climb, a visual of the silhouette and exhausts being obtained against the light northern sky from 4,000ft. The view was quarter astern and the e/a clearly identified as of the Me 210 type probably an Me 410.
>
> The Operator informed the pilot that the range was decreasing too rapidly. Pilot throttled back and opened fire from 200yds allowing one ring deflection as e/a was turning starboard.
>
> The starboard engine immediately blew up, flames spreading instantaneously to the fuselage. Pilot broke off at about 70yds easing the stick back to avoid debris as the e/a disintegrated and went down in flames.

Thirty-one-year-year-old Methner was posthumously promoted to Major. He was replaced as Gruppen Kommandeur by Hauptmann Kurt Heintz. Heintz had been awarded the Ritterkreuz with 9./KG 6 (formerly 9./LG 1) on 17 October 1942, and had been instructing with III./KG 101 prior to moving to V./KG 2 following his predecessor's death.

There would be one more loss in July 1943, when Oberleutnant Helmut Biermann of 14./KG 2 was shot down off Beachy Head on 30 July 1943. The victor was Wing Commander Geoff Park of 256 Squadron.

German records reveal that during July 1943, London, Ipswich, Felixstowe, Brighton and Chelmsford were all bombed by Me 410s in conventional bombing attacks. At least one intruder mission was carried out against airfields in the Cambridge/Newmarket area on 14 July 1943.

On 12 August 1943, Me 410A-1, 226, U5+AE of 14./KG 2 crashed at Le Mans due to engine failure having run out of fuel during an attack on Bournemouth. Leutnant Günther Schneke and Gefreiter Otto Kröger were both killed.

The first intruder kill by a Hornet, as the Me 410 was also known, occurred on the night of 10 August 1943. This involved Unteroffizier Johann Trenke of 16./KG 2, who shot down an Avro Lancaster of 115 Squadron. The bomber, which was being flown by Flying Officer John Erwin, disintegrated over farmland at East Hall Far, Boughton Monchelsea in Kent. All seven men on board were killed. A second claim for a Stirling by Leutnant Hermann Walther of 15./KG 2 cannot be matched to any RAF loss.

The same night a number of airfields were attacked, one of which was RAF Feltwell. Feltwell was the home of 192 Squadron, which reported the following:

> One Halifax [DK246 captained by Pilot Officer Arthur Willis] and one Wellington [HE498 captained by Flying Officer Alexander Davidson] of 192 Sqn carried out special duty operations tonight. The Halifax operated off the Frisian Islands and off the coast of Denmark taking off at 2224hrs and returning to base at 0512hrs. The Wellington operated over Germany in the vicinity of Nürnberg taking off at 2300hrs and returning to base at 0425hrs.
>
> At 0430hrs the aerodrome was attacked by an Me 210 [*sic*] which presumably followed our Wellington in and, taking advantage of the flare-path being lit, flew low over the aerodrome, attacked the flare-path with cannon fire and dropped two 100kg and one 500lb canister of Butterfly anti-personnel bombs. There were no casualties

Hauptmann Kurt Heintz took command of the V Gruppe following the death of Hauptmann Methner.

> and the only damage suffered was two craters on the airfield six feet deep and 12ft wide which did not render the aerodrome unserviceable.

The German pilot was probably Hauptmann Wilhelm Schmitter of 15./KG 2, whose claim to have damaged a number of aircraft was overly optimistic. A very experienced aviator, having flown with 1./Küstenfliegergruppe 706 from October 1937, at the start of the war he was an Unteroffizier on 1./Küstenfliegergruppe 906.

In October 1940, Schmitter was posted away to undergo further blind flying training being promoted to Leutnant in November 1940. He would move to 4./KG 40 (subordinate to I./KG 40) on 9 February 1941, flying the He 111, his first operational flight being on 3 May 1941.

Schmitter began converting to the Do 217 in July 1941, and he flew his first and last mission of 1941 on 7 September that year as he was injured in a car accident on 25 September. By this time he had flown at least 122 operational flights against Britain. He rejoined 4./KG 40 in January 1942, and, from 14 February 1942, restarted operational flying and carried out a number of special missions against land targets, most of the time being part of Stab II./KG 40. He would receive the Ehrenpokal in January 1942, the Deutsches Kreuz in Gold in May 1942, and the Ritterkreuz in September 1942. The Ritterkreuz came after one unsuccessful and two successful lone daylight attacks on Leamington Spa.

Promoted to Hauptmann in March 1943, Schmitter was given command of 5./KG 40. After converting to the Me 410, this became 15./KG 2 in June the same year. Between

Oberleutnant Fritz Sengschmitt, Staffelkapitän 14./KG 2, and Oberleutnant Wilhelm Schmitter, Staffelkapitän 15./KG 2. (*Jeremy Green*)

Oberst Dietrich Peltz, Angiffsführer England, visiting KG 2.

7 September 1941 and 18 May 1943, he had undertaken sixty operational flights with the Do 217.

Operations and successes were sporadic, and as the year progressed less intruder missions were completed, while more bombing and then pathfinder sorties against London (usually with two SC250 bombs) became the norm. This appears to coincide with the appointment of Oberst Dietrich Peltz as the commanding officer of IX Fliegerkorps in August 1943 after which he attempted to coordinate bombing attacks on England, apparently seeing the Hornet better suited as a bomber or pathfinder as opposed to an intruder.

August 1943 would prove to be a busier month for V./KG 2 with intruder, pathfinding and bombing missions being carried out at least on eight nights with up to fourteen aircraft. Targets ranged from Bournemouth in the south-west, to Colchester in the south-east, and as far north as Lincoln.

With this increase in operations, service losses were inevitable. On 12 August 1943, Leutnant Günther Schnecke and his Bordfunker from 14./KG 2 were killed when they suffered engine failure, due to a lack of fuel while returning from an attack on Bournemouth, and crashed at Le Mans. Eleven Me 410s were reported to have taken part in this diversionary attack; eight bombs exploded around 01.00 hours, killing thirteen civilians, and injuring a further eighteen.

Six days later, Oberleutnant Helmut Nieber and his Bordfunker of 15./KG 2 were injured when they suffered an engine fire returning from a major, but futile, attack on Lincoln

The tail of Feldwebel Walter Hartmann's Me 410A-1, which was shot down by Squadron Leader Geoff Howitt of 85 Squadron on 23 August 1943. (*Andy Saunders*)

Unteroffizier Hans-Johann Oertel of 14./KG 2, who was also shot down on 23 August 1943. (*via Simon Parry*)

Feldwebel Werner Benner of 16./KG 2 was killed in action on the night of 23 August 1943. (*via Simon Parry*)

Unteroffizier Hermann Reimers, Bordfunker to Feldwebel Benner. (*via Simon Parry*)

and crashed near Épinoy. Niebler was killed in an accident while leading 5./KG 51 on 29 May 1944.

The first combat losses came in the early hours of 23 August 1943, when fourteen aircraft carried out intruder attacks in the Cambridge area. Flight Lieutenant Clive Kirkland of 29 Squadron shot down the Me 410 flown by Unteroffizier Hans-Johann Oertel of 14./KG 2 twenty-five miles north-east of Foreness, albeit the night fighter crew thought they had attacked a Ju 88.

Twenty-five minutes before this, however, Squadron Leader Geoff Howitt of 85 Squadron had intercepted the Me

410 flown by Feldwebel Walter Hartmann of 16./KG 2:

> Pilot recognised the e/a as an Me 210-type which had extremely bright yellow exhausts. A strong searchlight beam now illuminated the e/a enabling pilot to get a perfect silhouette and showing up the crosses on the wings. Pilot now got dead astern and pulling the nose up slightly fired a short burst whereupon the e/a immediately burst into flames with a vivid flash and showers of burning pieces flew off in all directions. The e/a went down burning merrily and crashed near Harwich.

Squadron Leader Paul Arbon of 29 Squadron, who shot down Hauptmann Wilhelm Schmitter on 24 August 1943. (*via Ed McManus*)

Amazingly, the Bordfunker, Obergefreiter Michael Meurer, managed to bail out before the tail and wings broke away; the aircraft's remains crashed at Chemondiston. Meurer was the first member of V./KG 2 to be captured and he confirmed the identity of the new unit. He also stated the aircraft was brand new and had only been delivered to 16./KG 2 a few hours before being shot down. Other than that, he revealed little else to his interrogators.

The following night would see another series of Fernnachtjagd missions over East Anglia – and another air combat victory, though this would be achieved at a cost. Feldwebel Heinz Graeber, Bordfunker of Hauptmann Wilhelm Schmitter of 15./KG 2, would shoot down the Lancaster of 97 Sqn flown by Sergeant Cliff Chatten returning to Bourn from attacking Berlin. The Lancaster caught fire and the pilot, who had been wounded in the leg and ribs by gunfire, ordered the crew to bail out; the aircraft crashed near Shouldham, south-east of Swaffham. Sadly the rear gunner's body was found in the wreckage. Cliff Chatten would recover from his wounds and would later be commissioned and awarded the DSO and DFC.

Success for the intruders ended there, though, as a number of Mosquito night fighters had already begun to exact revenge. The first claim for an Me 410 that night went to Wing Commander Bob Mack of 29 Squadron, who shot down his victim forty miles east of RAF Manston at 23.22 hours.

This was followed by Flight Lieutenant Geoff Goodman of 29 Squadron near Dunkirk at 02.25 hours, and then Lieutenant Johann Rad of 85 Squadron off East Anglia fifteen minutes later. For its part, 15./KG 2 reported the loss of Leutnant Helmut Barzel and his Bordfunker, while 16./KG 2 would confirm the loss of Feldwebel Werner Benner that

Standing front left in the leather jacket is Oberleutnant Günter Näder, Staffelkapitän of 16./KG 2, who was killed on 4 September 1943.

night. Benner and his Bordfunker were believed to have bailed out; the pilot's body was later washed ashore in Belgium.

There would be one more claim and one more loss this night. Squadron Leader Paul Arbon and Flying Officer Alfred Ashcroft of 29 Squadron, both of whom were Battle of Britain veterans, took off from RAF Bradwell Bay at 02.23 hours. They were soon given a contact by Ground Controller Squadron Leader David Mawhood.

Flying at 2,000ft, they detected an aircraft slightly above them and dead ahead:

> Closed to 400ft and saw silhouette of Me 210. Opened fire at 150yds with four bursts total 5½ seconds and saw many strikes on port engine and fuselage. E/a turned slightly port and a further burst caused starboard engine to explode and e/a gave off much white smoke and lost height rapidly. Debris hit our aircraft. Visual was then lost but a large flash was seen on the sea 10 miles north of Knocke at 0333hrs

Fresh from shooting down Sergeant Chatten's Lancaster, Wilhelm Schmitter and Bordfunker Heinz Graeber were heading home over the sea at relatively low-level when Paul Arbon struck. Schmitter managed to ditch the crippled Me 410 during which Heinz Graeber sustained serious injuries, breaking both legs. Both men managed to get into dinghies and, having been able to send out a distress signal, were soon rescued. Schmitter was uninjured while Graeber went straight to hospital where, in October 1943,

Oberleutnant Günter Näder's replacement was Hauptmann Karl-Egon Frhr von Dalwigk zu Lichtenfels, seen here.

Hauptmann Karl-Egon Frhr von Dalwigk zu Lichtenfels is seen here on the left with V./KG 2.

he received the Ritterkreuz. After his left leg had to be amputated, Graeber never flew again on operations, while Wilhelm Schmitter would be flying again in exactly a month's time – but was not destined to see the year out.

There would be just one more loss in August 1943, when, on the last day of the month, Leutnant Carl Jukel of 14./KG 2 failed to return from a Fernnachtjagd mission against

Major Wolf-Dietrich Meister, far left, took command of 16./KG 2, then I./KG 51, and finally KG 51. Here he is talking to Hauptmann Hans-Joachim Grundmann who took command of 6./KG 51 in April 1944. Between them is Oberleutnant Bernd Sartor, Geschwader Adjutant.

airfields in the Lincoln area. There were no claims by night fighters that night and Jukel's body was later washed ashore in Holland a month later.

The first loss of the month occurred on 4 September 1943, when Deutsches Kreuz in Gold winner Oberleutnant Günter Näder Staffelkapitän of 16./KG 2 suffered engine failure returning to Schiphol while stalking RAF bombers which had been attacking Berlin. His Me 410 crashed at Zeist, killing him and his Bordfunker. He would be promoted to Hauptmann posthumously.

Leutnant Heinz-Günther Baack of 14./KG 51 claimed to have shot down a twin-engine aircraft near Lincoln during the night. However, this cannot be matched with any RAF losses.

Günter Näder was then replaced as Staffelkapitän by Hauptmann Egon Freiherr von Dalwigk zu Lichtenfels. He was a pre-war officer who had flown with 2./KG 255 (later 2./KG 51) from April 1937, and had been taken prisoner on 18 June 1940 when his Ju 88 suffered engine failure during an operational flight. He would then become an instructor on Luftkriegsschule 1 and 4 from February 1941 to September 1942, after which he became Staffelkapitän of 7./LG 1 (which a month later became 7./KG 6) by which time he had been promoted to Hauptmann.

Posted to Eprobungsstaffel Me 410 on 12 July 1943, he arrived on 16./KG 2 on 8 September 1943. He was the brother of Hauptmann Friedrich-Karl Freiherr von Dalwigk zu Lichtenfels, the Gruppenkommandeur of I./StG 77, who was shot down and killed on 9 July 1940 and would be awarded the Ritterkreuz and posthumously promoted to Major.

In total, there were eight nights in September 1943 when intruder missions were undertaken. One in particular came on the early hours of 16 September 1943, when an Me 410 from 15./KG 2, which was flown by Unteroffizier Hans-Willi Brogmus with Unteroffizier Helmut Lindemann as his Bordfunker, attacked the former RNAS airfield at Ford in West Sussex. They too had followed a landing aircraft in and then attacked.

The West Sussex County Council Action Officer's Minute Book reported that Ford was bombed at 02.40 hours on 16 September 1943. Two 50kg Sprengbombe Dickwandig/SD bombs were dropped; both exploded with no damage or casualties. The raider also dropped four AB23 SD2 bomb

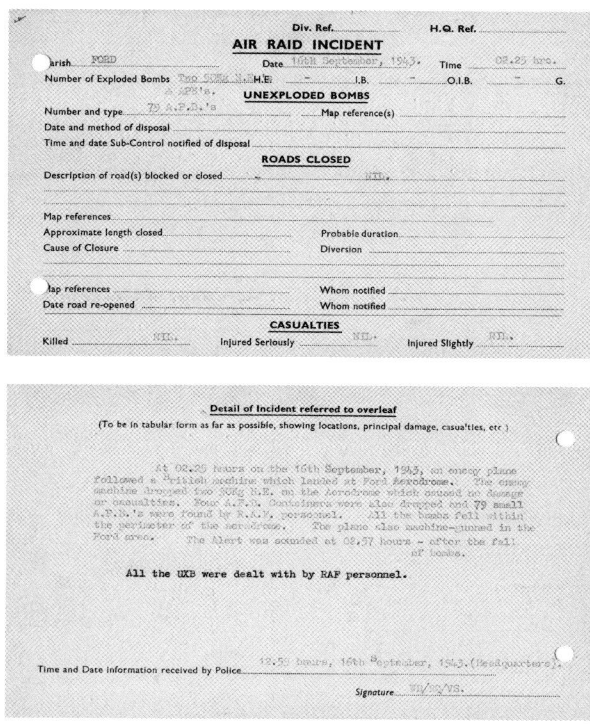

Div. Ref. H.Q. Ref.

AIR RAID INCIDENT

Parish FORD Date 16th September, 1943. Time 02.25 hrs.

Number of Exploded Bombs Two 50Kg H.E.'s H.E. - I.B. - O.I.B. - G.

4 APB's.

UNEXPLODED BOMBS

Number and type 79 A.P.B.'s Map reference(s)

Date and method of disposal

Time and date Sub-Control notified of disposal

ROADS CLOSED

Description of road(s) blocked or closed - NIL.

Map references

Approximate length closed Probable duration

Cause of Closure Diversion

Map references Whom notified

Date road re-opened Whom notified

CASUALTIES

Killed NIL. Injured Seriously NIL. Injured Slightly NIL.

Detail of Incident referred to overleaf

(To be in tabular form as far as possible, showing locations, principal damage, casualties, etc)

At 02.25 hours on the 16th September, 1943, an enemy plane followed a British machine which landed at Ford Aerodrome. The enemy machine dropped two 50Kg H.E. on the Aerodrome which caused no damage or casualties. Four A.P.B. Containers were also dropped and 79 small A.P.B.'s were found by R.A.F. personnel. All the bombs fell within the perimeter of the aerodrome. The plane also machine-gunned in the Ford area. The Alert was sounded at 02.57 hours - after the fall of bombs.

All the UXB were dealt with by RAF personnel.

Time and Date information received by Police 12.55 hours, 16th September, 1943.(Headquarters).

Signature WD/SQ/VS.

A Police incident card detailing the attack on Ford by 15./KG 2. (*Martin Mace/Historic Military Press*)

containers with twenty-three SD2 Butterfly bombs each. Of the latter, seventy-nine had been accounted for by the time the report was made at 16.00 hours; a search for the remainder was still underway. It was stated that there was no possibility of any having fallen outside the aerodrome.

As for Ford, recorded the following was recorded in its Operations Record Book:

> At 0225hrs an unidentified twin-engine enemy aircraft made a glide attack at 40ft. on Ford airfield. Three HE, approximately 50kg and several 2kg anti-personnel (Butterfly) bombs were dropped, 79 of which did not explode. There were no casualties. A Bomb Disposal Squad arrived from West Malling in charge of Flt Lts D H Bennett and C B Smith to deal with the unexploded anti-personnel bombs

The same night saw Oberfeldwebel Horst Müller of 15./KG 2 fail to return from an intruder mission, the latter stated as being in the Cambridge area. Apparently the Me 410s were following back RAF bombers which had attacked Montluçon. It would appear that he fell victim to a Mosquito of 29 Squadron that was crewed by Flying Officer Brian Jarvis and Flying Officer George Smith some thirty miles south-east of Beachy Head:

> A contact was obtained at two miles range at starboard and below crossing slightly to port. Mosquito lost height down to 2,000ft and increased speed and slowly closed in to 1,200ft range and obtained visual of four electric blue exhausts. On closing in further to about 500ft the target was seen to be weaving slightly up and down and a silhouette was seen and the aircraft identified as a Me 410.
>
> Fire was opened at 200yds from astern and below 1–1½ burst being given and the enemy aircraft immediately burst into flames and slowed up. The Mosquito overtook to starboard obtaining another excellent silhouette before aircraft spiralled down onto the sea where it was seen to burn furiously for a time and then subside.

Jarvis then set out to return to RAF Ford but because of the attack by Unteroffizier Brogmus they had to divert to RAF Tangmere. It is interesting to note that in combats with Me 410s so far, RAF night fighter pilots commented on the vivid exhaust flames emitted by the Me 410, a sure-fire means of identification.

The next recorded intruder mission occurred on the night of 22 September 1943, when fourteen aircraft took off to intercept RAF bombers returning from Hannover. Thirty-five-year-old Major Wolf-Dietrich Meister had recently been posted to 14./KG 2, which had previously been commanded by Ritterkreuz winner Oberleutnant Fritz Sengschmitt who had been posted to 2./ZG 26.

A pre-war officer with I./KG 252, Meister had flown operationally with 1./KG 2 in Poland in September 1939 before a being posted to a number of ground or staff tours. In May 1943, he was posted to Schlachtgeschwader 101 and two months later to I./KG 101. On 21 August 1943, he arrived on 14./KG 2 and would take command of the Staffel on 6 October 1943.

On the night of 22 September 1943, Meister claimed to have shot down a four-engine aircraft near Lincoln at 01.34 hours. This turned out to be a Lancaster of 57 Squadron flown by Australian Pilot Officer Gordon Duff; his bomber was attacked returning to RAF East Kirby and crashed at Sauls Field Farm, Spilsby. Its demise was attributed to 'enemy intruder action'. Two of the Lancaster's crew managed to bail out, though Duff and four others were killed. The following account appeared in HQ Bomber Command Routine Orders on 6 October 1943:

Oberleutnant Rudolf Abrahamczik of 14./KG 2, who shot down a Lancaster of 101 Squadron on 28 September 1943.

> The C-in-C wishes to bring to the notice of all ranks in the Command the courage and devotion to duty displayed by members of a crew of No.57 Sqn on the night of 22–23 September 1943 when returning from an attack on Hanover.
>
> A Lancaster aircraft captained by Plt Off Duff was attacked by an unidentified aircraft at 4,000ft when in the circuit at base. The Lancaster was set on fire by the fighter's first burst and a violent explosion occurred in the port wing. Plt Off Duff succeeded in retaining control and gave the order to abandon the aircraft which was burning along the port wing and was almost unmanageable.
>
> The Bomb Aimer and Flight Engineer bailed out safely at 2,000ft and 1,500ft respectively. Plt Off Duff remained at the controls and succeeded in keeping the aircraft level until at 1,000ft when it made a tight turn and dived into the ground. The two members of the crew who landed safely undoubtedly owe their lives to Plt Off Duff's efforts to give his crew the chance to abandon the aircraft.
>
> Throughout the entire incident, Flt Sgt Pryde engaged the aircraft with fire from the rear turret and was last seen to be still firing as the aircraft went into its last dive.

The operation that night was the first that Unteroffizier Hans-Willi Brogmus and Unteroffizier Helmut Lindemann of 15./KG 2 had flown since attacking Ford on 16 September 1943. They reported taking off from Vitry at 00.13 hours but were forced to land at Melsbroek at 01.50 hours as they were intercepted by a night fighter which had damaged their starboard engine. This was a Mosquito of 85 Squadron flown by Flight Lieutenant Cyril Houghton, with Flight Lieutenant Arthur Patston as his Nav/Rad. Once again, the Me 410's exhaust flames were a clear advantage to the RAF crew:

> Pilot got a visual of exhausts at 2,000ft range, e/a weaving very slightly but altering height. This made the exhausts difficult to follow as they kept disappearing but a

Oberleutnant Rudolf Abrahamczik, in the centre, talking to Hauptmann Walter Schmidt (Gr IA) and Oberleutnant Rudiger Thiemann (Gr NO). Behind them is Me 410A-1 U5+FE of 14./KG 2.

Another view of Oberleutnant Rudolf Abrahamczik talking to the same officers.

Formation flying being carried out by Me 410A-1s of 16./KG 2.

Another shot of the Me 410A-1s of 16./KG 2 in formation.

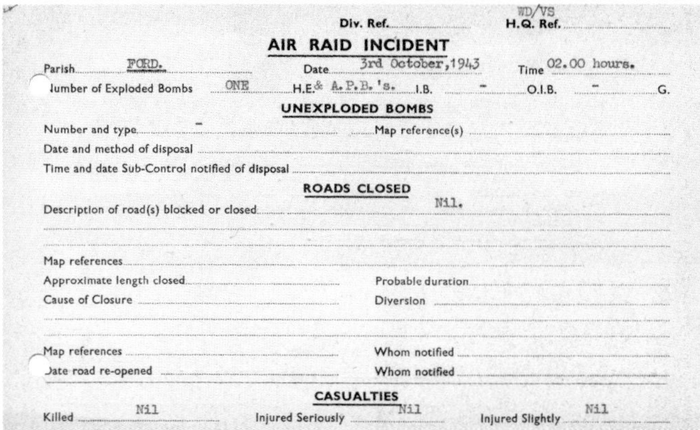

WD/VS
Div. Ref. H.Q. Ref.

AIR RAID INCIDENT

Parish FORD. Date 3rd October, 1943 Time 02.00 hours.
Number of Exploded Bombs ONE H.E.& A.P.B.'s. I.B. - O.I.B. - G.

UNEXPLODED BOMBS

Number and type - Map reference(s)
Date and method of disposal
Time and date Sub-Control notified of disposal

ROADS CLOSED

Description of road(s) blocked or closed Nil.

Map references
Approximate length closed Probable duration
Cause of Closure Diversion

Map references Whom notified
Date road re-opened Whom notified

CASUALTIES

Killed Nil Injured Seriously Nil Injured Slightly Nil

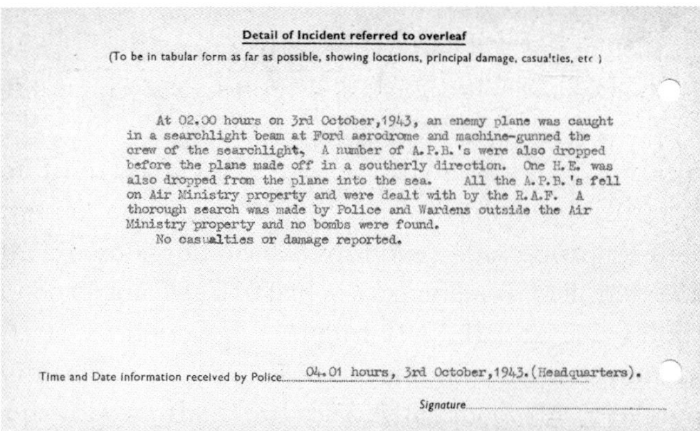

Detail of Incident referred to overleaf

(To be in tabular form as far as possible, showing locations, principal damage, casualties, etc.)

At 02.00 hours on 3rd October, 1943, an enemy plane was caught in a searchlight beam at Ford aerodrome and machine-gunned the crew of the searchlight. A number of A.P.B.'s were also dropped before the plane made off in a southerly direction. One H.E. was also dropped from the plane into the sea. All the A.P.B.'s fell on Air Ministry property and were dealt with by the R.A.F. A thorough search was made by Police and Wardens outside the Air Ministry property and no bombs were found.

No casualties or damage reported.

Time and Date information received by Police 04.01 hours, 3rd October, 1943. (Headquarters).

Signature

A second Police incident card detailing an attack on Ford, this time on 3 October 1943, by an unidentified Me 410 of V./KG 2. (*Martin Mace/Historic Military Press*)

A Me 410A-1 of V./KG 2.

> visual of the silhouette was obtained from about 200ft when the exhausts were clearly visible as four distinct flames.
>
> Pilot recognised e/a as an Me 410 and as the e/a began to peel off to starboard, a good plan view was seen. Pilot gave a short burst of deflection and observed strikes between starboard engine and fuselage followed by a huge yellowish-white explosion in the starboard engine. The e/a immediately swung in towards its turn and pilot had to pull up sharply to avoid a collision as the e/a disappeared underneath going down vertically and disappearing below the Mosquito.

For Brogmus and Lindemann, their luck would run out one month and eight days later.

There would be one more success for V./KG 2 when on 28 September 1943, Oberleutnant Rudolf Abrahamcik of 14./KG 2 shot down a Lancaster of 101 Squadron that, flown by Pilot Officer Desmond Skipper, was returning from bombing Hannover. They were on their way back to RAF Ludford Magna but had been instructed to divert to RAF Lindholme when Abrahamczik attacked them. The Lancaster crashed near Wickenby; all eight crew were killed.

Bordfunker Unteroffizier Gottfried Wendler of 15./KG 2 claimed to have damaged two bombers near Great Yarmouth this night. It is not known who his pilot was. Wendler was killed flying with Leutnant Rolf Proposch on 31 October 1943; a letter of commendation for the EK II was found on Wendler's body mentioning this combat and that he had taken part in five Fernnachtjagd operations.

Abrahamczik's victory would be the last confirmed Me 410 intruder kill by V./KG 2. The next claim came on 31 March 1944, by which time V./KG 2 had become II./KG 51.

October 1943 would herald a change for V./KG 2 with just two recorded Fernnachtjagd missions being flown at the start of the month, but there were eight bombing missions against London. There would also be at least three daylight fighter defence missions.

Unteroffizier Heinz Holzmann of 14./KG 2 would file two Fernnachtjagd claims in the Bedford area on 3 October 1943, and Oberfeldwebel Wilhelm Wessel of 16./KG 2 would report having damaged two aircraft on the same night. These cannot be matched to any RAF losses, and, in any case, were not confirmed by the Luftwaffe.

Major Wolf-Dietrich Meister, Staffelkapitän of 14./KG 2 since 6 October 1943, claimed a four-engine bomber in daylight on 9 October 1943, with another on 14 October 1943, as did Unteroffizier Heinz Holzmann of 14./KG 2 and Feldwebel Hermann Bolten of V./KG 2; the claims on 14 October 1943 were not confirmed. These daylight fighter missions show how misguided the Luftwaffe was in the employment of experienced aircrew, who specialised in night bomber missions, on daylight fighter missions, in an aircraft which would prove itself inferior to American day fighters.

Another change also came on 22 October 1943, when Major Wolf-Dietrich Meister became Kommandeur of the Me 410-equipped I./KG 51. On 11 October 1943, the then Kommandeur, Hauptmann Klaus Häberlen, was summoned to Germany where he was sacked by Reichsmarschall Herman Göring. He left his Gruppe four days later. Command of 14./KG 2 passed to Oberleutnant Rudolf Abrahamczik.

The remains of Leutnant Rolf Proposch's Me 410A-1 of 15./KG 2, which came down at Frimley Green on 31 October 1943. (*Andy Saunders*)

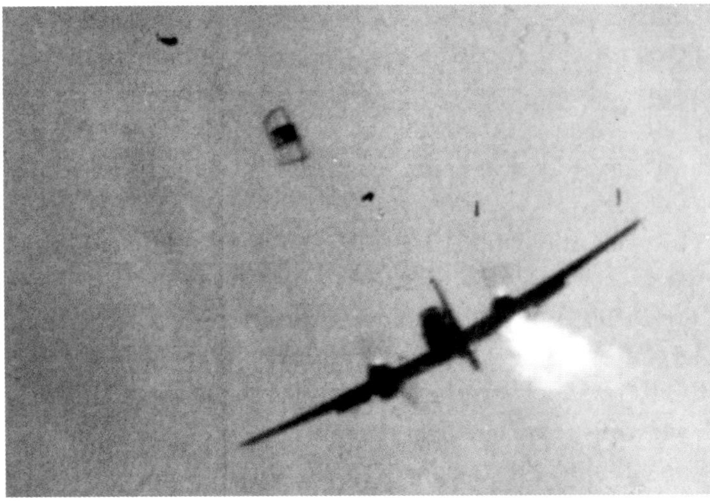

A camera gun still of the attack on Leutnant Heinz-Günther Baack's Me 410A-1, of 14./KG 2, on 5 November 1943. (*USAF*)

Me 410 losses in October 1943 were higher than previous months. On the night of 7 October, for example, Flying Officer Bernard Thwaites of 85 Squadron damaged the Me 410 flown by Feldwebel Wilhelm Sohn of 14./KG 2 so badly that it crashed at Sleydinge near Gent in Belgium killing both crew. The same night, Feldwebel Georg Slodczyk of 16./KG 2 failed to return. The body of his Bordfunker was found eleven miles south-west of Dungeness on 13 October 1943. There were RAF claims for Me 410s ten miles south of Hastings, off Gravesend and off Dungeness that night, so who shot this aircraft down cannot be said for certain, apart from the fact that the successful crew came from 85 Squadron.

Then on early hours of 18 October 1943, Squadron Leader Nigel Bunting shot down the Me 410 flown by Feldwebel Lothar Bleich of 15./KG 2. Bunting set the intruder on fire and it crashed at high speed and at a steep angle, exploding on impact near Brentwood killing both crew.

There would be two final losses on the last night of the month when Leutnant Rolf Proposch of 15./KG 2 was shot down by Flak while attacking London. His Me 410 crashed at Frimley Green in Surrey, killing him and his Bordfunker. As eluded to earlier, Unteroffizier Hans-Willi Brogmus of 15./KG 2 failed to return, though the cause for his loss not known. His usual Bordfunker, Unteroffizier Helmut Lindemann, was killed with him.

November 1943 would see just one night of intruder operations recorded – namely on the 4–5 November. Nine attacks on London were also carried out.

Unteroffizier Felix Hainzinger, Hauptmann Wilhelm Schmitter's Bordfunker. Both men were killed on 8 November 1943.

There were also two days when Tagjagd, or day fighter missions, were carried out; there were no casualties on 3 November 1943, but on 5 November 1943, two aircraft were shot down by American fighters. Leutnant Heinz-Günther Baack of 14./KG 2 managed to bail out near München-Gladbach, but his Bordfunker, Unteroffizier Georg Gillmann, was not so lucky. It is believed that they were shot down by Lieutenant Richard Stearns of the 350th Fighter Squadron/353rd Fighter Group, whose camera gun showed the Me 410's cockpit being jettisoned. The second loss was Unteroffizier Georg Baars of 14./KG 2, who, along with his Bordfunker, was killed when their aircraft was shot down near Rheydt. Why the Luftwaffe thought that night intruder pilots would be effective as day fighter pilots is, put simply, criminal. But in 1944, this would become far more commonplace.

Three nights later would see the most serious loss to date for V./KG 2. At 21.50 hours, Hauptmann Wilhelm Schmitter, together with his new Bordfunker, Unteroffizier Felix Hainzinger, lifted off from Schiphol to carry out a bombing attack on London. Target marking would be performed by a Ju 88S-1 of 7./KG 6 flown by Oberfeldwebel Karl Elpers, an experienced pilot who had been awarded the Deutsches Kreuz in Gold with 9./LG 1 in July 1942. The attack height was to be 7500m, descending to 5300m between 22.43 hours and 22.52 hours. The bomb load was mixed, but included fourteen SC250 Trialen bombs. One Me 410 did not take off for technical reasons. Crews reported that night fighters were active, spotting them at 22.41 hours, 22.43 hours and 22.50 hours.

Three Me 410 crews would fall victim to the RAF defenders that night. The first to be lost was Unteroffizier Heinz Holzmann and his Bordfunker, Unteroffizier Wilfried Fischer, of 14./KG 2. They were shot down twenty miles south of Beachy Head at 22.15 hours by

The crater created by Hauptmann Wilhelm Schmitter's crash, 8 November 1943. (*Andy Saunders*)

Flying Officer Russell Steward and Flying Officer George Main of 29 Squadron. Having got a visual of four yellow exhausts, they closed in for the kill:

> The target turned 100 degrees to port and fighter pulled up behind and identified the target as an Me 410 on good silhouette. At 900ft a one second burst with cannon was given from astern followed by a four second burst. Strikes were seen all over the e/a followed by an explosion and a large yellow glow and many sparks. The e/a flew up at a fierce angle and the fighter turned slightly to starboard. The e/a appeared to stall then dived to port aglow and disappeared into the cloud coincident with bright orange glow which lasted for 30 seconds.

The next loss was a serious one, when Squadron Leader Bill Maguire and Flying Officer Bill Jones shot down an Me 410 near Eastbourne:

> Closed range to 1,500ft where a visual was obtained on fairly bright pale blue twin exhaust flames. At 1,000ft range aircraft identified as Me 410 and Sqn Ldr Maguire opened fire at 200yds dead astern. Many strikes were observed coming from centre section. Broke away to starboard and watched aircraft go into a gentle dive on an even keel with no further evidence of fire so pilot attacked again closing to 150yds, further strikes and large orange glow in fuselage observed. Broke away to starboard to avoid flying wreckage and saw e/a go into a vertical dive trailing sparks and black and white smoke. E/a crashed on land near Eastbourne with bombs on board.

The Me 410 hit the ground at Hampden Park, north-east of Eastbourne, its bomb-load exploding on impact. The blast left a crater 100ft in diameter. Only a few fragments of aircraft were recovered. Of the two crew, Helmut Schmitter and his Bordfunker, there was not enough to bury. The loss of Schmitter, who would be awarded the Eichenlaub and posthumously promoted to Major, must have been a bitter blow to the Gruppe; it is not certain who immediately replaced him.

The final loss that night was Feldwebel Toni Knie and Unteroffizier Ignaz Aberl of 14./KG 2. The pair was shot down by Flying Officer Graeme Reed and his Nav/Rad, Flying

Flying Officer Terry Clark, a Nav/Rad in 488 Squadron, was involved in the shooting down of Leutnant Heinz-Günther Baack of 14./KG 2 on 20 December 1943.

Officer Ralph Bricker, of 488 Squadron, the Me 410 crashing into the sea off RAF Manston at 00.59 hours:

> I identified the e/a as an Me 410 with four very bright yellow exhausts. Outer exhausts were on ring of gun sight when I opened fire with two second burst of cannon from 250yds from slightly above and to starboard, the starboard engine caught fire but the e/a appeared to fly straight on with no evasive action or return fire.
>
> I gave a three second burst again from 250yds above and starboard. The e/a rolled over to port diving vertically and my Navigator saw the port wing buckle under and the aircraft disintegrate in flames into cloud. Contact was obtained eight miles east of Foulness Island and e/a's plot ceased 15 miles north of Manston."

To make matters worse, the Ju 88S-1 flown by Oberfeldwebel Karl Elpers also failed to return. The circumstances behind its loss are not known.

It would appear that another seven attacks on London by V./KG 2 would take place during the remainder of the month, but none were as eventful or as costly as the attack on 8–9 November 1943.

December 1943 was much quieter, with V./KG 2 concentrating on London. Attacks are recorded as taking place on just six nights. The only loss during this time was Leutnant Heinz-Günther Baack of 14./KG 2 on the night of 19 December 1943.

Baack had recovered from being shot down the previous month during a Tagjagd mission and was now flying with a new Bordfunker. The target that night was London, with attacks being made by six Me 410s between 02.30 hours and 02.36 hours. They were to drop a total of twelve SC250 Trialen bombs in a descending attack from 7500m to 5100m. Twelve Fw 190s from I./SKG 10 would then attack just over three hours later.

Returning Luftwaffe crews reported seeing a British night fighter shooting down an aircraft at 02.43 hours. This matches perfectly with the combat report filed by Pilot Officer Doug Robinson and Flying Officer Terry Clark DFM of 488 Squadron, who shot down an Me 410 near Rye at 02.40 hours:

> A contact was obtained at 12 o'clock range two miles with the e/a well above so pilot climbed to 25,000ft and obtained a visual on an Me 410, 2,000ft ahead and slightly below ... pilot closed to 250yds and opened fire with a two to three second burst but owing to vapour trails no strikes were seen.
>
> The e/a took violent evasive action, climbing and diving in tight turns but the searchlights illuminated and held the e/a and our pilot plainly saw the black crosses on the wings.
>
> A second attack was made from 150yds closing to 100yds, several short bursts during which strikes were seen on the port engine and fuselage a red glow appearing from the engine. Inaccurate tracer from the barbettes was passing above our aircraft and the pilot made his third attack from 100yds with a two second burst and pieces flew off the e/a which did a steep port turn and dived towards the ground.

> The visual was temporarily lost but the aircraft was seen to hit the ground and explode shortly afterwards.

The Me 410 hit the ground at Iden in East Sussex killing the pilot. However, the Bordfunker, Unteroffizier Michael Strasser, managed to bail out and was found twenty miles from the crash site suffering from severe injuries.

A police report submitted by Sergeant Fred Balcombe explains the finals moments of the plane and its crew:

> This plane was observed to come down in flames and crash in a meadow at a point south-west of Boonshill Farm House in the parish of Iden.
>
> On my arrival there I saw one member of the crew, Leutnant Heinz Baack, lying on the ground just clear of the machine and he was dead having sustained very severe facial injuries. The machine was badly wrecked and was on fire and pieces of this machine were scattered over a radius of about 100 to 150yds.
>
> I dispatched the dead airman to Rye Mortuary and continued the search for the missing airman and as he could not be found I caused the information to be sent to Divisional HQ and organised a search of the surrounding countryside.
>
> This airman, Michael Strasser, was found in the Kent area the same day and owing to his serious injuries was taken to the 105th General Hospital, Benenden in Kent where he now is.

Nineteen-year-old Baack had had an eventful time with V./KG 2. He was credited with shooting down an aircraft near Lincoln on 4 September 1943 (when he was still 18), as well as being shot down himself on 5 November 1943 – quite something for a pilot of his age and apparent inexperience.

The last recorded attack of 1943 by V./KG 2 was again against London on the night of 30 December. It was not particularly successful. One Me 410 was to act as a pathfinder dropping five LC50F flares on the target between 19.12 hours and 19.24 hours, from 6500m. However, this aircraft experienced problems with its bomb release mechanism. The four attacking Me 410s also arrived early and proceeded to drop eight SC250 bombs blind. Of interest, they were accompanied by a further Me 410 with a new crew who was flying for familiarisation and not carrying bombs.

January 1944 would see a big change in Luftwaffe air operations over the United Kingdom. On 7 December 1943, Josef Goebbels, the Reich Minister for Propaganda, had written:

> Göring has now gone west to prepare the reprisal attacks against England. For this we need about 200 heavy four-engined aircraft which will in one night fly to England twice and deliver a massive blow against the capital. Of course, we cannot carry out an attack like this often enough but it should serve as a reminder to the English that we are still around.

This statement arose from a conference held on 28 November 1943, in which Reichsmarschall Hermann Göring had stated the following to a meeting of senior Luftwaffe officers:

> Gentlemen, the matter I am now going to discuss with you is one of the strictest secrecy; the matter of the preparation and execution of reprisals against England, the first attack to be on London. First of all there are the units which General Peltz, Angriffsführer England, already has as the commander responsible for this operation. These units must now be replenished with aircraft more rapidly. The Director of Air Armaments is to do everything possible in a special effort in the next few days.

Göring then continued by saying:

> I have told the Führer we shall be ready in 14 days. It is absolutely necessary that we have 300 aircraft ready for the first operation. If I can have some 100 in the second raid and early in the morning about 150, then that is 550–600 sorties; that is our objective!

Despite his boast, this offensive, known as *Steinbock*, did not start until the night of 21 January 1944. That said, in the first three weeks of the month V./KG 2 was still active, albeit no Fernnachtjagd missions undertaken. Four nights saw attacks on London, while on 11 January 1944 Tagjagd missions were flown. During the latter, Feldwebel Hermann Bolten of Stab V./KG 2 was one of a number of pilots credited in shooting down a four-engine bomber.

Feldwebel Fredrich Hess of 16./KG 2, who was shot down on 2 January 1944. (*via Simon Parry*)

The same day saw Hauptmann Rudolf Balzer of 14./KG 2 be shot down; he and his Bordfunker were killed. Oberleutnant Hermann Walther of 16./KG 2 was also shot down. He bailed out wounded, while his Bordfunker survived without injury.

There would be four more losses before *Steinbock* began, with eight crew killed. The most unfortunate loss was that of Oberleutnant Helmut Schultze of 14./KG 2, who crashed at Marquise while returning from London on 3 January 1944. He and his Bordfunker were both killed.

Twenty-six-year-old Schultze had joined 13(Z)./LG 1, after training, on 6 February 1940. Then, two days into the Battle of France, he had been forced to crash-land at high speed near Chauvency-le-Chateâu.

Oberleutnant Helmut Schultze of 14./KG 2, seen here with V.(Z)/LG 1 in 1940.

Flight Lieutenant Jimmy Rawnsley and Wing Commander John Cunningham of 85 Squadron, the crew probably responsible for shooting down Oberleutnant Helmut Schultze on 3 January 1944. (*Andy Thomas*)

The Bf 110s of V(Z)./LG 1 had just bounced Hurricanes of 501 Squadron, when Schultze was, in turn, targeted by Sergeant Jérémie Bressieux of Groupe de Chasse I/5.

Schultze and his Bordfunker were captured, only to be released on 30 June 1940, after the French surrender. He then became an instructor at Fliegerschützenschule 1, followed by a period as instructor at Flugzeugführerschule (C) 6 at Kolberg, before he joined IV./KG 26 in August 1943. This was followed by IV./KG 2 in October 1943, at which point he must have converted to the Me 410.

Schultze was killed just over two months later. It is probable that he had fallen victim to Wing Commander John 'Cat's Eyes' Cunningham and Flight Lieutenant Jimmy Rawnsley of 85 Squadron:

Stabsfeldwebel Otto Runge, Bordfunker to Hauptmann Kurt Heintz of Stab V./KG 2, was killed in action on 22 January 1944. (*via Simon Parry*)

> At height of 18,000ft, pilot switched off the Nitrous Oxide and as he got down to 10,000ft, got a visual at 1,000ft range, the Operator with the aid of his Ross Night Glasses recognising an Me 410.
>
> Pilot closed in to about 250yds and fired a short burst from dead astern causing a large explosion followed by considerable flame along the fuselage. The e/a fell very sharply to port and was lost to view temporarily under port wing.

> On looking below pilot saw the French coast which he believed to be between Le Touquet and Berck and saw the Me 410 hit the ground with a violent explosion, lighting up the cloud with an orange glow.

The first night of *Steinbock* finally came on 21 January 1944. However, despite having flown two attacking waves, an incredible sixteen Ju 88s, two Ju 188s, eight He 177s, one Fw 190, one Me 410 and four Do 217s were lost, either to British defences, combat, or while crashing en route to or from the target. In terms of the human cost, seventy-four aircrew were killed or missing, fifteen captured and eight wounded or injured on the two raids this night. They had been a failure, with a loss rate of 10% – British defences and German inexperience, inaccuracy and naivety were to blame for this.

It was clear to the Luftwaffe that such losses would soon become unsustainable and an immediate result was no more double attacks in one night. Losses of both experienced and inexperienced aircrew would seriously impact German bombing effectiveness for the remainder of *Steinbock* and afterwards over Normandy.

The lone Me 410 which was lost was a notable one in that it was flown by Ritterkreuz winner Hauptmann Kurt Heintz, Gruppen Kommandeur of V./KG 2. British intelligence noted:

> It has now been established that the Me 410 which crashed at Lydd in Kent at 0450hrs on 22 January 1944 belonged to Stab V./KG 2. Both crew members, one of whom was a Hauptmann with the Ritterkreuz, were killed and it is possible that this aircraft was one of the pathfinders which were to light up the target for the He 177s.

Heintz had flown from the start of the war with II./KG 51, 8./KG 51, 9./LG 1 and II./KG 40. On operations since the start of the war, he had been awarded the Ritterkreuz as early as October 1942, by when he had flown 300 missions. His Bordfunker, Stabsfeldwebel Otto Runge, who was killed with him, had also been awarded the Deutsches Kreuz in Gold in September 1942 with 9./LG 1, and had presumably been flying with Heintz for some time.

In the wreckage of their aircraft, RAF investigators found a briefing note which gave the course to be followed that night:

1. Base [Vitry] to peak of climb
2. Peak to climb to beacon Liesa (St Valéry--sur-Somme)
3. Liesa to English coast
4. English coast to Ablauflinie
5. Cross Ablauflinie glide attack and release bombs
6. Fly to 51.39N 02.52E [midway between Southwold and The Hague]
7. 51.39N 02.52E to Ostend
8. Ostend to base

Heintz was replaced by Hauptmann Karl-Egon Frhr von Dalwigk zu Lichtenfels, who himself would be replaced by 25-year-old Hauptmann Dierk-Henning Vester as Staffelkapitän of 16./KG 2. Little is known about Vester's previous experience, apart from the fact that he and his Bordfunker had flown with 6./KG 40.

There would be two more nights of activity by V./KG 2 against London in January 1944, and on the 24th another Tagjagd for some crews. There would be no claims or losses, and for the time being it appeared that intruding missions were halted in preference for bombing, nuisance attacks and pathfinding.

February 1944 would see at least fourteen attacks on London. Some of these involved Me 410s dropping the massive SB 1000 or SD 1000 bombs.

The next casualties did not occur until 22 February, exactly a month after the loss of Hauptmann Heintz, when Feldwebel Hermann Bolten and his Bordfunker, Feldwebel Wilhelm Lohf, of 14./KG 2 were attacked by a night fighter during an operation against London. Their assailant was probably Flight Sergeant Tom Bryan and Feldwebel Basil Friis of 96 Squadron, who claimed an Me 410 destroyed. Bolten reported being hit in the port engine and crash-landed at Abbeville at 03.17 hours. This matches well with the RAF crew's combat report:

> I attacked from 150yds with two short bursts. Target was then dead ahead and slightly above now flying a fairly steady course, height 17,000ft. There were strikes in the port engine, the e/a took violent evasive action and returned my fire though his aim was wide. I followed him and fired another short burst with no results.
>
> E/a now throttled back violently and did a vertical bank to port. I overshot below him and noticed no exhaust flares were visible on the port engine … I lost my visual as he dived steeply away.

V./KG 2's part in the Baby Blitz, as *Steinbock* is also known, now changed, with the Gruppe becoming II./KG 51. Its crews, including its Executive Officers and aircraft, moved as well. The change was announced on 6 February 1944, but was not fully complete until early March 1944. It would appear that the 'U5' fuselage codes denoting KG 2 were retained until at least 22 March 1944, when they were replaced by KG 51's '9K'. It was at the end of the month that II./KG 51 recommenced intruder operations.

At the same time, I./KG 51, commanded by Hauptmann Hans Unrau, arrived at Saint-André in France. Unrau, who had been the Staffelkapitän of 1./KG 51, had taken command of the Gruppe from Major Wolf-Dietrich Meister, who became temporary Geschwader Kommodore around 15 February 1944. Meister would become permanent Kommodore two months later. He had taken over from Ritterkreuz winner Major Hanns Heise, who would then take command of KG 2.

The crews of I./KG 51 would fly pure bombing missions or pathfinding. Its first mission was believed to be against London on the night of 23 February 1944. One of the crews involved was Oberleutnant Eberhard Winkel and his Bordfunker, Feldwebel Adolf Schwachenwald, of 1./KG 51. The Gruppe's first combat losses came on the night

The remains of Unteroffizier Reinhard Eggers' Me 410A-1 of 14./KG 2 after its crash at Framfield, 23 February 1944. (*Andy Saunders*)

Unidentified aircrew gather round an Me 410A-1.

of 14 March 1944, when Deutsches Kreuz in Gold winner Oberleutnant Werner Pape of 1./KG 51 was killed in an accident while taking off from Saint-André to attack London. Leutnant Horst Eppendorf and Unteroffizier Günter Zaprodsky of 2./KG 51 were killed when they crash-landed near Beauvais on the return.

The last two losses for the old Geschwader came on the night of 22 February 1944. Four Me 410s were reported to have targeted London. The first aircraft to be lost was from 14./KG 2; it was flown by Unteroffizier Reinhard Eggers. It was intercepted by Squadron Leader Peter Caldwell of 96 Squadron. Eggers' fate was observed from the ground by policeman Sergeant W. Simpson, who subsequently wrote the following:

> This plane was attacked by a night fighter and was seen falling in flames [crashing at Framfield in Sussex]. When it crashed the bombs on board exploded throwing portions of wreckage and pieces of the bodies of the airmen 300yds away. Only small portions of bodies were found (sufficient to fill a sack quarter full).
>
> A military medical officer examined the hands and feet which were found and said without question they were from two different bodies. Also portions of the men's identity cards were found. The two occupants were Uffz Bernhard [*sic*] Eggers and Ogefr Stefan Bednorz.

A second Me 410 crashed fifteen minutes later. Flown by Leutnant Felix Müller of 16./KG 2 was plotted approaching High Wycombe in Buckinghamshire from the north, only to be engaged by a predicted 3.7-inch gun battery. The Me 410's engines were heard to rev up and the aircraft suddenly dived into the ground, killing its crew. Of interest is the fact that a document found on the Bordfunker's body gave the Feldpostnummer 52371, which RAF intelligence knew was used by 16./KG 2 and 6./KG 51.

With the confusion around V./KG 2 changing to II./KG 51, it appears that a third Me 410 was lost on this night, when Feldwebel Karl Müller and his Bordfunker, Unteroffizier Kurt Bein, recorded as being with both 16./KG 2 and 6./KG 51, failed to return. Their loss has been further confused with that of Leutnant Felix Müller, also of 16 Staffel. It would now appear that they fell victim to a Mosquito from 85 Squadron. Flying Officer Edward Hedgecoe and Flying Officer Norman Bamford claimed to have shot down an Me 410 thirty-five miles south of Dungeness at 00.32 hours, while Flight Lieutenant Branse Burbridge and Flying Officer Bill Skelton claimed another at 00.45 hours, also off Dungeness. Both Karl Müller and Kurt Bein had flown together with 9./KG 2 from late 1942 and at some stage had flown with 3./KG 2.

March 1944 would see very few missions flown by Me 410s. Surviving records indicate that on five nights only II./KG 51 carried out bombing attacks or Störangriff missions on London.

Then, on the night of 31 March 1944, it would appear that Fernnachtjagd missions recommenced. The first recorded kill of this new intruding phase was made by Major Wolf-Dietrich Meister, Acting Kommodore of KG 51, during the night of Bomber Command's disastrous Nürnberg attack. He was probably the pilot responsible for damaging the 12 Squadron Lancaster flown by Flight Sergeant Gus L'Estrange, who reported:

> Norwich area 0425hrs, 1500ft attacked by twin-engined aircraft. Rear Gunner [Sgt A Davenport] injured. Aircraft holed extensively in fuselage. Starboard outer u/s all hydraulics u/s.

A series of intruder sorties would be carried out in April 1944 with, it would appear, I./KG 51 being tasked with bombing London. The first mention of such attacks came on 11 April, when twelve aircraft carried out intruder missions in the Lincoln area, which saw three successful air combat victories.

The first of these was achieved by Leutnant Wolfgang Wenning of Stab II./KG 51, who claimed a Boeing B-17 Flying Fortress north of Ipswich. This was from the 413th BS/96th BG, flown by Lieutenant Don McGregor. This aircraft was en route to Snetterton Heath from

Leutnant Wolfgang Wenning of Stab II./KG 51, seen here while in training.

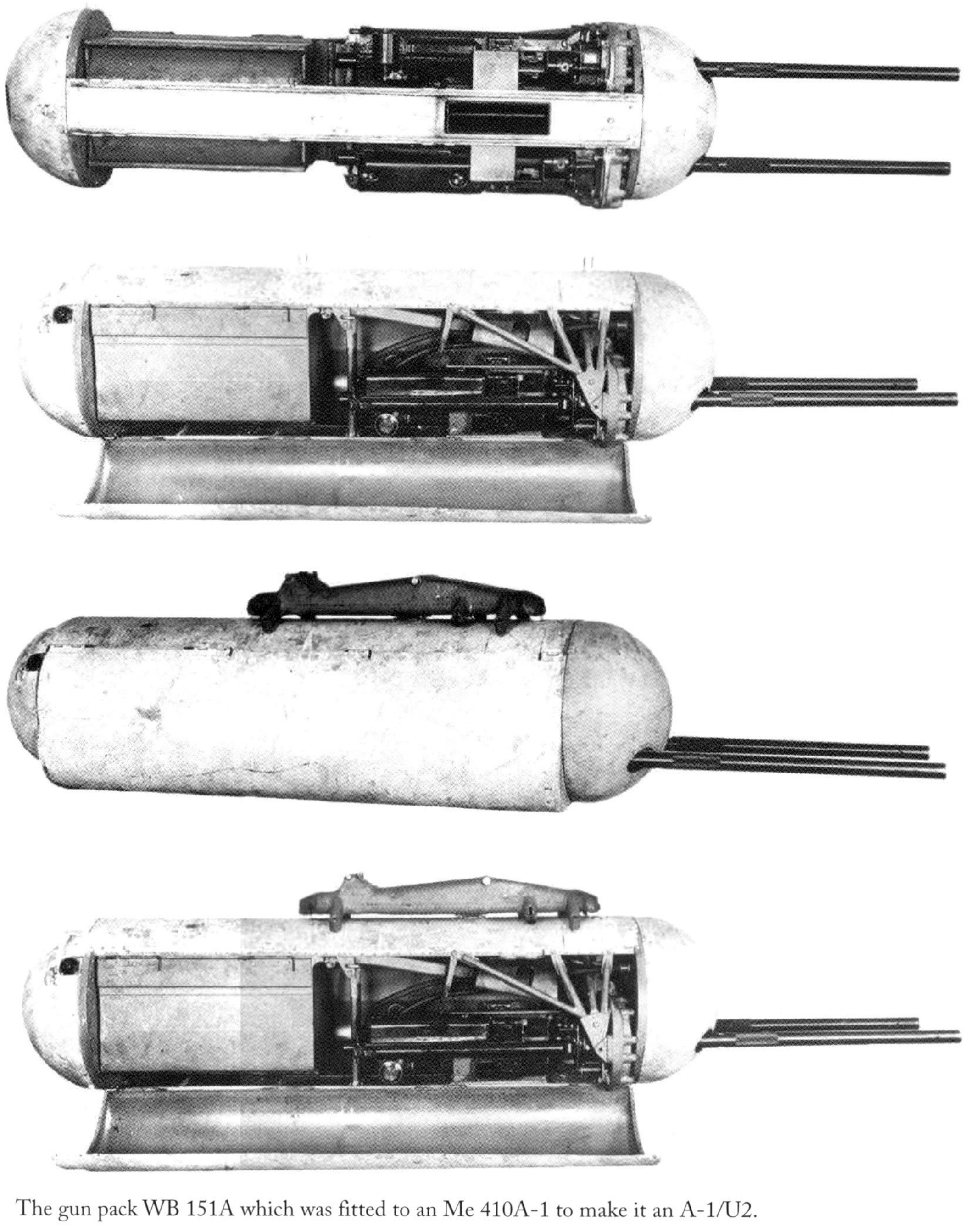

The gun pack WB 151A which was fitted to an Me 410A-1 to make it an A-1/U2.

Framlingham when it was shot down and crashed at Great Glemham in Suffolk, three of the crew being killed.

The second successful pilot that night was Hauptmann Dietrich Puttfarken, Staffelkapitän of 5./KG 51. It is believed that he shot down a Short Stirling of 1654 Heavy Conversion Unit, which was flown by Flight Sergeant Joe Nicholson, and, unusually, a Spitfire of 64 Squadron piloted by Flight Sergeant Gordon Maunders. The Stirling crashed in flames

A gun pack with two MK 103s seen fitted in the bomb bay of an Me 410B-2 of II./ZG 26.

Though not used by intruders, these B-2s have an additional fitting of two 20mm cannon in a bulged fairing.

at the Bassingham bombing range, the pilot and three crew members being killed. The remaining four men on board bailed out safely.

Maunders, meanwhile, had been about to land his Spitfire back at RAF Coltishall, with his navigation lights on, when he was attacked by Puttfarken who severely damaged the Spitfire's engine. Maunders felt a severe shock and throttled up, climbing to 4,000ft. However, the engine's temperature began to rise and it began to spark and flame. He then turned the Spitfire onto its back, but he initially couldn't bail out. It was when the aircraft went into a left-hand spin that he finally managed to escape, throwing himself out two miles north of base. Maunders landed safely at Randall's Farm, Skeyton, where he was given a cup of tea while he waited for the RAF to arrive.

At RAF Lakenheath, a Stirling of 149 Squadron was strafed shortly after landing from operations at 01.00 hours on 12 April 1944. It was taxying in on the perimeter track west of the airfield. Strangely this was not mentioned in the squadron records book, but was mentioned in the RAF Lakenheath record book.

Ritterkreuz winner Puttfarken had only recently arrived on II./KG 51, having been Staffelkapitän of 11./KG 51, and successfully converted to the Me 410 with ZG 101. He had flown all but seven of his operational flights on the Eastern Front, having been posted to I./KG 51 in August 1940. He had received the Frontflugspange in Gold in November 1941, and the Ritterkreuz, having flown 258 Feindflug (operational flights), on 7 October 1942, by which time he was leading 1./KG 51. He had also received the Ehrenpokal in December 1941 and Deutsches Kreuz in Gold in July 1942. However, both Wenning and Puttfarken would be dead before the end of April 1944.

It was about now that the newer version of the Me 410 began to make an impression with II./KG 51. The standard armament of the Me 410A-1 of two MG 17s and two MG 151/20s firing forward were bolstered by the fitment of a WB 151A weapons carrier into the bomb bay. This gave the aircraft an additional pair of MG 151/20s, the aircraft now being designated the Me 410 A-1/U2.

This conversion could be done by the unit and took up to ten hours to complete. The first four Me 410A-1/U2s were recorded on V./KG 2 in December 1943, and by February 1944 there would be eighteen A-1/U2s and four A-1s. In time, II./KG 51 would have a maximum of twenty-four A-1/U2s and no A-1s by April 1944, all of which coincided with the return to Fernnachtjagd missions. The Me 410A-1/U2 could no longer carry bombs in the bomb bay, but could carry four 50kg bombs extrernally, so it was logical that Fernnachtjagd missions now took precedence with II./KG 51.

Pilot Officer J.P. Cosgrove of 625 Squadron, who was killed by an intruder on 19 April 1944.

Both Wenning and Puttfarken would go on to claim two kills on the night of 18–19 April 1944. These were a Lancaster of 115 Squadron, this flown by Pilot Officer John Birnie, and a Halifax of 625 Squadron, that flown by Pilot Officer Joe Cosgrove RCAF. Both had been tasked to a raid on the city of Rouen. Birnie's Lancaster, LL667/R, is stated to have been shot down by an intruder while attempting to land at RAF Witchford at 02.10 hours. Cosgrove's Halifax, ME734, was brought down some twenty minutes later while in the process of landing at RAF Kelstern – some ninety miles further north. The two losses claimed the lives of all fourteen men onboard the bombers.

Birnie's Lancaster was not the only 115 Squadron aircraft to fall to the guns of an intruder that night. Also attempting to land at RAF Witchford, albeit a while later at 03.48 hours, was Flight Lieutenant Charlie Eddy's LL867/J. The victor in this case was Oberleutnant Klaus Bieber of 5./KG 51. No one in this Lancaster survived.

This has been Eddy's eleventh operational sortie, but his had already been a remarkable RAF career. On 19 March 1943, he had, for example, been wounded in the right leg by enemy action, injuries which led to him being admitted to the RAF hospital at Ely. Having returned to duty, his aircraft crashed while returning from a raid on Aachen on 13 July 1943. Eddy never knew that he was made an Additional Member of the Military Division of the Most Excellent Order of the British Empire for his gallantry that night, the citation for his MBE not being published in *The London Gazette* until 26 May 1944, some three weeks after his death:

> One night in July, 1943, this officer was the pilot and captain of an aircraft which crashed when attempting an emergency landing and burst into flames immediately. He received concussion and injuries to his scalp and spine.
>
> Despite his injuries, Flying Officer Eddy remained in the aircraft and assisted the bomb aimer from the overturned second pilot's seat. After getting clear of the aircraft, Flying Officer Eddy, on learning that one member of the crew was absent, re-entered the blazing wreckage and assisted a medical officer in a vain attempt to extricate the mid-upper gunner who was trapped in his turret. It was not until the heat, fumes and smoke had made a continuance of rescue work impossible that Flying Officer Eddy was persuaded to abandon his efforts.
>
> His face was scorched whilst he was attempting to rescue the gunner and he collapsed immediately after finally leaving the aircraft. Flying Officer Eddy showed gallantry in dangerous circumstances and his unselfishness was instrumental in saving the bomb aimer's life.

Returning to the events of night of 18–19 April 1944, one claim not filed by the Luftwaffe intruders was for a 25 Squadron Mosquito. While taxiing in at RAF Coltishall at 04.50 hours, the Mosquito was strafed by an Me 410 which flew over the airfield at high speed. Sub-Lieutenant James Adams and Sub-Lieutenant Horace Smith escaped without injury, but the Mosquito was hit in the port engine and both coolant systems. Some damage was caused to the taxiway, and in daylight spent 20mm and 13mm rounds were picked up on the airfield.

RAF Tuddenham also came under attack that night, more specially at 02.40 hours, as aircraft were landing. No damage was caused, but the incident was reported on by the BBC.

Flying Officer Keith Panter and Warrant Officer Bert Moggs of 25 Squadron claimed to have shot down an Me 410 some fifteen to twenty miles west of Ijmuiden in the Netherlands at 04.35 hours. The only casualty that night was Feldwebel Franz Dietrich of 6./KG 51, who force-landed near Bergen, a couple of miles north of Alkmaar, after having lost an engine; the cause for the engine failure was not recorded as being due to a night fighter. However, Panter's combat report provides some clues as to what might have happened:

Flight Lieutenant Don MacFadyen of 60 OTU, victim of an attack by Unteroffizier Franz Wachtler of 4./KG 51 on 12 April 1944. (*RCAF, via Andy Thomas*)

> Visual was obtained at 700ft to port and slightly above of target silhouetted against the light sky of the breaking dawn. We identified it immediately as a Me 410. We dropped back and turned to port until target was dead ahead and fired a one and a half second burst from 500ft.
>
> Strikes were scored on the port engine which exploded and set fire to the port mainplane. The e/a then flicked over onto its back and dived almost vertically still on fire. We watched it going down for a very brief period before it disappeared and it is believed that the e/a went into the sea.

It appears that there would be one more success that night, albeit that, once again, the German crew did not claim it. Unteroffizier Franz Wachtler and Bordfunker Unteroffizier Albert Wolk of 4./KG 51 had taken off from Eindhoven at 23.51 hours. His logbook states that the mission was a Nachtjagd in the Lincoln area, and that he shot at a Beaufighter. Seeing no results of his attack, he did not claim anything and landed back at Eindhoven at 02.42 hours.

Oberleutnant Richard Pahl, who was killed with 1./KG 51 on 19 April 1944.

However, that night a Mosquito of 60 OTU, crewed by Flight Lieutenant Don MacFadyen DFC and Flying Officer James Wright, had taken

Richard Pahl, in the centre, pictured with Leutnant Klaus Dold and Oberleutnant Johannes Richter of III./KG 51, during the Russian campaign in 1942. All three would be killed in action. (*Millett*)

off from RAF High Ercall on a night navigation exercise. They reported being damaged by a night fighter and bailed out without incident near Grantham. So, it would appear that the Wachtler crew had been successful after all. Don MacFadyen was instructing at 60 OTU having been awarded the DFC with 418 Squadron and would afterwards receive the DSO and a Bar to the DFC with 406 Squadron.

For II./KG 51, everything that been achieved so far in April 1944 had been done so without loss. This, though, was more than could be said for I./KG 51, which had, up to 22 April 1944, lost nine aircraft and sixteen aircrew killed or missing. In addition to the two losses over France on the night of 14 March 1944, the Me 410 of Unteroffizier Willi Krause of 2./KG 51 was damaged during combat with the Mosquito flown by Flying Officer Chris Nowell of 85 Squadron on 21 March 1944. Krause was killed when he crashed at Tancarville, near Le Havre.

Then on 24 March 1944, Feldwebel Joachim Hübener and his Bordfunker were killed in a take-off accident. Their aircraft crashed at Chavigny, near Saint-André.

The next loss occurred on 12 April 1944, when Leutnant Helmut Siol failed to return from an attack on London. His body, along with that of his Bordfunker, was later washed ashore in France. Two nights later, Squadron Leader Alastair Parker-Rees of 96 Squadron shot down Unteroffizier Heinz Zehmisch of 3./KG 51, the latter came down in the Channel off Dungeness. Feldwebel Karl-Heinz Bargstadt, also of 3 Staffel, crashed on landing at Vitry-en-Artois; both he and his Bordfunker were killed.

The remains of Richard Pahl's Me 410A-1 in Brighton. (*Andy Saunders*)

The final losses for I./KG 51 came on the nights of 19 and 20 April 1944. The first was a serious one for I./KG 51. This involved Oberleutnant Richard Pahl, Staffelkapitän of 1./KG 51, who was shot down off Brighton by Wing Commander Ed Crew of 96 Squadron while en route to attack London. His Me 410A-1 crashed into St Nicholas Churchyard in Brighton.

Oberfeldwebel Hans Frach of 6./KG 51 receiving the Ritterkreuz in October 1944.

Pahl was another highly experienced pilot. Having joined 8./KG 51 in mid-1941, he was wounded by Flak while serving with 9./KG 51 on 3 March 1942. Already awarded the Ehrenpokal and Deutsches Kreuz in Gold, Pahl was posthumously promoted to Hauptmann. The absence of bombs and the presence of flares in the wreckage would indicate Pahl was acting as a pathfinder.

The following night, Flight Lieutenant Clive Brooks of 456 Squadron brought down Leutnant Reinhold Witt of 1./KG 51, who had also been en route to London. The Me 410 crashed near Nuthurst in West Sussex killing both crew; the bomb load exploded thirty minutes later. The following account was published in the *West Sussex County Times*, under the headline 'Home Guard Seek Enemy Airman', on 21 April 1944:

> The two members of the crew of the German bomber which was shot down a few miles from the South Coast on Wednesday night were killed when their 'plane crashed in flames on farm land about half a mile away from a village, and exploded. There was no damage or casualties. A partly burned parachute found near the spot led to reports that one of the crew was at large and police and Home Guard search parties were called out.

The last recorded loss of a I./KG 51 Me 410 came on 15 May 1944, when Feldwebel Fritz Hanch of 2./KG 51 ran out of fuel and was injured force-landing near Caen. It is believed that he was one of six aircraft from I./KG 51 which acted as pathfinders loaded with SC1000 bombs (only five made it to the target area) for an abortive attack on Bristol on the night of 14 May 1944. It is possible that some Fernnachtjagd missions were also flown this night, as the airfield at Chilbolton in Hampshire was reported to have been attacked.

The part now played by I./KG 51 in further attacks on London is not known with any certainty, as the Gruppe would return to Germany around 23 May 1944 to begin its conversion to the Me 262. Indeed, the night after the unsuccessful Bristol operation seemingly marks the last for missions flown by the Me 410s of I./KG 51 before they departed to Germany.

For II./KG 51, after an initial period of success upon returning to intruding, the remainder of April 1944 would see one night of spectacular success. The month would also see losses, some of them serious, start to rise again.

Bordfunker Feldwebel Gustav Delp of 6./KG 51, flying with Leutnant Wolfgang Wenning, thought he had shot down a Republic P-47 Thunderbolt at dawn on 21 April 1944. This was, in fact a Miles Master of 7 (Pilot) Advanced Flying Unit being flown by Flying Officer James Banister, who was killed when he crashed near Peterborough. Delp had flown in Do 217s of 5./KG 2 and had been injured on 22 June 1942, when he bailed out of his damaged Do 217 on returning from an attack on Southampton. He had been awarded the Ehrenpokal and had received the Deutsches Kreuz in Gold in March 1944.

On the negative side for the Germans that night was the fact that Hauptmann Dierk-Henning Vester, Staffelkapitän of 6./KG 5, and his Bordfunker were both killed in an accident while taking off from Soesterberg.

The following night would see aircraft from II./KG 51 following a number of Consolidated B-24 Liberators back to their bases in Suffolk following a daylight attack on Hamm in Germany. A total of 804 USAAF bombers had taken off late in the afternoon to attack the railway marshalling yards in the city, which is located in the north-eastern part of the Ruhr area. The American bombers headed out over Lowestoft and returned via Clacton. There would also be a massive fighter escort throughout the mission. Of the attacking aircraft, 278 were B-24s from the 2nd Bomb Division; they were the last to take off, last to attack and last to land.

As they approached the English coast on their return, they must have been unaware that they were being stalked by around fourteen Me 410A-1/U2s of 6./KG 51. The first pilot to make a claim, off the coast at 22.04 hours, was Feldwebel Johann Trenke of 6./KG 51. This was believed to be the B-24 flown by Lieutenant Cherry Pitts of 715th BS/448th BG which came down into the sea off Hopton; there were no survivors.

The next loss came from 735th BS/453rd BS, the pilot in this instance being Lieutenant Jim Munsey. Munsey's B-24 is believed to have been attacked off the coast by Leutnant Wolfgang Wenning of Stab II./KG 51. Munsey ordered his crew to abandon their stricken bomber near Southwold, despite which the two pilots were killed when the B-24 crashed into Reydon Marshes.

Ten 'Halifaxes and B-17s' were claimed as being shot down between 22.05 hours and 22.26 hours that day. In reality, it was nine B-24s the of 389th, 448th, 453rd, 458th and 467th Bomb Groups that were lost. A number of unconfirmed claims were not allowed, even though another five B-24s were wrecked on landing or burnt out on the ground following being damaged in combat or bombed.

Even Feldwebel Gustav Delp, Wolfgang Wenning's Bordfunker, was credited with an aircraft south of Norwich. This is possibly the B-24 flown by 1st Lieutenant Stalie Reid of the 79th BS/467th BG which crashed at Barsham in Suffolk.

Oberleutnant Dietrich Puttfarken.

To add further insult to injury, a number of Allied airfields, such as Rackham, had 50kg bombs dropped on them.

A number of American gunners claimed to have hit Me 410s; two were lost to return fire. Gunners on Lieutenant F.T. Wilkerson's B-24, which was part of the 567th BS/389th BG, reported setting the Me 410 that attacked them on fire, before they themselves then crashed in flames at Cantley, Norfolk, at 22.17 hours.

The aircraft hit by Wilkerson's crew was presumably the Me 410 that dived into the ground at speed at Ashby St Mary, close to Cantley, at around 22.10 hours. The intruder exploded, scattering wreckage across an area of fifteen acres. Of the German crew very little was found to warrant a burial, but a cloth Deutsches Kreuz in Gold was picked up, as was something that proved the identities of the two men – Oberleutnant Klaus Krüger and his Bordfunker, Feldwebel Michael Reichardt. Both had received the Deutsches Kreuz in Gold with 7./KG 51.

The wreckage of 2nd Lieutenant Charles 'Red' Stilson's B-24 of 754th BS/458th BG near Horsham St Faith after crash-landing on 22 April 1944. (*USAF*)

A cloth Deutsches Kreuz in Gold, similar to that found in the wreckage of Oberleutnant Klaus Krüger's Me 410.

An Armstrong Whitworth Albermarle, similar to the 42 OTU aircraft shot down by Unteroffizier Walter Brügel of 4./KG 51.

Gunners on another B-24 of the 754th BS/458th BG, that piloted by Lieutenant Charles 'Red' Stilson, reported being attacked ten miles from Horsham St Faith. His gunners put up a fierce return fire, and on its second pass the Me 410 was hit – albeit the B-24 was already on fire by this point.

What actually happened to the second Me 410 lost that night cannot be stated for certain, except that it is known that Hauptmann Dietrich Puttfarken, the 5./KG 51 Staffelkapitän, and his Bordfunker, Oberfeldwebel Willi Lux, did not return. The loss of four of its airmen that night was a serious blow for II./KG 51. Puttfarken had received the Ritterkreuz, and all four had been awarded the Deutsches Kreuz in Gold and Ehrenpokal. Dietrich Puttfarken would be posthumously promoted to Major.

In its Operations Record Book, RAF Coltishall reported that at about 22.00 hours, a large force of returning Liberators was attacked by six intruders in its sector:

> They found the B-24s a sitting target as they were about to land at nearby aerodromes with navigation lights on. It is reported that 10 Liberators were shot down and five crashed on landing. Eight Mosquitoes of 25 Sqn were airborne during this phase of activity but no joy except many contacts on friendlies.

Despite these losses, a second wave of intruders set forth later that night. During these missions, Unteroffizier Walter Brügel of 4/KG 51 attacked an Armstrong Whitworth Albermarle of 42 OTU. Having taken off from RAF Ashbourne at 02.30 hours on a night navigation exercise, it was fatally hit and crashed at Holland Fen near Lowestoft. The pilot, Sergeant John Hutchinson, and two of the crew were killed; the other two onboard bailed out safely.

The remainder of April saw four more kills for the intruders, albeit one was pyrrhic. The first two claims came during the early hours of 25 April 1944, when II./KG 51 went after bombers returning from Karlsruhe.

The first casualty was Warrant Officer Murray McPherson RCAF of 626 Squadron, who was shot down by Unteroffizier Eberhard Baier of 6./KG 51. With his Lancaster, DV177, damaged, McPherson tried to divert to the USAAF base at Boxted. The did not make the airfield and crashed at Ipswich Road, Highwoods, Colchester, killing all on board.

The second aircraft to be lost was Halifax LK789 of 76 Squadron. Having shadowed his victim, Leutnant Wolfgang Wenning, the Technical Officer of Stab II./KG 51, eventually opened fire. Pilot Officer Douglas Dibbins seemingly attempted to force-land near Colony Farm, Manea, Cambridgeshire, but the bomber was destroyed in the crash that resulted. Only one of the seven-man crew survived.

Forty-eight hours later the intruders struck again, when eleven aircraft from II./KG 51 took off to carry out another Fernnachtjagd.

The first claim was filed by Feldwebel Johann Trenke of 6./KG 51. His combat was stated to have occurred over RAF Mildenhall, but it cannot be matched to any corresponding Allied loss.

Five minutes later, and much further to the west, a second engagement took place, but which was not reported on by the German crew. With his Bordfunker, Feldwebel Gustav Delp, Leutnant Wolfgang Wenning of Stab II./KG 51 had patrolled as far as Rugby when they spotted around four aircraft in the circuit of RAF Church Lawford. The pair promptly headed in for the attack.

Pilot Officer Moore of 18 (P) AFU, who was killed when he collided with Leutnant Wolfgang Wenning of Stab II./KG 51 on 27 April 1944.

Wenning opened fire on an Airspeed Oxford of 18 (P) AFU Unit. At the controls of the latter was Canadian Pilot Officer Gregor Moore. The Oxford began to break in the air – at which point the Me 410 collided with it. Both aircraft crashed at Mitchells Farm, Frankton, killing all three aircrew. Gregor Moore had joined 18 (P) AFU in January 1944. Just eleven days prior to his death he had celebrated his 20th birthday.

With Wenning's Me 410/U2 being the first to foil on UK soil, the wreckage was understandably of great interest to the RAF investigators. Their findings, published in Report No. 8/130 on 4 May 1944, read as follows:

> At 0430hrs on 27 April 1944 an Me 410 on intruder operations crashed at Manor Farm, Frankton near Rugby after being in collision with an Airspeed Oxford. This aircraft is of interest, being the first of the sub-type 'F' [presumably Fern for long range – *Author*]. Its principal difference between this and other Me 410s examined is an increase in armament 4 x MG 151/20 being installed in the nose instead of the usual two.

Identification Markings:	9K+Z? (Z black outlined in yellow). On the base of the tail-fin 42 was painted in black and below this on the fuselage 750 in black on a white background.
Camouflage:	Blue-grey on top surfaces, spray painted black on the under surfaces.
Armament:	Nose 4 x MG 151 20mm; 2 x MG 17 7.92mm calibre.
Barbettes:	2 x MG 131 13mm calibre. The two extra MG 151s were mounted in the bomb bay.
Internal equipment and special points:	The radio identified was FuG 10P, FuG 16, FuBl 2, FuG 25A and FuG 101A. Since the aircraft was operating on a free-lance intruder patrol, it is not obvious why the FuG 25A was carried. All the instruments were destroyed. Two 66 gallon external drop tanks were carried, this being the first occasion on which extra

> tanks have been seen on an Me 410. They were carried on special mountings fitted with an explosive charge for sheering the single retaining bolt, this being the only method of dropping the tank. On fighter-bombers such as the Fw 190 the extra tanks are carried on mountings similar to bomb carriers from which they can be released mechanically.

Aged 21, Wenning had been an up and coming ace, he and his Bordfunker having already claimed six aircraft destroyed while serving with II./KG 51. Having finished his flying training, he had been posted to IV./KG 2 on 1 June 1943. He received the EK I on 24 January 1944, and Frontflugspange in Bronze on 2 February 1944; he would be posthumously promoted to Oberleutnant.

There was one further claim before April 1944 was over. This occurred when, twenty-four hours after Wenning's loss, Unteroffizier Artur Döhler of 5./KG 51 reported shooting down an aircraft over the North Sea, south-east of Ipswich. The identity of his victim cannot be stated with any certainty.

With I./KG 51 soon to return to Germany, May 1944 would be quieter. That said, in addition to the usual tasks, both I and II./KG 51 undertook Nachtjagd missions. For example, Oberleutnant Georg Csurusky, the new Staffelkapitän of 1./KG 51, was credited with shooting down a Halifax south-west of La Ferrière on the night of 6-7 May 1944. This is believed to actually be Lancaster ND449 of 156 Squadron that was flown by Flight Lieutenant Henry Churchill DFC and Bar. Churchill and two of his crew were killed; the other four evaded capture.

On the following night a Halifax of 138 (Special Duties) Squadron, LL280 flown by Wing Commander Bill Russell DFC and Bar, was brought down to the north-west of Tours. These were the only victories claimed by I./KG 51 while operating the Me 410.

The first recorded mission for the month of May for II./KG 51 came on the night of the 8th, when a number of aircraft carried out night fighter sorties in the Évreux area. Then on the night of 11 May 1944, four Me 410s carried out what was described as 'harassing raids on ground organisation and intruder night fighting', albeit two aircraft returned early with technical problems.

Oberleutnant Georg Csurusky of 1./KG 51.

The following night saw eight Me 410s carrying out Fernnachtjagd in a large area south of The Wash and north of the Humber. A

Mosquitoes of 105 Squadron, similar to those damaged by an intruder on 23 May 1944.

An air-to-air shot of a de Havilland Mosquito of 105 Squadron.

number of aircraft were apparently attacked near Kettering, Wyton and Bury St Edmunds, but no RAF aircraft can be matched to these reports, albeit Bomber Command was active that night.

Unteroffizier Walter Brügel of 4./KG 51 filed a claim for a four-engine aircraft near Brestedt (which is in Schleswig-Holstein in northern Germany) at 02.38 hours. As is so often the case, this cannot be matched to any Allied aircraft. Some reports state his claim was in the Bury St Edmunds area; these, again, cannot be linked to any specific incident.

Apart from the Bristol attack on the night of 14 May 1944, the next major series of intruder attacks came on the night of 21 May 1944. On this occasion, a force of ten Me 410 roamed the skies in the Cambridge-Norwich-Ipswich areas. Unteroffizier Eberhard Baier and Feldwebel Johann Trenke of 6./KG 51 each claimed two bombers. Only one victim can be positively attributed to Baier – this being Lancaster NN695 of 619 Squadron. Flown by Flying Officer Bob Redshaw, it was caught by the Me 410 near RAF East Wretham while returning from Duisburg. Of the seven men on board, only one is believed to have survived.

That night, II./KG 51 also reported attacking at least eight other aircraft, but without any results.

The following night, another eight Me 410s carried out a similar attack in the same area. Between them they claimed to have attacked four aircraft and bombed at least four airfields. RAF Bourn and RAF Great Ashfield reported being attacked by intruders at 03.20 hours and 03.45 hours respectively. Two 105 Squadron Mosquitoes were damaged at Bourn, the intruder involved possibly being Leutnant Martin Kneis of 4./KG 51, who noted attacking an airfield at 03.32 hours.

A Lancaster of 582 Squadron, being flown by Squadron Leader Harold Heney, was attacked near the airfield at Little Staughton in Bedfordshire at 03.10 hours:

Squadron Leader Reg Harrison, ninth from the right in the front row, and his Nav/Rad, Flying Officer Reg Horrex, behind Harrison's right shoulder, of 151 Squadron. (*Kelsey*)

> Lost height making for base as there were many airfields put on navigation lights. At 0310hrs height 2,500ft attacked by enemy intruder from rear and below. The rear turret being u/s we were a sitting shot but corkscrewed to starboard and evaded the fighter but not until he was able to rake us with fire.
>
> Fortunately no crew were injured but hydraulics were shot away and we were forced to use emergency undercarriage and flaps system making a good landing at base. Aircraft Category AC because of enemy fighter, Flak and an incendiary.

Around the same time, an Avro Anson of 13 OTU was also attacked by an intruder. It was destroyed in a crash-landing at Little Staughton at 03.10 hours. Flying Officer Paul Davidson was badly wounded by a 20mm cannon round. He would succumb to his injuries on 26 May 1944.

At 03.25 hours on 25 May 1944, RAF Tuddenham again received attention from an intruder:

> A twin-engined aircraft believed to be an Me 410 shot up the Station from 600ft with cannon and machine gun – four small bombs were also dropped. Damage was chiefly to crops and a few broken windows in the NAAFI and tailor's shop. There were no casualties.

Losses for II./KG 51 in May 1944 were relatively light. With the build up to the invasion of Normandy, more RAF intruders were starting to make their presence felt over Occupied Europe than in previous months.

As part of this increasing activity, Oberleutnant Klaus Bieber and his Bordfunker of 5./KG 51 were killed when they were shot down by an RAF intruder barely a mile north-east of Beauvais at 00.30 hours on 12 May 1944. We cannot be certain who was responsible for this casualty, though Squadron Leader Reg Harrison and Flying Officer Edwin Horrex of 151 Squadron duly claimed what they thought was a Ju 188 about fifty miles east of Saint-André at 01.50 hours. This, they stated, had been carrying 'drop tanks or bombs under each wing outboard'. However, Ju 188s, or Ju 88s for that matter, did not carry such tanks on bombing missions. It is possible that Bieber's Me 410 was the victim of Flight

Wing Commander Mike White-Boycott of 25 Squadron.

Lieutenant Harry White and Flying Officer Mike Allen of 141 Squadron, who destroyed a Ju 88 north of Amiens at 23.50 hours.

The next losses did not occur until the night of 28–29 May 1944. Just before midnight, twelve aircraft took off to carry out Fernnachtjagd in the Wash-Norwich-Ipswich-Cambridge area. Things started badly for II./KG 51, when two Me 410s of 5 Staffel, those flown by Oberleutnant Helmut Niebler, the Staffelführer, and Unteroffizier Artur Döhler, collided on take-off from Gilze-Rijen. Niebler and his Bordfunker were killed, while the other two crew were injured. Niebler had been with 4./KG 40 and then 15./KG 2 and had been injured in an accident on 18 August 1943, while returning from an attack on Lincoln.

The rest of the intruders pressed on with the night's mission. They duly reported no encounters with RAF aircraft, though they successfully carried out attacks on a number of airfields which included Deopham Green, Oakington and Tuddenham. German records note that one Me 410 was listed as overdue; this was because Feldwebel Ernst Dietrich and Unteroffizier Walter Schaknies of 6./KG 51 had been shot down by Wing Commander Mike Wight-Boycott and Flight Lieutenant Douglas Reid of 25 Squadron. Wight-Boycott later posted this combat report:

> When I was at 1,000ft I got a visual on four bright exhausts at a range of 1,200ft against a dark hazy background. I approached to about 700ft and established that the aircraft had a very tall fin and a distinct hump. This was verified by my Nav through night binoculars and we both agreed that it was an Me 410.
>
> By this time my altimeter showed below sea-level and I dropped back slightly and to the port side opening fire with a ½ second burst. Strikes were seen about the port wing root and immediately after the aircraft blew up with a blinding flash and passed under my port wing.

Aircrew of 25 Squadron seen at RAF Coltishall in 1944.

> As I turned to port I saw the aircraft blazing on the water in two portions which were lying close to each other (the time and position was 0336hrs east of Cromer). The e/a could be seen burning on the water from 20 miles away. The Bandit did not appear to take any evasive action barring a leisurely weave and flying very low over the sea.

The last two nights in May 1944 saw more Fernnachtjagd missions in the usual areas around East Anglia. These, though, ended with little, if any, results.

Events in June 1944 saw a shift in emphasis following the Allies' invasion of France. Despite this, II./KG 51, carrying out missions either over the UK or the Normandy beachhead, suffered heavily at the hands of Allied intruders, night fighters and Flak.

The first casualty was Leutnant Martin Knies of 4./KG 51 who was wounded near Neuilly-sur-Seine during the early hours of 3 June 1944. While the Luftwaffe loss report states this was as a result of a night fighter, Kneis' own logbook says it was due to return fire from a bomber he had been attacking.

Flying Officer Tom Wright and Pilot Officer Len Ambery of 239 Squadron did report to have damaged the starboard engine a Bf 110 while supporting bombers attacking Trappes that night. Their claim was at around the right time, and noted the following:

> Aircraft was closing rapidly so throttled right back and at 5–6,000ft height at 150–100yds range gave a two second burst. Aircraft broke off immediately narrowly missing e/a's tail unit and on looking back flames were seen coming from e/a's starboard engine.

Three nights later what must have been the first German air combat loss of Operation *Overlord* occurred. The actual purpose of 4./KG 51's Oberfeldwebel Hermann Bolten's flight on 6 June 1944 was either a night fighter sortie, in response to Bomber Command's attacks on the gun batteries, or a long range intruder sortie over England. However, as he was returning to Saint-André, he was unaware that someone else was in the circuit.

At the controls of a 605 Squadron Mosquito, Flying Officer Roy Lelong and Flight Sergeant John McLaren had taken off from Manston in Kent to support the airborne landings. They had patrolled the Luftwaffe airfields at Évreux and Saint-André, only to find them unlit and inactive. However, at 01.30 hours, they noticed that the landing lights at the latter had suddenly been turned on – only to be almost immediately extinguished.

Seizing the opportunity, they dropped four bombs on the airfield. The lights then came on again after which the RAF crew spotted an aircraft:

> The pilot obtained a visual on an aircraft at 1,000ft silhouetted against cloud [which] helped him to recognise it as an Me 410. The aircraft was carrying no lights. Fg Off Lelong then flew in a steady climb to just underneath the enemy aircraft and confirmed it as an Me 410, he then throttled back and pulled up to dead astern and

> at a range of 150yds, opened fire. Strikes were seen around the cockpit area and the aircraft then burst into flames.
>
> It then lost height slowly in a spiral dive and finally crashed about seven miles SE of Evreux airfields. Fg Off Lelong then lost height and took photographs of the aircraft burning on the ground. Five minutes later the aircraft exploded and pieces continued to burn.

Surviving records for 4./KG 51 state that on returning to Saint-André from an operational flight, Bolten's Me 410 was attacked by a night fighter and spun into the ground from just 100m. Bolten was seriously injured and never flew again during the war. His long-standing Bordfunker, Feldwebel Wilhelm Lohf, was killed in the crash.

The night of 6 June 1944, saw attacks being made on targets in the beachhead area without results or loss. The following night would be different.

Leutnant Werner Mehls of 6./KG 51 recorded taking off from Soesterberg at 23.06 hours, his Me 410 laden with eight SD70 bombs destined for targets in the Raum C area. Airfields at Framlingham and Tuddenham reported being attacked, the latter stating:

> Prior to the return of four Stirlings [from 90 Squadron] on special duties, two Fortresses and a Liberator of the 8th USAAF landed here. They had been sent away from their own base owing to intruder activity. Just as the last American landed an unidentified intruder flew over the airfield firing cannon and machine guns and dropping anti-personnel bombs some of which did not explode. There were no casualties but two smaller explosions at the intersection of two runways left us with only the short runway serviceable.
>
> When our Stirlings returned, the first one [Warrant Officer S.F.T. Wright] landed without any trouble but the second one [flown by Flight Sergeant A.C.G. Hodges] overshot and bogged itself this putting the airfield completely unserviceable.
>
> The two remaining aircraft [one flown by Flight Sergeant P.D. Kelsey] were sent over to Newmarket and K [Sergeant D.C.M. Page] who had been badly shot up by fighter and Flak had to make a crash-landing as his undercarriage was damaged and his tyres badly holed. This was successfully carried out without any casualties.

Hauptmann Werner Düro of 4./KG 51, who was shot down on 8 June 1944.

The cost to II./KG 51 that night was heavy. These included 4 Staffel, which lost the aircraft flown by Staffelkapitän Hauptmann Werner Düro and

The remains of Feldwebel Siegfried Schönberger's Me 410A-1 of 6./KG 51, which crashed on 13 June 1944. (*Andy Saunders*)

Fahnenjunker-Unteroffizier Karl-Heinz Mono, and 6 Staffel, the victim in this case being Feldwebel Hans-Erich Seemann.

Claims for Me 410s were submitted by at least two RAF crews that night. Flight Lieutenant Douglas Greaves of 25 Squadron, reported that his attack was made off Happisburgh at 00.20 hours. Meanwhile, Pilot Officer Desmond Tull of 219 Squadron got his victim ten miles east of Harwich at 00.30 hours. No other German aircraft were lost that night, so the claim for a Ju 188 off Harwich at 23.59 hours, which was made by Squadron Leader Pat Burke of 219 Squadron, probably relates to the third Me 410 casualty.

Twenty-three-year-old Werner Düro was another experienced pilot. He joined Oberleutnant Hans-Joachim Grundmann's 6./KG 51 in August 1941, then took command of 5./KG 51 in December 1942, taking the place of Oberleutnant Harald Nebelung who had been killed in action on 17 November 1942. Düro then moved to Stab/KG 51 in February 1943, where he acted as Geschwader Adjutant, Major beim Stabe and Ia. He took command of 4./KG 51 at the start of April 1944, his first Staffelkapitän, Hauptmann Hans-Joachim Grundmann, replacing him as Geschwader Ia. Having flown 223 operational flights by July 1943, Düro had been awarded the Frontflugspange in Gold and Ehrenpokal in June 1942 and three months later the Deutsches Kreuz in Gold. He had taken part in the attack on B-24s on 22 April 1944, during which he claimed his only victory of the war.

The remainder of June 1944 saw a myriad of different missions for the Me 410s. These included Fernnachtjagd, attacks over Seine Bay, and Strassenjagd (attacks against Allied vehicles in the beachhead area). There was a new task on the night of 12 June 1944 when II./KG 51 carried out a recce over London, apparently a precursor of the first V1 attacks. During the recce, Feldwebel Siegfried Schönberger and Unteroffizier Kurt Quatfasel of

Flying Officer Mike Gloster of 219 Squadron.

Oberfähnrich Friedrich Jirmann of 5./KG 51 was shot down by Flight Lieutenant George Jameson of 488 Squadron on 25 June 1944.

6./KG 51 had the misfortune of being hit by Flak over the Thames Estuary and as they were flying at just 400ft, dived into the ground near Barking in Essex. Both men were killed.

There were a series of other losses this month. Feldwebel Friedrich Fix and his Bordfunker from 5./KG 51 were killed returning from a Fernnachtjagd when their Me 410 crashed near Oudendijk in the Netherlands. Then, on 15 June 1944, Feldwebel Heinrich Ramm of 5./KG 51 failed to return from another Fernnachtjagd. He is believed to have been shot down off Harwich by Flying Officer Mike Gloster of 219 Squadron. Gloster and his Nav/Rad, Flying Officer Reg Wall, had been vectored onto what they thought was a Ju 88:

> I got a visual on four exhausts and silhouette at 3,000ft against light eastern sky identified as a Ju 88 from slightly below and astern, closed to 500ft and opened fire with two second burst, no return fire or evasive action, another burst and strikes seen on port engine which caught fire, target then went into thin cloud.
>
> Still following on AI target reduced speed, I flew alongside to see results and burning pieces were falling off and as the fire did not seem to be spreading I got behind for another burst and before I could fire, two white objects, I think parachutes, came away from the e/a. It then banked sharply to port and dived steeply into the sea. I followed him down to 1,500ft and saw it explode on the sea burning for a short time.

No other Ju 88 was lost off the UK this night. If Ramm and his Bordfunker, Unteroffizier Karl Seeland, had managed to bail out, they were never rescued and their bodies were never found

Finally, there would be one more Me 410 combat for June 1944 – it was the first over the Normandy beaches. Oberfähnrich Friedrich Jirmann had joined 13./KG 2 at Coulommiers from Fluzeugführerschule (C) 18 in October 1943, but did not join 5./KG 51 at Soesterberg until May 1944. During the early hours of 25 June 1944, he and his Bordfunker, Gefreiter Alwin Dreher, were tasked to undertake a Strassenjagd over Normandy. However, they were spotted twenty miles southwest of Bayeux by a very experienced RAF crew – that of Flight Lieutenant Bill Jameson and Flying Officer Norman Crookes of 488 Squadron.

Jameson and Crookes had taken off from RAF Zeals in Somerset at 02.25 hours, and arrived over Bayeux to begin their patrol at 03.05 hours. Just under an hour later, GCI directed them towards a target flying west and dropping flares:

> Visual was obtained on two very bright exhausts, silver/white, which on closing was seen to be two exhausts on each engine in approximately the same position as a Mosquitoes exhaust. We closed in to about 300yds and attempted to identify. At this time the e/a fired off another flare.
>
> The e/a was flying away from the dawn and on looking through night glasses my Nav thought it was probably a Mosquito; no resin lights [dim rear facing lights on trailing edge of the Mosquito wing tips, just outboard of the ailerons.], IFF (Identification Friend or Foe] or Type F [forward firing infra-red lamp in which target aircraft, if friendly, received a warning it had been illuminated] were showing.

Oberfähnrich Friedrich Jirmann and his Bordfunker, Gefreiter Alwin Dreher.

Jamie Jameson and Norman Crookes of 488 Squadron.

Leutnant Karl-Heinz Friedrich of 5./KG 51, who shot down a B-24 on 28 June 1944, but mistook it for a Stirling.

> We closed and coming underneath from the beam at 100yds range identified it as an Me 410 with long-range tanks outboard of the engines. We dropped back again to 150yds dead astern where I opened fire with a three quarter second burst. I was at 6,000ft. Strikes were seen on the centre of the fuselage and pieces fell away. The e/a continued straight and level. Two more half second bursts from dead astern and more strikes seen with more pieces falling away. The e/a dived steeply downwards hitting the ground about 10 seconds later with a vivid flash.

Friedrich Jirmann had very little to say about the combat:

> I can confirm events which are described in the RAF combat report. We had spotted our opponent and turned to get out of the light of the dawn. I then tried to find the British nightfighter but to no avail. Suddenly the Me 410 was hit by a burst of fire and baling out was the only alternative. Unfortunately Dreher's parachute did not open.

The Me 410 crashed near Dangy, south-west of Bayeux, where Dreher's body was found. Being behind German lines, Jirmann was taken to a German hospital in Le Mans. He returned to II./KG 51 the following month, by which time it was based at Clastres, to the north-east of Paris, from where it operated for much of July and early August 1944.

If all appeared negative for II./KG 51 following the Allied invasion, at least one night of Fernnachtjagd operations did meet with success. Though claims were submitted for Allied bombers in the early hours of 13 June (two) and 17 June (also two), these cannot be positively matched with RAF losses. However, things would be different during the early hours of 28 June 1944.

The first claim that night, for a four-engine aircraft near Newmarket, was made by Leutnant Anselm Markau of 4./KG 51. This was Lancaster NE145 of 90 Squadron flown by Pilot Officer Cyril Todd. Having taken off from RAF Tuddenham to attack the V1 facility at Biennais in France, the Lancaster crashed at Canada Farm, Icklingham, Suffolk during its return. All on board were killed.

The second claim was made by Leutnant Karl-Heinz Friedrich of 5./KG 51, for what he thought was a Stirling west of Letchworth. In fact, he had attacked a B-24 of the 850th BS/801st BG. Piloted by 1st Lieutenant Bill Huenekens, the Liberator was on a night navigation exercise went it was attacked. Crashing west of Eaton Socon, the pilot and two crew were killed. The death toll would have been higher if it was not for navigator, 2nd Lieutenant Robert Callahan, who was awarded the Silver Star for saving the life of the bombardier, 2nd Lieutenant Robert Sanders:

> The airplane in which Lt Callahan was flying burst into flames as a result of an attack by an enemy intruder aircraft. When the flames began to engulf the whole plane, the pilot gave the order to bail out.
>
> Just as Lt Callahan was preparing to jump, he noticed the bombardier's parachute was out of his reach and on fire. Acting with coolness and courage, he instructed the

bombardier to lock his arms about him and they would jump together using one parachute.

Although at a fairly low altitude, Lt Callahan delayed pulling the ripcord in order to lessen the shock which might have broken the bombardier's grip on him. Lt Callahan sustained a broken ankle on landing.

The last casualty attributable to an intruder was Sergeant Walter Smith of 90 Squadron, seen here, on 28 June 1944.

The final claim that night was made by Unteroffizier Franz Wachtler of 4./KG 51, this being for a Lancaster near Saffron Walden. This was another 90 Squadron aircraft. Flown by Flight Lieutenant Alec Burton DFC, his Lancaster was damaged by gunfire while landing at Tuddenham. The 20-year-old Canadian rear gunner, Sergeant Walter Smith, was killed.

Burton was on his third tour of operations. Having been awarded the DFC with 70 Squadron in 1942, he would be awarded the DSO in September 1944. Walter Smith was the last casualty over UK attributable to intruders of II./KG 51, as, from now on, all bar one of the German losses (which included Markau and Wachtler) and two air combat claims would

Leutnant Karl Denk of 5./KG 51, who was killed on 6 July 1944.

Another picture of Leutnant Karl Denk of 5./KG 51.

occur over France. Within a month, II./KG 51 would then cease flying operations on the Me 410, and was also withdrawn to Germany for conversion to the Me 262.

Surviving records for II./KG 51 for July 1944 show quite a number of attacks over the Normandy beaches – at least sixteen – but there was still the occasional attack against mainland UK targets.

Fahnenjunker-Feldwebel Heinz Ebeling of 4./KG 51, who was killed in an accident on 25 July 1944.

The first losses did not come until the early hours of 6 July 1944, when Unteroffizier Hans-Joachim Ziegler of 6./KG 51 and Leutnant Karl Denk of 5./KG 51 failed to return from a Strassenjagd. The former crashed at Villers-Bocage, the latter at La Neuvre-Lyre south-west of Évreux. There were two RAF claims that night. The first, by Flight Lieutenant Charles Ramsay of 264 Squadron, occurred near Falaise at 02.45 hours, the second, by Warrant Officer Jeff Moore of 604 (County of Middlesex) Squadron, some miles west-south-west of Caen at 02.35 hours. Three German aircrew were killed; Ziegler's Bordfunker bailed out and was captured.

The following night the experienced crew of Unteroffizier Franz Wachtler and Unteroffizier Albert Wolk of 4./KG 51 suffered an engine fire while en route for an attack on the beachhead. Both survived, albeit injured, when their Me 410 crashed near Cormeilles. It was Wolk's 52nd Feindflug; he would never fly operationally again.

The following night saw attacks being made on London and Allied forward airfields. The London attack was uneventful, though Leutnant Anselm Markau of 4./KG 51 failed to return. He and his Bordfunker were buried in a German military cemetery near Elbeuf, south of Rouen. The only claim for an Me 410 that night was made by Squadron Leader Ian March of 410 Squadron whose victim was stated to have exploded in the air over the south-west suburbs of Paris, quite some distance away.

Unfortunately the losses, either through combat or due to accident, continued as the final full month of operations progressed. Unteroffizier Johann Reisser and his Bordfunker from 5./KG 51 were killed returning from an attack on Allied forward airfields on 13 July. Their aircraft crashed near Resnescourt. Two nights later, Leutnant Heinz Pieper of 4./KG 51 failed to return from attacking resupply lines in the beachhead area. Pieper had very little combat experience and had only been awarded the EK II; no trace of him or his Bordfunker, Unteroffizier Eugen Büchner, who had celebrated his 31st birthday two weeks before, were ever found. The following night Unteroffizier Martin Golde of 6./KG 51 belly-landed his Flak damaged Me 410 at Coulommiers. Both he and Unteroffizier Ernst Jorda were uninjured.

The final loss came as a result of what appeared to be one final night of intruder missions over Britain. Tuesday, 25 July 1944, started badly when Fahnenjunker-Feldwebel Heinz Ebeling and his Bordfunker were killed in an accident while talking off from Clastres. While what happened over England cannot be said for sure, it is known that Unteroffizier Walter Brügel and his Bordfunker, Unteroffizier Rudolf Sperlich, of 4./KG 51 had been tasked to carry out an intruder mission in Raum C. They had apparently turned back for home when they were spotted by a Mosquito of 515 Squadron, itself returning from an intruder mission of the Böblingen/Stuttgart area.

The RAF intruder was crewed by the former Dambuster Squadron Leader Micky Martin DSO, DFC and his Nav/Rad, Flying Officer John Smith. Whether in error or as an aid to recognition by German anti-aircraft batteries, the Me 410 was burning navigation and tail lights which made it easy to spot. The RAF crew's combat report records the Me 410's demise near Knocke in Belgium:

> The enemy aircraft was obviously unaware of the Mosquito's presence and as the range was opened to about 70yds slightly below and astern, the tail light of the Me 410 literally blotted out the spot on the ring sight. This inconvenience was adjusted with no trouble at all and the ring sight moved to the Hun's starboard engine, a short burst of cannon setting the engine well alight.
>
> This obviously shook the Hun and he speedily dived to port but an almost instantaneous short second burst of cannon fire directed at the port wing blew the wing off and the enemy aircraft, burning well, went down in a screaming dive and was seen to crash on the sea and continued burning.

Oberleutnant Werner Mehls of 6./KG 51 records bombing attacks on Allied troops on the nights of 26, 27 and 28 July 1944, but II./KG 51's time flying the Me 410 was not yet coming to an end.

On 1 August 1944, while on an operational flight, Leutnant Uwe Laas of 5./KG 51 was forced to bail out of his Me 410. His parachute failed to open and he was killed south-east of Villers-Cotterêts. The same night, Bordfunker Obergefreiter Erwin Herbig was injured in a crash-landing at Rosières. Then, on 3 August 1944, the Staffelführer of 6./KG 51 was killed on a training flight in southern Germany. That same date, Oberfeldwebel Wilhelm Wessel and Feldwebel Günter Reese of 4./KG 51 were both injured when they suffered an engine failure on an operational sortie and crash-landed at Chauny.

On 5 August 1944, Oberfähnrich Walter Fink of 4./KG 51 failed to return from attacking Allied resupply routes. He and his Bordfunker, Unteroffizier Otto Morcinek, were killed when their Me 410 crashed at Chapelle de Saint-Quentin-d'Elle, near Berigny to the north-east of Saint-Lô. No Me 410s were claimed that night, but it is possible that this last combat loss of a II./KG 51 Me 410 was due to Flying Officer Andy Shaw and his Nav/Rad, Flight Sergeant Len Wyman, of 488 Squadron who claimed what they thought was a Ju 188 ten miles north-east of Saint-Lô.

A Me 410A-1 of 6./KG 51 that was found abandoned at Saint-André by the RCAF.

An Me 410 of ZG 26 that was found abandoned in Norway at the end of the war in Europe.

A second Me 410 that was found abandoned in Norway after the German surrender.

Two successful pilots from 6./KG 51 – Fahnenjunker-Feldwebel Johann Trenke and Oberfeldwebel Hans Frach.

Only two complete Me 410s have survived. This Me 410 A-1/U2 is currently at the RAF Museum Midlands at Cosford near Wolverhampton.

A few sporadic attacks then took place on various nights against Allied ground targets. It was on 14 August 1944, following a series of air attacks against Clastres, that II./KG 51 received orders to relocate to Schwäbisch-Hall in Baden-Württemberg. There, as already mentioned, they were to begin the process of converting to the Me 262.

The last recorded operational flights by an Me 410 occurred on the night of 15 August 1944. Undertaken by 6./KG 51, these involved Oberleutnant Hans-Georg Lamle carrying out a Strassenjagd, while Feldwebel Johann Trenke and Unteroffizier Martin Golde carried out armed reconnaissances.

The exploits of the Me 410 Fernnachtjäger over the UK and north-west Europe were at last over. However, the cost had been high – V./KG 2 lost thirty-four aircraft in combat or on combat operations, while II./KG 51 lost twenty-eight. Added to that the nine aircraft lost by I./KG 51 between 15 March and 15 May 1944, a total of seventy-one Me 410s were lost over the UK, France, Belgium and the Netherlands. In terms of aircrew, sixty-one were killed or missing with V./KG 2, with two taken prisoner, forty-four killed with II./KG 51 and sixteen with I./KG 51.

Thirty-five Allied aircraft can be confirmed as shot down by the Me 410 Fernnachtjäger. One might ask whether, in the overall scheme of things, it was worth the effort and bloodshed on the German side. When compared to the successes of the Nachtjäger over Germany, one cannot help asking what was the point of it all?

Between September 1943 and June 1944, the official availability of Me 410s in the bomber role, according to the Luftwaffe records, ranged from thirty-five in September 1943, to a maximum of ninety-three in January 1944. From then, the numbers decreased to just twenty-six in June 1944.

In terms of aircraft casualties, 113 were lost in combat or accidents not due to enemy action, with another 105 suffering varying degrees of damage, either as a result of enemy action or in non-combat accidents. It is, therefore, not surprising the Me 410 failed in its task over the United Kingdom.

Epilogue

To say that intruder missions over Britain had ceased in the summer of 1944 is not strictly true. There were subsequently some instances where a German night fighter might have followed an aircraft further west than it should have. This is what possibly happened to the Stirling of 196 Squadron flown by Flight Lieutenant Ralph Campbell on the night of 21 February 1945. The wireless operator, Flight Sergeant Sid McQuillan, recalled what happened:

> It was on the evening of 21 February 1945 when we took off from Shepherds Grove at 1821hrs. The target was described as Rees, Germany, 24 x 500lb bombs tactical. The operation was successful but I cannot remember if we encountered enemy activity on the way out or back until we reached base at 2230hrs.
>
> We had no indication that intruders were in the area until the Ju 88 struck. At that time we were on the final approach to landing when we were raked by cannon fire, presumably a fuel line was severed because the plane burst into flames immediately.
>
> As you can imagine we were too low to bail out and therefore had to stick with it, the fire seemed to be in the centre section where the Engineer and I had our stations. I made a grab for the fire extinguisher with my left hand but it was already extremely hot and I could not hold it which I imagine was the reason for my left hand being more severely burnt than the right. Fortunately the controls were not damaged and the pilot was able to make a normal landing. I had already opened the astrodome through which the Engineer and I made our escape as soon as the plane came to a halt.
>
> The report states that the Rear Gunner [WO1 John McGovern] failed to get out and was burnt to death. The Engineer and I received severe burns, the Navigator had superficial hand burns, the pilot and Bomb Aimer had no injuries, the fire had not worked its way forward until after the landing.

There were no German claims for shooting down of this Stirling.

The skies above Britain were by now a very dangerous place to be, but that did not prevent Operation *Gisela* and Operation *Adelheid* going ahead; the latter being a smaller-scale operation. On the night of 3 March 1945, 142 (post-war analysis would say this was more like eighty) Ju 88s followed back bombers which had been attacking Ladbergen and Kamen. Night fighters had already claimed nine RAF bombers over Germany and would go on to claim another sixteen off the English coast or over mainland north-east England (many more were damaged). However, twenty-three night fighters were lost and seven more damaged.

Warrant Officer J.B. McGovern of 196 Squadron, who was killed by an intruder while his Stirling was landing at RAF Shepherd's Grove, 21 February 1945.

Hauptmann Johann Dreher of 12./NJG 3, who was killed during Operation *Gisela* on 3–4 March 1945.

The remains of Oberfeldwebel Leo Zimmermann's Ju 88G-6 of 5./NJG 4, which flew into the ground near Metfield in Suffolk while attacking a B-24 on 4 March 1945.

One of the casualties was Ritterkreuz winner Hauptmann Johann Dreher, Staffelkapitän of 13./NJG 3. He and his crew were killed when he flew into Dunnington Lodge Farm near RAF Elvington near York while trying to shoot down landing RAF bombers. Sadly Richard Moll, his wife, Ellen, and pregnant daughter-in-law, Violet, were all fatally injured.

Feldwebel Heinz Hommel, seen here in 1942, of 7./NJG 2.

On the night of 17 March 1945, ten Ju 88 Gs carried out another operation. Claims were filed by Feldwebel Heinz Hommel of 7./NJG 2, for a Lancaster near Louth, Feldwebel Rudolf Haupt of 8./NJG 2, for a Mosquito near York, and Feldwebel Rudi Morenz of 5./NJG 2, for a Lancaster and Halifax over Pocklington airfield.

It is believed that Heinz Hommel accounted for the Lancaster of 550 Squadron flown by Pilot Officer Alf Lockyer which, because there were no operations that night, was on a training flight. It was this crew's first flight with 550 Squadron; only the flight engineer, Sergeant Ted Drawbridge, survived when the aircraft crashed at Rimswell near Withernsea.

Hommel was a very experienced Ju 88 fighter pilot who had flown with V./KG 40 (later I./ZG 1) over the Bay of Biscay between 1942 and 1944. Two of his crew, the Beobachter, Unteroffizier Ernst Götz, and Bordfunker, Unteroffizier Hans Namhoff, were equally experienced, only the SN-2 radar operator, Obergefreiter Krewer, was not as experienced. Hommel's Gruppen Kommandeur, Hauptmann Heinz Ferger (who would be shot down and mortally wounded landing at Lübeck-Blankensee on the night of 9 April 1945, by Pilot Officer Don McFayden of 406 Squadron), wrote the following:

> During the mission in the night of 17/18 March 1945, the crew of Fw Hommel, 7./NJG 2, has shown a high degree of flying skills, consideration, courage and daringness.
>
> When attacking a Lancaster flying over England, the port engine of his aircraft cut out. Despite this defect, he pursued the turning enemy and shot it down in flames. After this air victory, Fw Hommel looked for a worthwhile target for his bombs and then dropped them into the main street of an English city with good success.
>
> The crew then returned, flying on one engine, to the base where the pilot carried out a perfect landing.
>
> I would like to express my full recognition to Fw Hommel and his crew for the excellent fighting and flying performance proven during this mission.

Feldwebel Heinz Hommel (left) and his crew in 1942.

After shooting down the bomber, Hommel dropped two AB500 bomb containers, which contained SD10A bombs, on Hull. The sirens there sounded at 21.36 hours, the bombs being dropped at 21.50 hours. The area affected was very close to a large cinema from which the patrons were just leaving. Of the seventy-four bombs, a small number, not more than six, fell on or very near the pavement crowded with people. One of the six failed to explode; at least two of them fell on previously damaged property, leaving only three which were likely to have caused the casualties. The remainder of the bombs fell approximately half of them on previously damaged houses or vacant land and the other half in small clusters on houses or in the yards attached to houses. These small clusters bursting together in a confined area gave the impression of small calibre high explosive bombs.

Sadly, there were fofty-four casualties, of which twelve were fatal.

It is believed that Rudi Morenz damaged two aircraft from 1664 Heavy Conversion Unit while the Mosquito cannot be matched to any losses.

Three nights later, Fernnachtjäger returned for a final time. A Stirling of 620 Squadron, that flown by Squadron Leader George Whitty DFC, was apparently attacked and crashed at Ford Farm, Great Dunmow, at 21.22 hours. The Stirling came down alongside an old Roman road leading to the village of Great Dunmow. It hit trees, passed under power lines, slid along the ground for some 125 yards and then struck a bank close to the village, where it exploded on impact. Six of the crew perished in the crash, while the rear gunner died of his injuries before he could be admitted to hospital. The dead included the Great Dunmow Special Air Service Liaison Officer, Captain George Slater.

A Court of Inquiry at the time concluded that the crash had not been caused by 'damage to the aircraft in the air', taking the view that the Captain had probably been watching the airfield lights instead of his instruments. However, research into the event some fifty years later revealed that contrary to the Court's findings, it was common knowledge amongst many on the base that the Stirling had been shot down by an enemy intruder as after releasing a Horsa glider, an aircraft had been seen following the Stirling across the field and cannon fire was clearly heard by a number of people immediately prior to the crash.

The second loss that night was a Halifax of 1665 Heavy Conversion Unit, flown by Pilot Officer Peter Nettlefield. This was shot down by an intruder and crashed at Elton near Peterborough at 22.40 hours, with the pilot and two crew being killed. It is believed that Feldwebel Rudi Morenz of 5./NJG 2 was responsible for shooting down both of these aircraft.

From the night of 24 March 1945, much of the Nachtjagd was now used almost exclusively in the Nachtschlacht role against the Allied forces crossing the Rhine and beyond. It would, therefore, appear that for the last two nights of Fernnachtjäger attacks, the Germans emerged the victors. But for the campaign as a whole, it was a hollow victory.

Appendices

Appendix I	Commanders II./NJG 1; I./NJG 2 (July 1940–October 1941)	142
Appendix II	I./NJG 2 Leading Intruder Pilots, October 1940–November 1941	143
Appendix III	Report on Night Fighting over Eastern England, 10–11 May 1941	144
Appendix IV	Report on Night Operations, 28–29 June 1941	146
Appendix V	Report on Night Operations Against England, by Fernnachtjäger, 23–24 July 1941	147
Appendix VI	Report on Night Operations Against England, by Fernnachtjäger, 7–8 August 1941	148
Appendix VII	Report on Night Operations Against England, by Fernnachtjäger, 1–2 September 1941	150
Appendix VIII	Report on Night Operations Against Eastern England, by Fernnachtjäger, 12–13 October 1941	152
Appendix IX	Intruder Claims, July 1940–October 1941	153
Appendix X	II./NJG 1 and 1, 2, 3, 4./NJG 2 Combat Losses/Accidents on Operations, August 1940–October 1941	161
Appendix XI	II./NJG 1 and 2./NJG 2 Dornier Do 17Z-10 Claims, September 1940–May 1941	171
Appendix XII	V./KG 2, I./KG 51 and II./KG 51 Executives, June 1943–August 1944	173
Appendix XIII	Deutsches Kreuz in Gold Winners Who Flew the Me 410 with V./KG 2, and I and II./KG 51	176
Appendix XIV	Known Messerschmitt Me 410 Operations Over The UK with V./KG 2 and II./KG 51	177
Appendix XV	Messerschmitt Me 410 Claims, N.W. Europe, August 1943–August 1944	188
Appendix XVI	Messerschmitt Me 410 Combat Losses, N.W. Europe, June 1943–August 1944	193

Appendix I

Commanders II./NJG 1; I./NJG 2 (July 1940–October 1941)

Gruppen Kommandeur	
Major Karl-Heinz Heyse	27 July 1940–†23 November 1940
Hauptmann Karl Hülshoff	To Komm NJG 2 1 November 1941
Hauptmann Rolf Jung	
Staffel Kapitän 1./NJG 2	
Oberleutnant Herbert Bönsch	To Stab./NJG 2 November 1941
Oberleutnant Albert Schulz	November 1941 to November 1942 (became 5./NJG 2)
Staffel Kapitän 2./NJG 2	
Oberleutnant Hans-Georg Schütze	To September 1940?
Hauptmann Rolf Jung	To Gr Kdr I./NJG 2 November 1941
Oberleutnant/Hauptmann Heinz Harmstorf	†22 July 1942
Staffel Kapitän 3./NJG 2	
Hauptmann Karl Hülshoff	To Gr Kdr I./NJG 2 23 Nov 40
Oberleutnant Ulrich Meyer	†21 December 1940
Oberleutnant Paul Semrau	
Staffel Kapitän 4./NJG 2 (joins I./NJG 2 to end of Feb 42)	
Oberleutnant Paul Zimmermann	†17 October 1940
Oberleutnant Paul Bohn	†26 June 1941
Oberleutnant Hans-Georg Schütze	†18 May 1942

Appendix II

I./NJG 2 Leading Intruder Pilots, October 1940–November 1941

Ofw Wilhelm Beier	3./NJG 2	14		RK
Fw Alfons Köster	3./NJG 2	11	†7 January 45	DKiG, RK
Ofw Peter Laufs	1./NJG 2	10	†27January 1942	DKiG
Lt Hans Hahn	3./NJG 2	12	†11 October 1941	RK
Lt Heinz Völker	3./NJG 2	9	†22 July 1941	
Oblt Paul Semrau	3./NJG 2	9	†8 February 1945	DKiG, EL
Ofw Heinz Strüning	1./NJG 2	9	†25 December 1944	EP, DKiG, EL
Ofw Hermann Sommer	2./NJG 2	9	†11 February 1944	DKiG
Oblt Kurt Herrmann	1./NJG 2	9	PoW 11 March 1941	EP, DKiG
Oblt Herbert Bönsch	1./NJG2	7	†1 August 1942	DKiG
Ofw Rolf Bussmann	3./NJG 2	6		EP, DKiG
Oblt Paul Bohn	4./NJG 2	5	†26 June 1941	
Hptm Karl Hülshoff	Stab I./NJG 2	4		DKiG
Oblt Albert Schulz	2./NJG 2	4	†30 January 1944	DKiG

Appendix III

Report on Night Fighting over Eastern England, 10–11 May 1941

23.19 hours	Wellington shot down 2500m 150km north-east of Cromer. 2 crew jumped by parachute and afterwards it crashed in flames. Despite failure of port engine after hit by enemy fire, the crew succeeded in returning to home base on one engine and made a smooth landing.
00.01 hours	Attack on Feltwell airfield from 600m with 8 x SD50 and 32 incendiaries. The crew observed a hit by four bombs and afterwards an explosion in a hangar which was completely burnt.
00.25 hours	10 x SD50 released from 1500m on railway facilities at Scarborough. Small fire was perceived.
00.30 hours	Attack on Peterborough airfield from 100m with 2 x SC50 on the edge and accommodation struck. A large fire was caused.
00.30 hours	8 x SD50 released on Watton airfield from 3000m and afterwards a large fire started.
01.30 hours	8 x SD50 and 36 incendiaries released on Dotterell airfield. A strong fire was seen.
02.30 hours	10 x SD50 released from 2000m on Middlesbrough docks facilities. As a result several fires were seen.
03.30 hours	Attack on East Wretham airfield from 2000m with 8 x SD50. The crew afterwards observed fires on the edge.
03.46 hours	Bristol Blenheim shot down at 1000m 50km east of Scarborough. Crashed into the sea in flames
04.25 hours	Attack on a Vickers Wellington at 300m 60km south-east of Spurn Head. The enemy aircraft was hit by a long burst and hit in the middle of the fuselage and right wing. In a right curve from the opponent's point of view. Shooting down was probable however it was not seen.

Oberleutnant Heinz Harmstorf	1./NJG 2	Wellington	23.19 hours
Oberfeldwebel Wilhelm Beier	3./NJG 2	Blenheim	03.46 hours

Wellington R1445/103 Sqn (Fg Off C W Harper). On the return trip [from Hamburg], encountered twin-engined aircraft at 600yds on the port beam. Rear Gunner opened fire and the aircraft turned away. Took off 2155hrs landed 0555hrs

Wellington R1395/103 Sqn (Plt Off E C Ball). On the return trip [from Emden] was attacked in succession by an Me 109, two Me 110s and a Ju 88. The crew was unable to recall details owing to the rapidity of the attacks. An Me 110 was shot down in flames. Attention was directed at a Ju 88 at 10,000ft which broke off the attack with smoke and flames issuing from the starboard engine. The Wellington's starboard engine was partially disabled and all spare gear was jettisoned. A good landing was made at base Took off 2330hrs landed 0455hrs.

Appendix IV

Report on Night Operations, 28–29 June 1941

NIGHTFIGHTER DIVISION

9 aircraft of which:
  Six aircraft in Raum B, C and F
  3 aircraft twilight fighter sortie over the sea

1 Ju 88 Raum B 0200hrs attack from 1800m locality of Lincoln with 8 x SD50. Nothing observed.

1 Ju 88 Raum B 0115hrs attack on Coningsby airfield with 8 x SD50. Nothing observed. 0200hrs attacked by single-engined night fighter at 1800m over northern coast of Raum C. Defence by moveable machine guns. Own aircraft retreated after attack into cloud.

1 Ju 88 Raum C 0130hrs attacked Norwich from 2000m with 4 x SC50 and 4 x SD50. Nothing observed.

1 Ju 88 Raum F 0055hrs attacked airfield at Leamington from 600m with 5 x SC50 and 5 x SD50. Because of heavy Flak effects not observed.

2 Ju 88 no enemy contact and did not bomb.

3 Ju 88 twilight fighter sortie over the sea no enemy contact.

Appendix V

Report on Night Operations Against England, by Fernnachtjäger, 23–24 July 1941

7 aircraft in Raum B, C and F.

1 Ju 88 (Raum B) at 0305hrs attacked from 1000m with 10 SD 50 Digby airfield. Nothing to report.

1 Ju 88 (Raum C) at 0315hrs attacked from 1500m with 10 SD50 Feltwell airfield. Two explosions and six medium persistent fires seen.

1 Ju 88 (Raum C) at 0310hrs attack from 700m with 10 SD550 Honnington airfield. Two explosions and two large persistent fires seen.

1 Ju 88 (Raum B) at 0137hrs attack from 1200m with 10 SC50 against protected searchlight emplacement, probably Scampton. Bright flames seen.

1 Ju 88 (Raum B). Airfield due to haze not found 0430hrs attacked Great Yarmouth from 1000m with eight SD50. Three medium fires to the east of the town seen. 0430hrs attacked by night fighter over Great Yarmouth. Enemy aircraft dodged due to haze.

1 Ju 88 (Raum C) engine failure 0338hrs attacked Flak emplacement at Great Yarmouth from 2300m with 10 SC50. Nothing observed.

1 Ju 88 missing.

Ju 88 C-2, 0854, R4+LM of 4./NJG 2. Ogefr Heinrich Ladiges (F), Ogefr Friedrich Heinemann (BF) and Fw Josef Beblo (BM) killed. At 0042hrs five 50kg bombs were dropped on RAF Elsham by an aircraft flying from south-east towards Humber at 10,000ft. At 0050hrs, two more sticks of 50kg bombs were dropped on RAF Elsham by an aircraft flying due north at 6,000ft. At 0110hrs, this aircraft was seen to burst into flames, crash at Bonby, Lincolnshire and explode. Believed hit by AA Battery Z2 while over Scunthorpe. Crew formerly with 1./KGr 126.

Appendix VI

Report on Night Operations Against England, by Fernnachtjäger, 7–8 August 1941

9 aircraft in Raum B, C and F.

1 aircraft twilight patrol.

1 Ju 88 (Raum F) 0001hrs contact with Wellington at 2200m over Norwich Catton. After cannon fire aircraft flew into cloud. 0127hrs Wellington shot down on fire at 1800m in Quadrant 05 Ost/2320.

1 Do 17 (Raum F) 2345hrs at 2000m attacked by enemy night fighter east of Norwich. Escaped by diving away. 0015hrs second attack by night fighter at 1800m. Evaded attack.

1 Ju 88 (Raum B) 0031hrs attacked a landing four-engined aircraft at 300m above Waddington. Hits in fuselage seen further effects not observed. 0032hrs attacked Waddington from 200m with 10 x SD50. Explosions on runway, hangars and accommodation. Three strong explosions.

1 Ju 88 (Raum B south and Raum C north) 0150hrs from 100m attacked Raynham airfield with 10 x SD50. Results not observed. 0212hrs shot down a Whitley taking off from Marham airfield at 100m. Crash and destroyed aircraft seen on the ground.

1 Ju 88 (Raum B) no enemy contact. At 0207hrs attacked Hemswell with 10 x SD50. Seven explosions on runway. 3 bombs LZZ [delayed action fuzes].

1 Ju 88 (Raum C) 0055hrs contact with Handley Page in Quadrant 05 Ost/3370. Aircraft fell away to left into cloud after being hit. 0117hrs contact with Whitley at 3200m in Quadrant 05 Ost/1380. Aircraft burned after hits in port engine and flew into cloud. 0145hrs attacked Wattingham [sic] airfield from 800m. Detonations on north of the runway.

1 Ju 88 (Raum C) engine failure aborted. Emergency bombing against Norwich. Results not seen.

1 Ju 88 (Raum C) radio failure aborted.

1 Ju 88 (Raum B) 0320hrs burning victory Bristol Blenheim from 1800m in Quadrant 05 Ost/0342. Crash seen. 0344hrs Halifax shot down from 2500m in Quadrant 05 Ost/1424. Crash seen. 0348hrs burning victory Vickers Wellington from 2500m in Quadrant 05 Ost/14521. Crash seen. 0322 attacked Raynham airfield from 1500m with 10 SD50. Nothing observed.

1 Ju 88 twilight patrol no results.

Claims:

Lt Hans Schulz	2./NJG 2	Wellington	0127hrs	
Fw Alfons Köster	3./NJG 2	Whitley	0242hrs	
Ofw Wilhelm Beier	3./NJG 2	Blenheim	0320hrs	
Ofw Wilhelm Beier	3./NJG 2	Halifax	0344hrs	
Ofw Wilhelm Beier	3./NJG 2	Wellington	0348hrs	Unidentified

Wellington X9601/101 Sqn (Plt Off L A Rickinson) attacked by Ju 88 0120hrs. Sgt E Elliott (2P) wounded; Sgt E C Thompson bailed out and his body washed ashore at Borkum 7 Sep 41 Ac landed safely at RAF Oakington 0205hrs.

Wellington Z8810/101 Sqn (Plt Off B G Cook) attacked by night fighter. Sgt W L Lackie slightly wounded. Landed RAF Oakington 0614hrs.

Wellington T2965/103 Sqn (Plt Off J W Purcivall) attacked by Ju 88 on way out at 10,000ft, 0135hrs. Ac received hits from cannon shell and tracer. A large hole was made in the fuselage above the tail wheel. The oxygen pipes were cut. The Rear Gunner however fired several bursts into the fighter and it was seen diving away. [Note: German times are the same as British times]

Appendix VII

Report on Night Operations Against England, by Fernnachtjäger, 1–2 September 1941

8 aircraft against airfields.

1 aircraft in Raum C.

Acklington Airfield
1 Ju 88. No enemy contact. 2340hrs 8 x SC50 from 250m. Three violent explosions on south of the airfield, long persistent fire.

1 Ju 88. No enemy contact. Because of heavy flak at Acklington, not attacked. 2348hrs 10 x SC50 from 200m against an airfield 3km north-west of Acklington. Impacts and a large fire in accommodation.

Newcastle Ouston Airfield
1 Ju 88. No enemy contact. 2328hrs 4 x SC50 and 4 x SD50 from 1000m. Hits on hangars.
1 Ju 88. No enemy contact. 2345hrs 10 x SC50form 2000m. Impacts observed.
1 Ju 88. No enemy contact. Targeted airfield heavy flak not attacked. 0035hrs 5 x SC50 and 5 x SD50 from 2500m against Newcastle. Effects not seen.

Usworth Airfield
1 Ju 88. 2240hrs attacked by Bristol Blenheim [sic] over Hull. Own aircraft not hit escaped into darkness. Targeted airfield of Usworth not attacked due to heavy Flak. 2350hrs 10 x SD50 from 1400m against Newcastle. Three large dark red luminous fires seen. 0008hrs one barrage balloon shot down in flames over Hull from 1800m.

[Note: Blenheim was probably Beaufighter of 406 Sqn crewed by Wg Cdr D G Morris/Fg Off G B Houghton]

1 Ju 88. No enemy contact. Targeted airfield not attacked due to heavy Flak. 0015hrs 6 x SD50 and 72 x B1 E1 dropped from 1800m on RAF Waddington. Effects not seen.

1 Ju 88 overdue. Last radio transmission 0046hrs.

1 Ju 88 (Raum C). No enemy contact. No bombing.

Ju 88C-4, 0592, R4+CM of 4./NJG 2. Failed to return. Fw Walter Kleine (F) and Fw Helmuth Fiedler (BM) missing; Fw Hans Engmann (BF) killed, body washed ashore in Holland

Wg Cdr J C Cunningham DSO DFC/Wg Cdr R B Lees DFC, 604 Sqn: 'Time up from Coltishall 2050hrs, landed 0025hrs. GCI Control Neatishead (Flt Lt Donald). Whilst patrolling at 10,000ft on a vector of 280 degrees about 12 miles off coast north-east of Cromer pilot was taken over by GCI who informed pilot of a Bandit flying at 10,000ft on a course 110 degrees. As Beaufighter was being vectored on to Bandit and on a course of 150 degrees it passed through Bandit's slipstream. After a final vector of 120 degrees contact was obtained at maximum range. Range was closed to about 3,000ft when the Bandit which was flying at 210 to 215 degrees apparently saw the Beaufighter and proceeded to make a complete circuit to the right at the same time flying into very thin cloud layer at about 8,000ft (during the course of the manoeuvre contact was maintained at an average range of 4,000ft. Bandit finally settled down to a steady course of 140 degrees magnetic apparently in a shallow dive as a silhouette (at a range of about 2,000ft) was obtained when Beaufighter was closing in at a speed of about 230mph. Final approach to the Bandit was from beneath and from the left which was moon down from the Bandit. Exhaust flames were seen from a distance of 1,500ft and the Bandit identified as a Ju 88. Pilot eased up and fired from a range of 150yds astern and practically level. Pilot saw a large flash which appeared to come from either the fuselage at a point between the starboard engine and the fuselage. Pilot pulled away to the left and after about a minute observed further flashes from the Ju 88 which was now beneath and left of Beaufighter. About a minute later the Ju 88 hit the sea and burst into flames. Place of combat was about 25–30 miles east of Winterton. Time of combat 2355hrs.'

[Note: German times were one hour ahead of British]

Appendix VIII

Report on Night Operations Against Eastern England, by Fernnachtjäger, 12–13 October 1941

02.30 hours	An unidentified airfield in the region of The Wash was attacked from 800m altitude with 10 x SD50. Five fires observed.
03.14 hours	Newmarket airfield attacked with 8 x SC50. The crew saw two fires. Furthermore without observation of the effects.
22.50 hours	An airfield probably Newton with 180 x SD2 from 2200m altitude.
00.20 hours	Church Fenton airfield with 10 x SD50 LZZ from 800m altitude.
00.30 hours	Church Fenton again with 5 x SD50 and 5 x SD50 LZZ from 1400m altitude. Five explosions on the edge of the airfield.
00.45 hours	Church Fenton again with 8 x SC50 and 72 incendiaries from 1300m altitude. Airfield was lit up by all attacks.
00.25 hours	Kirton in Lindsey airfield with 5 x SC50 and 5 x SD50 from 500m altitude. Bombs landed on runway.
00.45 hours	Leconfield airfield with 6 x SC50 and 72 incendiaries from 800m altitude. Bombs landed away from runway.
02.50 hours	Airfield north of Lincoln with 60 incendiaries from 200m altitude. Because of searchlights effect not seen.
00.40 hours	Factory north of Ipswich (alternative target) with 190 x SD2 from 1400m altitude. The crew saw good hits but further effects not seen. Factory was protected by balloons at 1300m.
01.50 hours	Harbour facilities at Cromer with 180 x SD2 from 1300m altitude. Effects not seen.
02.25 hours	Grimsby town from 2000m altitude with 8 x SD50 no effects observed.
02.00 hours	Harbour facilities south of Skegness from 1200m with 10 x SC50. Crew observed one explosion.

Appendix IX

Intruder Claims, July 1940–October 1941

23 Jul 40	2230hrs	Fw Otto Wiese	4./NJG 1	Wellington	100km W. Texel
23 Jul 40	2230hrs	Fw Gustav Schramm	4./NJG 1	Wellington	100km W. Texel
17 Aug 40	2300hrs	Fw Peter Laufs	4./NJG 1	Hurricane	Lowestoft
27 Aug 40	2130hrs	Ofw Merbach	Stab II./NJG 1	Hurricane	Grimsby
8 Sep 40	2300hrs	Lt Kurt Herrmann	4./NJG 1	Blenheim	Waddington
10 Sep 40	2315hrs	Fw Hermann Sommer	5./NJG 1	Blenheim	Waddington (Blenheim R3905/15 Sqn (Plt Off J. Kee) damaged)
20 Oct 40	2130hrs	Hptm Karl Hülshoff	3./NJG 2	Hampden	Dishforth
24 Oct 40	2205hrs	Lt Kurt Herrmann	1./NJG 2	Blenheim	Hemswell (unidentified Beaufort damaged)
24 Oct 40	2210hrs	Lt Kurt Herrmann	1./NJG 2	Blenheim	Hemswell (Blenheim P4858/17 OTU damaged)
24 Oct 40	2302hrs	Fw Hans Hahn	3./NJG 2	Wellington	Linton on Ouse (Whitley P5073/102 Sqn (Plt Off A.G. Davies)
28 Oct 40	0030hrs	Lt Heinz Völker	2./NJG 2	Hampden	Scampton (Hampden X3027/49 Sqn (Fg Off J.R. Bufton)
23 Nov 40	1830hrs	Hptm Karl Hülshoff	3./NJG 2	Wellington	80km W. Scheveningen (possibly T2471/214 Sqn (Sgt S.C. Chester))
23 Nov 40	1845hrs	Lt Kurt Herrmann	1./NJG 2		Hampden 75km N.E. The Wash
23 Nov 40	1850hrs	Fw Heinz Strüning	1./NJG 2	Wellington	50km W. Scheveningen (see above)
17 Dec 40	0400hrs	Oblt Paul Bohn	4./NJG 2		Hampden Scampton
17 Dec 40	0636hrs	Fw Wilhelm Beier	3./NJG 2		Hurricane 5km E. Spilsby
21 Dec 40	0900hrs	Uffz Gerhard Blum	1./NJG 2		Blenheim Kings Lynn

22 Dec 40	2115hrs	Lt Heinz Völker	2./NJG 2	Blenheim	50km E. Aldeburgh
1 Jan 41	1840hrs	Lt Rudolf Stradner	1./NJG 2	Wellington	70km E. Lowestoft
2 Jan 41	1845hrs	Uffz Helmut Arnold	1./NJG 2	Wellington	50km E. Happisburgh
2 Jan 41	1902hrs	Fw Hans Hahn	3./NJG 2	Whitley	50km E. Withernsea (T4227/102 Sqn (Fg Off D.C.F. Coutts)
3 Jan 41	1850hrs	Lt Gerhard Böhme	3./NJG 2	Whitley	30km S.E. Flamborough Head (T4234/10 Sqn (Plt Off G. Williams) damaged)
16 Jan 41	0230hrs	Oblt Albert Schulz	2./NJG 2	Blenheim	Church Fenton (Defiant L7002/54 OTU (Plt Off H.G.S. Wyrill)
16 Jan 41	0245hrs	Oblt Albert Schulz	2./NJG 2	Blenheim	Church Fenton (Defiant N1542/54 OTU (Flt Lt R.J.B. Burns) damaged)
11 Feb 41	0110hrs	Oblt Albert Schulz	2./NJG 2	Blenheim	West Raynham
11 Feb 41	0230hrs	Hptm Rolf Jung	2./NJG 2	Wellington	West Raynham (Wellington R1084/115 Sqn (Sgt H. Rodgers))
11 Feb 41	0415hrs	Oblt Paul Semrau	3./NJG 2	Blenheim	Feltwell (R3658/21 Sqn (Sqn Ldr J. Sabine)
11 Feb 41	0420hrs	Oblt Paul Semrau	3./NJG 2	Blenheim	Feltwell (Z5877/21 Sqn (Sgt A. Chattaway))
11 Feb 41	0649hrs	Oblt Kurt Herrmann	1./NJG 2	Hampden	Waddington (AD719/49 Sqn (Sgt J. Butterworth)
11 Feb 41	0658hrs	Oblt Kurt Herrmann	1./NJG 2	Hampden	Waddington (P1164/144 Sqn (Sgt W. McVie) damaged)
15 Feb 41	0730hrs	Fw Heinz Strüning	1./NJG 2	Hudson	75km E. Great Yarmouth (N7318/206 Sqn (Sqn Ldr O. Dias) undamaged)
15 Feb 41	1958hrs	Fw Heinz Strüning	1./NJG 2	Wellington	65km ENE.Southend
16 Feb 41	0125hrs	Oblt Herbert Bönsch	1./NJG 2	Blenheim	Waddington (Oxford R6076/2FTS (Fg Off R.M. Hackney) or V3244/2 FTS (Fg Off M.E. Blackstone) damaged)
25 Feb 41	2344hrs	Fw Ernst Ziebarth	2./NJG 2	Wellington	Waddington (R1009/218 Sqn (Sgt R. Hoos)
27 Feb 41	0010hrs	Oblt Herbert Bönsch	1./NJG 2	Blenheim	Scampton

27 Feb 41	0140hrs	Oblt Kurt Herrmann	1./NJG 2	Blenheim	Waddington (Oxford R6107/2 CFS (Fg Off D.M. Egan)
2 Mar 41	0255hrs	Oblt Herbert Bönsch	1./NJG 2	Blenheim	Scampton
12 Mar 41	2210hrs	Fw Heinz Mittelstädt	2./NJG 2	Blenheim	N. Wells (possibly Wellington P9226/311 Sqn damaged)
13 Mar 41	0115hrs	Fw Hans Hahn	3./NJG 2	Blenheim	Leeming (Blenheim L6835/54 OTU (Plt Off M.G. Calvert))
13 Mar 41	2200hrs	Fw Hans Hahn	3./NJG 2	Hudson	Waddington (Manchester L7319/207 Sqn (Fg Off H.V. Matthews))
18 Mar 41	0653hrs	Fw Peter Laufs	1./NJG 2	Wellington	Cromer (X3161/221 Sqn (Plt Off Robinson) damaged)
18 Mar 41	0720hrs	Lt Rudolf Pfeiffer	1./NJG 2	Wellington	Mildenhall (R1474/149 Sqn (Sgt R. Warren))
4 Apr 41	0120hrs	Lt Heinz Völker	3./NJG 2	Wellington	West Raynham (R1470/115 Sqn (Sgt C.M. Thompson)
8 Apr 41	0120hrs	Lt Hans Feuerbaum	2./NJG 2	Hudson	Wells (206 Sqn (Plt Off C.R. Alexander) damaged)
8 Apr 41	0123hrs	Lt Hans Feuerbaum	2./NJG 2	Hampden	Wells (Z6478/51 Sqn (Plt Off G.R. Mattey) damaged)
8 Apr 41	0140hrs	Fw Hans Hahn	3./NJG 2	Hampden	Upwood (P2092/14 OTU (Sgt R.J. Holborow))
8 Apr 41	2250hrs	Hptm Karl Hülshoff	Stab I./NJG 2	Wellington	50km E. Bridlington (P9230/311 Sqn (Plt Off J. Hrncir) damaged
8 Apr 41	2300hrs	Hptm Karl Hülshoff	Stab I./NJG 2	Hampden	30km N. Scarborough
8 Apr 41	2345hrs	Fw Hans Hahn	3./NJG 2	Wellington	Wellingore (Beaufighter R2250/29 Sqn (Flt Lt G.P. Gibson) damaged)
9 Apr 41	2315hrs	Uffz Hans Berschwinger	4./NJG 2	Wellington	Marham (R1049/221 Sqn (Plt Off P.C. Brown))
10 Apr 41	0130hrs	Fw Peter Laufs	1./NJG 2	Wellington	Wells
10 Apr 41	0130hrs	Oblt Albert Schulz	2./NJG 2	Wellington	Cambridge (L4253/11 OTU (Sgt G.D.H. Dutton)

10 Apr 41	0255hrs	Ofw Wilhelm Beier	3./NJG 2	Whitley	Chelmsford
10 Apr 41	0500hrs	Uffz Alfons Köster	3./NJG 2	Single-engine	
16 Apr 41	2303hrs	Lt Heinz Völker	3./NJG 2	Hampden	Finningley
17 Apr 41	0144hrs	Fw Hans Hahn	3./NJG 2	Hampden	SE.Waddington (AD761/144 Sqn (Sgt H. Kirby))
21 Apr 41	0332hrs	Fw Hans Hahn	3./NJG 2	Hampden	Digby (Battle P6674/12 FTS (Sgt R. Kilbuern))
24 Apr 41	0135hrs	Fw Vincenz Giessübel	2./NJG 2	Twin-engine	Wellington N2912/11 OTU (Sgt P.H.Nicholls)
25 Apr 41	0035hrs	Lt Heinz Völker	3./NJG 2	Blenheim	Lindholme (L1320/54 OTU (Sgt A. Spurgin))
25 Apr 41	0037hrs	Lt Heinz Völker	3./NJG 2	Blenheim	Lindholme (L1478/54 OTU (Sgt G.W. Attenborough) damaged)
25 Apr 41	0044hrs	Lt Heinz Völker	3./NJG 2	Blenheim	Lindholme (K7132/54 OTU (Flt Lt R.W. Denison))
25 Apr 41	0050hrs	Ofw Herbert Biehne (BF)	3./NJG 2	Blenheim	Lindholme
26 Apr 41	0330hrs	Lt Rudolf Pfeiffer	4./NJG 2	Singe-engine	Hemswell (Defiant N1568/54 OTU (Sgt F.C. Crozier))
30 Apr 41	0015hrs	Ofw Hermann Sommer	2./NJG 2	Blenheim	Tollerton (Oxford L9686/2 CFS (LAC Patrick))
30 Apr 41	0020hrs	Ofw Hermann Sommer	2./NJG 2	Blenheim	Tollerton
30 Apr 41	0050hrs	Ofw Hermann Sommer	2./NJG 2	Blenheim	Hucknall
30 Apr 41	0130hrs	Ofw Hermann Sommer	2./NJG 2	Beaufort	Bircham Newton
3 May 41	0315hrs	Lt Hans Feuerbaum	2./NJG 2	Hampden	Church Fenton (Whitley Z6641/77 Sqn (Sgt Mills) damaged)
4 May 41	0246hrs	Ofw Hans Hahn	3./NJG 2	Fulmar	Stoke Holy Cross (Spitfire P7699/222 Sqn (Pl Off P.B. Klee))
5 May 41	0113hrs	Ofw Hans Hahn	3./NJG 2	Blenheim	Feltwell (Hurricane P3866/257 Sqn (Sgt R. G. Parrott))
5 May 41	0430hrs	Uffz Bittner	2./NJG 2	Blenheim	35km N.W. Great Yarmouth
7 May 41	0248hrs	Fw Heinz Strüning	1./NJG 2	Wellington	Peterborough (R3227/11 OTU (Fg Off T.J. Warner))
8 May 41	0022hrs	Uffz Alfons Köster	3./NJG 2	Wellington	5km W. Southend

8 May 41	0120hrs	Oblt Paul Semrau	3./NJG 2	Wellington	5km S. Grantham (Oxford W6636/14 FTS (Fg Off R.P. Davey))
8 May 41	0250hrs	Ofw Wilhelm Beier	3./NJG 2	Wellington	Wells
8 May 41	2330hrs	Uffz Alfons Köster	3./NJG 2	Blenheim	E. Mablethorpe (Wellington R1397/103 Sqn (Plt Off Anderson) damaged)
9 May 41	2330hrs	Fw Heinz Strüning	1./NJG 2	Wellington	NE Clacton
10 May 41	2334hrs	Oblt Heinz Harmstorf	1./NJG 2	Wellington	150km N.E. Cromer
11 May 41	0340hrs	Ofw Wilhelm Beier	3./NJG 2	Blenheim	50km E. Scarborough (Wellington R1445/103 Sqn (Plt Off Harper) damaged
16 May 41	2330hrs	Ofw Hermann Sommer	2./NJG 2	Wellington	Wells
18 May 41	0219hrs	Oblt Paul Semrau	3./NJG 2	Blenheim	5km S. Grantham (Battle R7363/12 FTS (Fg Off B.K. Thomas)
4 Jun 41	0135hrs	Ofw Wilhelm Beier	3./NJG 2	Blenheim	20km S.E. Lowestoft
12 Jun 41	0207hrs	Uffz Alfons Köster	3./NJG 2	Hampden	N.W. London (Hampden 1341/16 OTU (Plt Off L.B. Gunter) or Anson N5014/16 OTU (Plt Off D.G.D. Buckley) or Anson R6961/16 OTU (Plt Off D.C. Adams) all damaged)
12 Jun 41	0400hrs	Oblt Paul Bohn	4./NJG 2	Wellington	N.E. Bacton
12 Jun 41	0410hrs	Oblt Paul Bohn	4./NJG 2	Whitley	N.E. Bacton
13 Jun 41	0041hrs	Ofw Wilhelm Beier	3./NJG 2	Defiant	Thornaby
13 Jun 41	0110hrs	Oblt Paul Semrau	3./NJG 2	Halifax	Finningley (Wellington R1708/25 OTU (Sgt W.R.L. Collyer))
16 Jun 41	2400hrs	Ofw Rolf Bussmann	3./NJG 2	Wellington	N. Cromer
17 Jun 41	0006hrs	Ofw Rolf Bussmann	3./NJG 2	Wellington	N.W. Cromer
17 Jun 41	0313hrs	Oblt Herbert Bönsch	1./NJG 2	Wellington	120km E. Harwich
17 Jun 41	0335hrs	Fw Helmut Arnold	1./NJG 2	Whitley	50km N. Ostende (possibly Z6492/78 Sqn (Plt Off D.S.W. Lake))
17 Jun 41	0335hrs	Ofw Hermann Sommer	2./NJG 2	Wellington	30km S.W. Lowestoft

17 Jun 41	0410hrs	Ofw Otto Glas (BF)	2./NJG 2	Wellington	20km E. Lowestoft
17 Jun 41	2400hrs	Oblt Herbert Bönsch	1./NJG 2	Wellington	115km E. Cromer (W5378/142 Sqn (Flt Lt A Gosman) damaged)
19 Jun 41	0425hrs	Oblt Paul Semrau	3./NJG 2	Whitley	90km N.E. Great Yarmouth (possibly W6560/78 Sqn (Flt Sgt V.H. Marks))
21 Jun 41	0020hrs	Oblt Paul Bohn	4./NJG 2	Wellington	200km E. Spurn Head (possibly R1713/218 Sqn (Sgt M.J. Fraser))
23 Jun 41	0013hrs	Oblt Herbert Bönsch	1./NJG 2	Wellington	75km N.E. Great Yarmouth
26 Jun 41	0015hrs	Oblt Paul Bohn	4./NJG 2	Whitley	50km E. Raum B
26 Jun 41	0135hrs	Ofw Hermann Jung	2./NJG 2	Wellington	75km E. Harwich
27 Jun 41	2345hrs	Fw Robert Lüddecke	3./NJG 2	Wellington	40km S.E. Eastbourne
27 Jun 41	2355hrs	Ofw Hermann Sommer	2./NJG 2	Wellington	70km E. Great Yarmouth
30 Jun 41	0350hrs	Fw Helmut Arnold	1./NJG 2	Wellington	60km E. Bacton
30 Jun 41	0414hrs	Ofw Hermann Jung	2./NJG 2	Wellington	200km E.S.E. Grimsby
5 Jul 41	0100hrs	Ofw Peter Laufs	1./NJG 2	Single-engine	Wells. Spitfire P8085/452 Sqn (Sgt A.G. Costello))
5 Jul 41	0150hrs	Ofw Heinz Strüning	1./NG 2	Wellington	10km E. Nottingham
6 Jul 41	0308hrs	Ofw Wilhelm Beier	3./NJG 2	Wellington	110km N.N.E. Texel
6 Jul 41	0336hrs	Ofw Wilhelm Beier	3./NJG 2	Blenheim	100km W. Texel
6 Jul 41	?	Ofw Rolf Bussmann	3./NJG 2	Wellington	65km N.E. Great Yarmouth
6 Jul 41	2324hrs	Ofw Wilhelm Beier	3./NJG 2	Whitley	60km N.E. Bacton. Possibly Hampden AD856/49 Sqn (Sgt J. Flint)
6 Jul 41	2324hrs	Ofw Wilhelm Beier	3./NJG 2	Whitley	60km N.E. Bacton (see above)
7 Jul 41	0004hrs	Fw Heinrich Barth	3./NJG 2	Blenheim	30km E. Great Yarmouth. Possibly Wellington R1471/115 Sqn (Sqn Ldr Knight) damaged)
7 Jul 41	0312hrs	Oblt Paul Semrau	3./NJG 2	Blenheim	Wells (Z6041/500 Sqn (Fg Off A Leeson))
8 Jul 41	0009hrs	Fw Hans Berschwinger	4./NJG 2	Whitley	N.W. Sheffield
9 Jul 41	0301hrs	Lt Heinz Schulz	2./NJG 2	Hampden	5km N.E. Feltwell
15 Jul 41	0125hrs	Fw Alfons Köster	3./NJG 2	Blenheim	Wyton

15 Jul 41	0130hrs	Fw Alfons Köster	3./NJG 2	Blenheim	Wyton
15 Jul 41	0430hrs	Unknown		Blenheim	Unconfirmed
16 Jul 41	0225hrs	Unknown	I./NJG 2	Swordfish	Upwood (Tiger Moth R4962/22 EFTS (LAC S.J. Hassall))
18 Jul 41	0250hrs	Oblt Paul Semrau	3./NJG 2	Blenheim	Digby (Wellington N2840/301 Sqn (Fg Off B. Kuzian))
18 Jul 41	0302hrs	Ofw Wilhelm Beier	3./NJG 2	Beaufort	120km N.E. Great Yarmouth
19 Jul 41	0040hrs	Oblt Hans-Georg Schütze	4./NJG 2	Twin-engine	Wyton (possibly X3619/11 OTU (damaged)
19 Jul 41	0050hrs	Oblt Hans-Georg Schütze	4./NJG 2	Twin-engine	Wyton (see above)
22 Jul 41	0119hrs	Lt Heinz Volker	3./NJG 2	Wellington	SW.Cambridge (Collided with R1334/11 OTU (Flt Sgt W.A. Hannah))
28 Jul 41	0346hrs	Lt Dr Lothar Bisang	2./NJG 2	Blenheim	Raum C (Oxford V3685/2 FTS (LAC R.S. Smith))
30 Jul 41	0036hrs	Fw Helmut Arnold	1./NJG 2	Whitley	Hemswell (possibly Oxford T1064/54 OTU (Sgt C.C. Woodward))
8 Aug 41	0139hrs	Lt Heinz Schulz	2./NJG 2	Wellington	70km N.E. Great Yarmouth (possibly X9601/101 Sqn (Plt Off L.A. Rickinson) or T2965/103 Sqn (Plt Off J.W. Purcivall) damaged)
8 Aug 41	0242hrs	Fw Alfons Köster	3./NJG 2	Whitley	Marham
8 Aug 41	0320hrs	Ofw Wilhelm Beier	3./NJG 2	Blenheim	East Dereham
8 Aug 41	0344hrs	Ofw Wilhelm Beier	3./NJG 2	Halifax	200km E. Withernsea
8 Aug 41	0348hrs	Ofw Wilhelm Beier	3./NJG 2	Wellington	200km E. Flamborough Head
13 Aug 41	0110hrs	Ofw Rolf Bussmann	3./NJG 2	Wellington	Oxford (Oxford R6156/15 SFTS (Flt Sgt E. Julin-Olsen or Oxford W6229/15 SFTS (LAC C.P. Blair))
13 Aug 41	0119hrs	Ofw Rolf Bussmann	3./NJG 2	Wellington	Oxford (see above)
13 Aug 41	0139hrs	Ofw Rolf Bussmann	3./NJG 2	Wellington	Oxford
13 Aug 41	0319hrs	Ofw Peter Laufs	1./NJG 2	Wellington	Coltishall (T2563/115 Sqn (Plt Off Woods))

15 Aug 41	0520hrs	Ofw Robert Lüddecke	1./NJG 2	Wellington	20km E. Humber Estuary (W5536/12 Sqn (Sgt A. Cameron))
15 Aug 41	0530hrs	Ofw Robert Lüddecke	1./NJG 2	Wellington	20km E. Humber Estuary
17 Aug 41	0044hrs	Lt Hans Hahn	3./NJG 2	Wellington	Scunthorpe (W5532/104 Sqn (Sgt W.T.R. Stephenson))
19 Aug 41	0120hrs	Ofw Heinz Strüning	1./NJG 2	Blenheim	Grantham
19 Aug 41	0200hrs	Ofw Heinz Strüning	1./NJG 2	Blenheim	Grantham
20 Aug 41	0239hrs	Fw Alfons Köster	3./NJG 2	Blenheim	20km W. Lincoln (possibly Wellington N3005/11 OTU (Flt Sgt C.G. Andrews))
1 Sep 41	0233hrs	Fw Alfons Köster	3./NJG 2	Wellington	Oxford (AnsonN5074/16 OTU (Flt Sgt O.C. Mairies))
1 Sep 41	0343hrs	Fw Alfons Köster	3./NJG 2	Hampden	Hatfield (Wellington R1411/99 Sqn (Plt Off G.S. Eccles))
20 Sep 41	2344hrs	Oblt Paul Semrau	3./NJG 2	Hampden	7km N.E. Upper Heyford (P5314/16 OTU (Sgt N. Van der Merwe))
30 Sep 41	2246hrs	Ofw Rolf Bussmann	3./NJG 2	Blenheim	Winthorpe
3 Oct 41	2341hrs	Fw Alfons Köster	3./NJG 2	Stirling	Cambridge (N6085/7 Sqn (Sqn Ldr D.I. McLeod))
11 Oct 41	2110hrs	Lt Hans Hahn	3./NJG 2	Oxford	Grantham (collided with AB767/12 FTS (Sgt T.D. Graham))
12 Oct 41	2130hrs	Ofw Heinz Strüning	1./NJG 2	Blenheim	Upwood (R3617/51 OTU (Sgt F. Filmer)

Appendix X

II./NJG 1 and 1, 2, 3, 4./NJG 2 Combat Losses/Accidents on Operations, August 1940–October 1941

Date	*Unit*	*Aircraft Details*	*Crew*	*Fate*
18 Aug 40	4./NJG 1	Ju 88C-2, 0245, 4D+HZ	Ofw Fritz Zenkel-F-+ Fw Gustav Schramm-BF-+ Gefr Hans Roth-BM-+	Missing over North Sea. Possibly shot down in combat with Wellington of 37 Sqn (Fg Off A. Hough)
16 Sep 40	1./NJG 2	Ju 88C-2, 0190, R4+AH	Fw Werner Palm-F-+ Gefr Hans Reinisch-BF-+ Gefr Rudolf Haberland-BM-+	Missing over North Sea. Pilot's body washed ashore in Denmark
14 Oct 40	2./NJG 2	Do 17Z-10, 2851, R4+DK	Uffz Erich Götz-F-inj Uffz Georg Herden-BF-inj Uffz Kurt Dreher-BM-inj	Crashed on landing at Gilze Rijen 0547hrs
17 Oct 40	4./NJG 2	Bf 110D-0, 3385, 3M+AH	Oblt Paul Zimmermann-F-St Kap-+ Gefr Walter Makowski-BF-+	Crashed at Capelle/Dongen on return from combat mission

Date	*Unit*	*Aircraft Details*	*Crew*	*Fate*
17 Oct 40	3./NJG 2	Ju 88C-2, 0251, R4+EL	-	Landing accident at Gilze-Rijen returning from operations
20 Oct 40	3./NJG 2	Ju 88C-2, 0278	Fw Kurt Schlicht-F-inj Uffz Wilhelm Marschall-BF-uninj Gefr Hans Nitz-BM-uninj	Landing accident at Eindhoven returning from operations
1 Nov 40	3./NJG 2	Ju 88C-4, 0349, R4+OL	Uffz Matthias Lang-F-+ Gefr Heinz Linke-BF-+ Gefr Wilhelm Gerardi-BM-+	Missing from operations
9 Nov 40	2./NJG 2	Do 17Z-7, 2817, R4+HK	Ofw Herbert Schmidt-F-uninj Ofw Paul Rosenberger-BF-uninj Uffz karl Lang-BM-inj	Damaged by Flak over Lincoln and crash-landed at Gilze-Rijen 0900hrs
23 Nov 40	Stab I./NJG 2	Ju 88C-4, 0347, R4+BB	Maj Karl-Heinrich Heyse-F-Gr Kdr-+ Uffz Richard Fiedler-BF-+ Uffz Herbert Bauda-BM-+	Missing from operations over North Sea
23 Nov 40	3./NJG 2	Ju 88C-4, 0373, R4+TK	Ofw Kurt Schlicht-F-+ Uffz Wilhelm Marschall-BF-+ Gefr Hans Nitz-BM-+	Missing from operations over North Sea. Bodies later washed ashore. One of these possibly lost in combat with Hampden of 61 Sqn (Sgt R. Oakley)

Date	*Unit*	*Aircraft Details*	*Crew*	*Fate*
23 Nov 40	I./NJG 2	Ju 88C	2 groundcrew killed	Exploded while being prepared for operations
21 Dec 40	3./NJG 2	Ju 88C-2, 0272, R4+KL	Oblt Ulrich Meyer-F-St Kap-+ Fw Fritz Schöttke-BF-+ Ogefr Wilhelm Schneider-BM-+	Shot down by Flak attacking RAF Manby and crashed at South Cockerington, 0815hrs
21 Dec 40	1./NJG 2	Ju 88C-2, 0182, R4+TH	Gefr Kurt Ludescher-F-+ Gefr Friedrich Rohde-BF-+ Gefr Heinrich Dempewolf-BM-+	Crashed at Gilze-Rijen on return from operations
1 Jan 41	1./NJG 2	Ju 88C-2, 0254, R4+KH	Lt Rudolf Stradner-F-uninj Uffz Wilhelm Krieg-BF-uninj Uffz Max Oswald-BM-uninj	Damaged in combat with Wellington possibly from 301 Sqn
9 Jan 41	3./NJG 2	Ju88C-2, 0227, R4+CL	Uffz Otto Kräher-F-+ Uffz Martin Stachowski-BF-+ Uffz Josef Diwok-BM-+	Missing from operations
4 Feb 41	2./NJG 2	Do 17Z-10, 2859, R4+BK	Oblt Otto-Heinrich Häuser-F-+ Fw Gerhard Palm-BF-+ Fw Johannes Quade-BM-+	Missing from operations
15 Feb 41	1./NJG 2	Ju 88C-2, 0239, R4+FH	Oblt Herbert Bönsch-F-St Kap-uninj Uffz Otto Böttcher-BF-uninj Fw August Willi-BM-uninj	Damaged in combat

Date	*Unit*	*Aircraft Details*	*Crew*	*Fate*
24 Feb 41	3./NJG 2	Ju 88C-4, 0544	Fw Johannes Schuster-F-+ Fw Franz Fuchs-BF-+ Gefr Kurt Masepohl-BM-+	Crashed Gut Valkenburg 6km SW Gilze-Rijen, 0020hrs returning from operations
27 Feb 41	3./NJG 2	Ju 88C-4, 0371	Oblt Heinz Semrau-F & crew uninj	Damaged in combat and force-landed at Gilze-Rijen
2 Mar 41	I./NJG 2	Ju 88C-4, 0377	-	Damaged in combat and force-landed at Gilze-Rijen
2 Mar 41	I./NJG 2	Ju 88C-4, 0375	-	Damaged in combat and force-landed at Gilze-Rijen
10 Mar 41	1./NJG 2	Ju 88C-4, 0343, R4+CH	Oblt Kurt Herrmann-F-POW Uffz Engelbert Böttner-BF-POW Fw Wilhelm Rüppel-BM-POW	Suffered engine failure and crash-landed at Hay Green, Terrington St Clement, 2350hrs
14 Mar 41	4./NJG 2	Ju 88C-4, 0604, R4+GM	Gefr Hans Körner-F-+ Gefr Karl Spangenberg-BF-+ Uffz Willi Gebhardt-BM-+	Shot down by Wg Cdr S.C Widdows, 29 Sqn and crashed at Dovendale, Tathwell, Lincs 0330hrs
31 Mar 41	4./NJG 2	Ju88C-4, 0618, R4+HM	Gefr Ottomar Krüger-F-+ Gefr August Kronewitter-BF-+ Gefr Heinrich Kellner-BM-+	Reported at 2315hrs that it had suffered engine failure 90km east of Flamborough Head

Date	*Unit*	*Aircraft Details*	*Crew*	*Fate*
9 Apr 41	4./NJG 2	Ju 88C-2, 0776, R4+CM	Gefr Franz Brotz-F-+ Uffz Willi Lindla-BF-POW Gefr Ewald Gorld-BM-POW	Shot down by Sgt S Bennett, 25 Sqn and crashed Burley-Langham Road, Oakham, Rutland 2210hrs
17 Apr 41	4./NJG 2	Ju 88C-4, 0345, R4+BM	Ogefr Wilhelm Beetz-F-+ Gefr Rudolf Kronika-BF-+ Gefr Johann Mittag-BM-+	Crashed due to unknown reasons at Gedney Hill, Thorney, Cambs 2123hrs
18 Apr 41	3./NJG 2	Ju 88C-2, 0732	Uffz Will Keller-F-+ Gefr Gerhard Wawra-BF-+ Uffz Helmut Heese-BM-+	Crashed at Dongen after having taken off from Gilze-Rijen on operational flight
18 Apr 41	I./NJG 2	Ju 88C-2, 0767	-	Force-landed at Gilze-Rijen after suffering technical problems on operations
24 Apr 41	2./NJG 2	Do 17Z-10	Fw Henrich Schwöbel-F-wounded Uffz Eduard Funke-BM-wounded	Wounded in combat with RAF bomber
6 May 41	I./NJG 2	Ju 88C-2, 0740	-	Damaged in combat
8 May 41	2./NJG 2	Do 17Z-10, 2843, R4+GK	Fw Wilhelm Lettenmeier-F-+ Uffz Georg Herden-BF-POW Uffz Herbert Thomas-BM-POW	Shot down by Plt Off D W Thompson, 25 Sqn and crashed at Carrington, Boston, Lincs, 0030hrs

Date	*Unit*	*Aircraft Details*	*Crew*	*Fate*
27 May 41	2./NJG 2	Ju 88C-4, 0359, R4+MK	Ofw Hermann Sommer-F-wounded Fw Otto Glass-BF-unwounded Ofw Johann Reinnagel-BM-wounded	Damaged in a ferry flight from Brest by Bf 109 and force-landed at Lannion
4 Jun 41	2./NJG 2	Ju 88C-4, 0570, R4+LK	Lt Johannes Feuerbaum-F-+ Gefr Gerhard Denzien-BF-+ Gefr Rudolf Peters-BM-+	Flew into hillside at Hutton Malgrave, Whitby 0030hrs
14 Jun 41	4./NJG 2	Ju 88C-4, 0550, R4+DM	Uffz Richard Hoffmann-F-POW Gefr Johann Reisinger-BF-+ Fw Peter Mayer-BM-POW	Shot down by Sqn Ldr H P Pleasance, 25 Sqn and crashed at Narford, Norfolk 0020hrs
14 Jun 41	4./NJG 2	Ju 88C-4, 0335, R4+AM	Uffz Helmut Bähner-F-+ Uffz Jakob Ried-BF-+ Uffz Heinz Schulz-BM-+	Shot down by Plt Off D W Thompson, 25 Sqn and crashed at Wingland Marsh, Terrington St Clement, Norfolk 0020hrs
14 Jun 41	4./NJG 2	Ju 88C-2, 0785, R4+JM	Uffz Vitus Alt-F-+ Uffz Hans-Georg Suckow-BF-+ Uffz Erwin Korn-BM-+	Hit sea circling dinghy containing crew from He 111 of 8./KG 4 which had ditched 75km N.W. Schouwen
21 Jun 41	I./NJG 2	Ju 88C-2, 0756	-	Damaged in combat and landed at Bergen

Date	*Unit*	*Aircraft Details*	*Crew*	*Fate*
22 Jun 41	1./NJG 2	Ju 88C-2, 0827, R4+JH	Ofw Otto Wiese-F-+ Uffz Heinrich Beul-BF-POW Gefr Hermann Mandel-BM-+	Shot down by Fg Off M.J. Herrick, 25 Sqn and crashed at Haynes Farm, Deeping St James, Lincs 0125hrs
24 Jun 41	2./NJG 2	Ju 88C-2	Lt Hans Schulz-F-uninj Uffz Wolfgang Pusch-BF-uninj Ogefr Ernst Idzick-BM-uninj	Suffered engine failure and ditched off Dutch coast; crew rescued by Seenotdienst
26 Jun 41	4./NJG 2	Ju 88C-2, 0794, R4+GM	Oblt Paul Bohn-F-St Kap-+ Fw Hans Engmann-BF-uninj Fw Walter Lindner-BM-uninj	Damaged in combat 0015 hrs and pilot killed. Crew bailed out over Charleville and aircraft crashed near Milan, Italy
9 Jul 41	1./NJG 2	Ju 88C-2, 0848, R4+MH	Lt Rudolf Stradner-F-+ Uffz Wilhelm Krieg-BF-+ Uffz Max Oswald-BM-+	Reported returning on one engine 0330hrs but ditched off Dutch coast. Body of BF washed ashore at Wittdün, Amrum 18 Aug 41
14 Jul 41	3./NJG 2	Ju 88C-4, 0636	Oblt Paul Semrau-F-St Kap-unwounded Gefr Johann Hantusch-BF-W Ogefr Georg Faulhaber-BM-W	Damaged in combat

Date	*Unit*	*Aircraft Details*	*Crew*	*Fate*
22 Jul 41	3./NJG 2	Ju 88C-2, 0842, R4+BL	Lt Heinz Völker-F-+ Uffz Herbert Indenbirken-BF-+ Fw Andreas Würstl-BM-+	Collided with Wellington of 10 OTU (Sgt W.A. Stewart) and crashed at Ashwell, Herts 0130hrs
24 Jul 41	4./NJG 2	Ju 88C-2, 0854, R4+LM	Ogefr Heinrich Ladiges-F-+ Ogefr Friedrich Heinemann-BF-+ Fw Josef Beblo-BM-+	Hit by Flak near Hull and crashed at Bonby, Lincs 0110hrs
28 Jul 41	2./NJG 2	Ju 88C-2, 0724, R4+KK	Lt Dr Lothar Bisang-F-+ Gefr Werner Ulbricht-BF-+ Gefr Fritz Rosenstock-BM-+	Dived into ground at Vine Farm, Wivenhoe, Essex 0420hrs believed trying to evade 85 Sqn Havoc or searchlights
31 Jul 41	3./NJG 2	Ju 88C-2, 0764	Lt Hans Hahn-F-inj Uffz Ernst Meissler-BF-uninj Uffz Helmut Scheidt-BM-inj	Take off accident
31 Jul 41	I./NJG 2	Ju 88C-2, 0748	-	Engine failure and force-landed near Moerdijk
12 Aug 41	Stab I./NJG 2	Ju 88C-2, 0845	Maj Karl Hülshoff-F-Gr Kdr-unwounded Ofw Willi Meyer-BF-wounded Ofw Paul Licht-BM-wounded	Damaged in combat with Sqn Ldr H.M. Stephen, 234 Sqn, 122hrs and force-landed at Steenbergen

Date	*Unit*	*Aircraft Details*	*Crew*	*Fate*
13 Aug 41	I./NJG 2	Ju 88C-4, 0375	-	Landing accident, Gilze-Rijen
17 Aug 41	4./NJG 2	Ju 88C-2, 0851, R4+HM	Lt Rudolf Pfeiffer-F-+ Gefr Otto Schierling-BF-+ Uffz Adolf Ranke-BM-+	Missing from operations; last radio message 2332hrs. BF's body discovered in North Sea 26 Aug 41 and buried at sea
24 Aug 41	1./NJG 2	Ju 88C-4, 0612, R4+FH	Gefr Lippert & crew uninj	Landing accident Gilze-Rijen
1 Sep 41	4./NJG 2	Ju 88C-4, 0592, R4+CM	Fw Walter Kleine-F-+ Fw Hans Engmann-BF-+ Fw Helmut Fiedler-BM-+	Shot down by Wg Cdr J. Cunningham, 604 Sqn east of Winterton, Norfolk, 2355hrs. BF's body washed ashore in Holland
4 Sep 41	3./NJG 2	Ju88C-4, 0337, R4+OL	Lt Hans Hahn-F-uninj Uffz Ernst Meissler-BF-uninj Fw Vlau (?)-BM-uninj	Accident Gilze-Rijen
5 Sep 41	1./NJG 2	Ju88C-4, 0377, R4+BH	-	Undercarriage collapsed Gilze-Rijen
15 Sep 41	I./NJG 2	Ju 88C-4, 0585	-	Written off in accident Gilze-Rijen
15 Sep 41	1./NJG 2	Ju 88C-2, 0779, R4+LH	-	Damaged in accident Gilze-Rijen

Date	*Unit*	*Aircraft Details*	*Crew*	*Fate*
16 Sep 41	1./NJG 2	Ju 88C-4, 0384, R4+DH	Ofw Willi Reisgies & crew uninj	Hit obstacle on take-off from Gilze-Rijen and totally destroyed
16 Sep 41	1./NJG 2	Ju 88C-2, 0839, R4+NH	Ofw Erwin Viel-F-POW Uffz Engelbert Wegener-BF-+ Ofw Heinrich Welker-BM-POW	Shot down by Sqn Ldr G.L. Raphael, 85 Sqn and crashed off Clacton, 2125hrs
19 Sep 41	2./NJG 2	Do 17Z-10, 2867	-	Undercarriage collapsed, Gilze-Rijen
3 Oct 41	4./NJG 2	Ju 88C -2, 0791	Fw Hans Berschwinger & crew uninj	Force-landed at Cadzand on Dutch/Belgian border short of fuel returning from operations.
11 Oct 41	3./NJG 2	Ju 88C-4, 0351, R4+NL	Lt Hans Hahn-F-+ Uffz Ernst Meissner-BF-+ Uffz Helmut Scheidt-BM-+	Collided with Oxford of 12 FTS (Sgt T.D. Graham) and crashed at Barrowby, Grantham, Lincs 2130hrs

Appendix XI

II./NJG 1 and 2./NJG 2 Dornier Do 17Z-10 Claims, September 1940–May 1941

Units operated a mixture of Ju 88Cs and Do 17Z-10s until the latter was replaced by the former by spring/summer 1941. It is speculation, apart from where indicated in bold, that the aircraft being flown was a Do 17Z-10.

Date	Pilot	Type	Time	Details	Notes
8 Sep 40	**Fw Hermann Sommer (5./NJG 1)**	**Blenheim**	**2315**	**Waddington**	**R3905/15 Sqn (Plt Off J Kee) dam RAF Wyton damaged**
16 Oct 1940	**Lt Ludwig Becker (4./NJG 1)**	**Wellington**	**2125**	**Oosterwolde**	**L7844/311 Sqn (Plt Off B Landa)**
17 Oct 40	**Uffz Werner Fick (4./NJG 1)**	**Wellington**	**0030**	**Ijsselmeer**	**Damaged**
28 Oct 40	**Lt Heinz Völker**	**Hampden**	**0030**	**Near Scampton**	**X3027/49 Sqn (Plt Off J R Bufton); crashed off Skegness**
22 Dec 40	**Lt Heinz Völker**	**Blenheim**	**2115**	**50km E.Aldeburgh**	
16 Jan 41	**Oblt Albert Schulz**		**0230**	**Church Fenton**	**Defiant L7002/54 OTU (Plt Off H G S Wyrill)**
	Oblt Albert Schulz		**0245**		**Defiant N1542/54 OTU (Flt Lt R J B Burns) damaged**
11 Feb 41	**Oblt Albert Schulz**		**0110**	**West Raynham**	
	Hptm Rolf Jung	**Wellington**	**0230**		**R1084/115 Sqn (Sgt H Rodgers)**
25 Feb 41	Fw Ernst Ziebarth		2340	Marham	R1009/218 Sqn (Sgt R Hoos)
12 Mar 41	Fw Heinz Mittelstädt		2210	Wells-next-to-the-Sea	Probably P9226/311 Sqn (damaged)
8 Apr 41	**Lt Hans Feuerbaum**	**Hudson**	**0120**		**206 Sqn (Plt Off C R Alexander) damaged near Langham**

<table>
<tr><th>Date</th><th>Pilot</th><th>Type</th><th>Time</th><th>Details</th><th>Notes</th></tr>
<tr><td>8 Apr 41</td><td>Lt Hans Feuerbaum</td><td>Hereford</td><td>0123</td><td>Wells-next-to-the-Sea</td><td>Probably Whitley Z6478/51 Sqn (Plt Off G R Mattey) damaged east of Scarborough, pilot wounded</td></tr>
<tr><td>10 Apr 41</td><td>Oblt Albert Schulz</td><td rowspan="2">Wellington</td><td>0130</td><td>Cambridge</td><td>Possibly L4253/11 OTU (Sgt G D H Dutton)</td></tr>
<tr><td>24 Apr 41</td><td>Fw Vincenz Giessübel</td><td>0155</td><td>Marham</td><td>N2912/11 OTU (Sgt P H Nicholls)</td></tr>
<tr><td>3 May 41</td><td>Lt Hans Feuerbaum</td><td>Hereford</td><td>0315</td><td>Church Fenton</td><td>Whitley Z6641/77 Sqn (Sgt Mills) dam Topcliffe</td></tr>
<tr><td>5 May 41</td><td>Uffz Bittner</td><td>Blenheim/Beaufighter</td><td>0415</td><td>35 km NW Great Yarmouth</td><td></td></tr>
</table>

Fw Hermann Sommer	Awarded Deutsches Kreuz in Gold (DKiG) 24 Apr 42 Ehrenpokal (EP) 1 Nov 43 + with 3./NJG 102 11 Feb 44.
Lt Ludwig Becker	Awarded EP 2 Mar 42, DKiG 4 May 42, Ritterkreuz 1 Jul 42, Eichenlaub 26 Feb 43 +with 12./NJG 1 26 Feb 43.
Uffz Werner Fick	+ with 2./NJG 1 24–25 Apr 44.
Lt Heinz Völker	+ with 3./NJG 2 22 Jul 41.
Oblt Albert Schulz	Awarded DKiG 21 Aug 42 +I./NJG 2 30 Jan 44.
Hptm Rolf Jung	Awarded EP 7 Sep 42; survived.
Fw Ernst Ziebarth	+22 Dec 41 with 2./NJG 2.
Fw Heinz Mittelstädt	+Blindflugschule 8 5 Dec 42
Lt Hans Feuerbaum	+4 Jun 41 with 2./NJG 2.
Fw Vincenz Giessübel	Survived.
Uffz Bittner	Fate and full name unknown

Appendix XII

V./KG 2, I./KG 51 and II./KG 51 Executives, June 1943–August 1944

I./KG 51

Converts from Ju 88 to Me 410 Aug 43. Starts converting to Me 262 May 1944.

Gr Kdr	
Maj Klaus Häberlen	Removed from post 15 Oct 43
Maj Wolf-Dietrich Meister	22 Oct 43 44 to Stellv Komm KG 51, 15 Feb 44
Maj Hans Unrau	From Feb 44
St Kap 1./KG *51*	
Hptm Hans Unrau	To Kdr
Oblt Richard Pahl	†19 Apr 44
Hptm Georg Csursky	From 28 Jul 44
St Kap 2./KG *51*	
Hptm Gerhard Müller	
St Kap 3./KG *51*	
Hptm Hans Gutzmer	

V./KG 2 & II./KG 51

Converts from II./KG 40 to V./KG 2 with Me 410 Jun-Jul 1943; re-designated II./KG 51 1 Mar 44 (commencing 6 Feb 44). Converts to Me 262 Aug 44

Gr Kdr:	
Hptm Friedrich Wilhelm Methner	17 Jun 43 - †16 Jul 43
Hptm Kurt Heintz	†22 Jan 44
Hptm Karl-Egon Frhr von Dalwigk zu Lichtenfels	17 Feb 44 - 5 Oct 44
Hptm Hans-Joachim Grundmann	
Gr IA:	
Hptm Walter Schmidt	†3 Aug 44
Lt Erwin Diekmann	

Gr NO:
Oblt Rudiger Thiemann

Gr TO:
Lt Wolfgang Wenning †24 Apr 44

Maj Beim Stab:
Hptm Wilhelm Ammich

Gr Adj:
Oblt Willi Berberich
Oblt Hermann Walther (stellv)

St Kap 14./KG 2
Formed from 4./KG 40 and re-designated 4./KG 51

Oblt Fritz Sengschmitt	to 2./ZG 26 Aug 43
Maj Wolf-Dietrich Meister	6 Oct 43 - 22 Oct 43 to I./KG 51
Hptm Rudolf Abrahamczik	to Apr 44
Hptm Werner Düero	1 Apr 44 - †8 Jun 44
Oblt Hermann Walther	
Hptm Helmut Brocke	†7 Dec 44
Oblt Hans-Georg Lamle	†26 Dec 44

St Kap 15./KG 2
Formed from 5./KG 40 and 5./KG 51

Hptm Wilhelm Schmitter	†8 Nov 43
[?]	
Oblt Dietrich Puttfarken	25 Mar 44 - †23 Apr 44
Oblt Helmut Niebler (St Fhr)	†29 May 44
Oblt Wolfgang Baetz	
Hptm Eberhard Winkel	wounded 2 Nov 44
Hptm Fritz Abel	†2 Mar 45

St Kap 16./KG 2
Formed from 5./KG 2 and re-designated 6./KG 51

Oblt Günter Näder	†4 Sep 43
Hptm Karl-Egon Frhr von Dalwigk zu Lichtenfels	8 Sep 43 to Gr Kdr 17 Feb 44
Oblt Hermann Walther (stellv)	Wounded 11. Jan 44

Hptm Dierk-Henning Vester	†21 Apr 44
Oblt Walter Schmidt (St Fhr)	† 3 Aug 44
Hptm Hans-Joachim Grundmann	to Gr Kdr

Erprobungskommando Me 210

Became 16./KG 6 1 Sep 42, then 11./ZG 1 Oct 42 then Erprobungsstaffel Me 410 Dec 42 then 13./KG 2 Jun 43

Oblt Walter Maurer	PoW 6 Sep 42
Lt Walter Lardy (St Fhr)	
Hptm Kurt Heintz	?
Hptm Karl-Egon Frhr von Dalwigk zu Lichtenfels	12 Jul 43 - 8 Sep 43

13./KG 2

Became 12./KG 51 Feb 44

Oblt Ewald Limberg	20 Jun 43	Feb 44
Hptm Rudolf Abrahamczik		

Appendix XIII

Deutsches Kreuz in Gold Winners Who Flew the Me 410 with V./KG 2, and I and II./KG 51

	Awarded With	*Date*	*Fate*
Oblt Karl-Günther Näder (F)	5./KG 2	2 Dec 42	†4 Sep 43
Uffz Walter Borlik (BF)	14./KG 2	5 Feb 44	
Fw Gustav Delp (BF)	16./KG 2	20 Mar 44	†27 Apr 44
Ofw Wilhelm Haase (F)	16./KG 2	20 Mar 44	
Ofw Hermann Kempenich (BF)	16./KG 2	20 Mar 44	
Ofw Willi Lux (BF)	I./KG 51	4 Aug 42	†22 Apr 44
Oblt Dietrich Puttfarken (F)*	I./KG 51	2 Jul 42	†22 Apr 44
Oblt Heinz Unrau (F)*	1./KG 51	12 Jan 43	
Lt Helmut Brocke (F)	1./KG 51	3 Oct 42	†7 Dec 44
Uffz Adolf Schwachenwald (BF)	1./KG 51	1 Apr 43	
Lt Eberhard Winkel (F)	1./KG 51	1 Apr 43	†21 Mar 45
Lt Werner Pape (F)	2./KG 51	12 Apr 43	†14 Mar 44
Hptm Hans-Joachim Grundmann (F)	II./KG 51	13 Aug 42	
Oblt Werner Düro (F)	6./KG 51	21 Aug 42	†8 Jun 44
Lt Klaus Krüger (F)	7./KG 51	17 Oct 43	†22 Apr 44
Fw Michael Reichardt (BF)	7./KG 51	5 Feb 44	†22 Apr 44
Oblt Richard Pahl (F)	8./KG 51	12 Dec 43	†19 Apr 44
FhfFw Johann Trenke (F)*	6./KG 51	01 Oct 44	
Lt Hans Gutzmer (F)	9./KG 51	1 Mar 43	
Ofw Heinz Gräber (BF)*	II./KG 40	21 Aug 42	w. 24 Aug 43
Hptm Friedrich-Wilhelm Methner (F)	II./KG 40	5 Nov 42	†16 Jul 43
Oblt Wilhelm Schmitter (F)*	II./KG 40	18 May 42	†8 Nov 43
Ofw Hans Frach (F)	4./KG 40	27 Oct 42	
Lt Rudolf Abrahamczik (F)*	6./KG 40	12 Jan 43	
Hptm Kurt Heintz (F)*	9./LG 1	10 Jul 42	†22 Jan 44
Ofw Otto Runge (BF)	9./LG 1	24 Sep 42	†22 Jan 44

* Indicates also awarded Ritterkreuz

Appendix XIV

Known Messerschmitt Me 410 Operations Over The UK With V./KG 2 and II./KG 51

Flugbuch:
Oblt Rudolf Abrahamczik, 14./KG 2 & 4./KG 51
Fw Hermann Bolten, 14./KG 2 & 4./KG 51
Oblt Werner Mehls, 6./KG 51
Uffz Heinz Holzmann, 14.KG 2
Uffz Franz Wachtler, 4./KG 51
Hptm Wilhelm Schmitter, 15./KG 2
Uffz Hans-Willi Brogmus, 15./KG 2
Fw Wilhelm Sohn, 14./KG 2

Mid June	Lechfeld > Merville > Evreux
18 Jun 43	First mission. 12 Me 410 0030–0040hr Portsmouth, 22 SC 250.
22 Jun 43	12 Me 410 Southampton. 1 Me 410 attacked Chichester, 10 Me 410 attacked main target 0300hrs 18 SC250, 1 PC1000.
22/23 Jun 43	12 Me 410, Störangriff London, 20 SC250.
13 Jul 43	9 Me 410 Störangriff London. 0245–0255hrs. 8 Me 410 10 SC250 und 24 SC50. 1 Me 410 bombed. 1277/05 Ost, (Farnborough)
14 Jul 43	10 Me 410 Cambridge. 2 Me 410 0018–0028hrs airfields at Cambridge and Newmarket. 2 Me 410 bombed Ipswich and Felixstowe. 4 Me 410 0330–0344hrs bombed Mildenhall, Cambridge, Waterbeach.
16 Jul 43	10 Me 410 Störangriff London. 8 Me 410 0035–0256hrs London, 10 SC250 & 2 SC50. 1 Me 410 Chelmsford.
26 Jul 43	London 10 ac
28/29 Jul 43	9 Me 410, Störangriff London. 4 Mark C50 (rot), 4 SC50 und 14 SC250 (Trialen).
30 Jul 43	V./KG 2 8 Me 410 Störangriff Brighton, 16 SC250 (Trialen) 0108–0115hrs.

Date	TO Times	Pilot	Target	Details
11 Aug 43	0324–0542	Schmitter	Fernnachtjagd	Cambridge; 2 aircraft probably destroyed on ground (8 ac 21 SC50 35 AB23 Feltwell)
11 Aug 43	0001–0204	Holzmann	Bournemouth	2 x SC250
12 Aug 43	2315–0030	Schmitter	Colchester	Beleuchter; 3 Markers + 4 SC50 (11 ac Fernnachtjagd, 4 Me 410 Colchester, Ipswich & Felixstowe)
12 Aug 43	2317–0043	Holzmann	Colchester	2 x SC250
15 Aug 43	0055–0220	Holzmann	Portsmouth	2 x SX250
16 Aug 43	0058–0216	Schmitter	Portsmouth	2 x SC250 (20 ac)
16 Aug 43	0058–0222	Brogmus	Portsmouth	8 x SC50
18 Aug 43	0012–0250	Schmitter	Colchester	Beleuchter. 4 Marker C50 + 4 SD50 (13 ac)
18 Aug 43	0027–0155	Abrahamczik	Colchester	
18 Aug 43	0019–0227	Brogmus	Colchester	4 x SC50 4 x SD50
23 Aug 43	0218–0350	Schmitter	Fernnachtjagd	Cambridge. 5 AB23 + 3 SD50 (14 ac)
23 Aug 43	0203–0434	Holzmann	Fernnachtjagd	Cambridge
24 Aug 43	0252–0350	Schmitter	Fernnachtjagd	Shot down Lancaster (EE105/97 Sqn (Sgt C S Chatten) but is then shot down by 29 Sqn & ditched off Belgian coast (alternative target Wymondham, Bacton, Sudbury)
31 Aug/1 Sep			Lincoln	Airfields
4 Sep 43	0242–0510	Abrahamczik	Fernnachtjagd	
4 Sep 43	0245–0330	Brogmus	Fernnachtjagd	Returned early with engine problems
7 Sep 43	0342–0510	Abrahamczik	Fernnachtjagd	(10 ac; Colchester, Southend & Canterbury bombed)
7 Sep 43	0343–0512	Brogmus	Lincoln	5 x AB23 3 x SD50

Date	TO Times	Pilot	Target	Details
8/9 Sep 43			Fernnachtjagd	14 Me 410. Airfields near Cambridge and Ramsgate.
16 Sep 43	0240–0404	Brogmus	Selsey Bill	5 x AB23 3 x SD50. Attacked RNAS Ford (Petersfield attacked)
23 Sep 43	0039–0047	Bolten	Fernnachtjagd	Returned early technical problems (14 ac)
23 Sep 43	0013–0150	Brogmus	Fernnachtjad	Damaged by 85 Sqn off Orfordness 2350hrs
23 Sep 43	0034–0258	Sohn	Nachtjagd	Lincoln
23 Sep 43	2034–2235	Bolten	Fernnachtjagd	Lincoln
24 Sep 43	0032–0230	Abrahamczik	Airfields	(13 ac 4 ac airfields Lincoln, Norwich & London, 6 ac targets between Cambridge and Norwich)
24 Sep 43	0034–0220	Sohn	Nachtjagd	Cambridge
24 Sep 43	0012–0240	Schmitter	Fernnachtjagd	Cambridge. 5 AB23
+3 SD50				
28 Sep 43	0025–0248	Abrahamczik	Airfields Lincoln	Stirling shot down (Lancaster ED410/101 Sqn (Plt Off D W Skipper); 4 other aircraft attacked (10 ac)
28 Sep 43	0028–0408	Bolten	Fernnachtjagd	Lincoln
3 Oct 43				12 Me 410 attacked airfields near Cambridge, 0235–0318hrs. 5 Me 410 attacked, 4 Me 410 attacked airfields south of London, 2 Me 410 Cambridge (575 SD2 und 15 SD50), 1 Me 410 attacked Norwich

Date	TO Times	Pilot	Target	Details
4 Oct 43	0010–0209	Bolten	Fernnachtjagd	Lincoln (16 ac 0014–0055hrs)
5 Oct 43	0007–0223	Bolten	Fernnachtjagd	Lincoln (13 ac)
7 Oct 43	2114–2248	Bolten	London	
7 Oct 43	2122–2350	Schmitter	London	2 x SC250
9 Oct 43			Tagjagd	
14 Oct 43	1405–1546	Bolten	Tagjagd	Shot down 4-engined bomber c.1600hrs
14 Oct 43	1608–1638	Abrahamczik	Tagjagd	Returned early with oxygen problems
17/18 Oct 43			London	8 Me 410
18 Oct 43	1542–1742	Bolten	Tagjagd	Frankfurt-Schweinfurt
18 Oct 43	1550–1755	Abrahamczik	Tagjagd	
18 Oct 43	2215–2335	Schmitter	London	2 x SC250 (4 ac)
21 Oct 43			London	9 Me 410 0051 0118hrs.
22 Oct 43	1847–2054	Schmitter	London	2 x SC250 (11 ac)
25 Oct 43	1857–2007	Bolten	London	3 Me 410 1935–1942hrs
30 Oct 43	1907–2057	Bolten	London	6 Me 410 2014–2017hrs
31 Oct 43			London	7 Me 410, 2233–2245hrs
3 Nov 43	1355–1446	Abrahamczik	Tagjagd	Hamburg/ Wilhelmshaven (8 ac TO 1305hrs)
4 Nov 43	2025–2200	Schmitter	London	2 x SC250 (9 ac)
4 Nov 43	2030–2210	Abrahamczik	Nachtjagd	
5 Nov 43	1235–1523	Abrahamczik	Tagjagd	2 aircraft shot down (8 ac)
6/7 Nov 43			London	8 Me 410 Störangriff.
8 Nov 43	2150–2243	Schmitter	London	Shot down by 85 Sqn. 7 ac 2243–2252hrs
19 Nov 43			London	6 Me 410 Störangriff 1905–1922hrs 10 SC250 (Trialen).
20 Nov 43	1917–2123	Abrahamczik	London	8 Me 410 2025–2137hrs

Date	TO Times	Pilot	Target	Details
25 Nov 43	1810–2024	Abrahamczik	London	8 Me 410 1900–1906hrs
26 Nov 43	2015–2150	Abrahamczik	London	4 Me 410 2057–2112hrs
28 Nov 43	0100–0247	Abrahamczik	London	Nightfighters
29/30 Nov 43			London	4 Me 410 Störangriff 6 SC250 (Trialen).
1 Dec 43			London	3 Me 410 Störangriff TO 1925hrs.
1 Dec 43	1925–2100	Abrahamczik	London	
10 Dec 43	1857–2037	Abrahamczik	London	
19/20 Dec 43			London	7 Me 410 Störangriff
20 Dec 43	0143–0303	Abrahamczik	London	
21 Dec 43	0116–0300	Abrahamczik	London	(8 ac)
21 Dec 43	1810–2003	Abrahamczik	London	(3 ac-2 London 1 Bedford)
30 Dec 43	1821–1841	Bolten	Störangriff	Returned early technical (3 ac)
2 Jan 44	2258–0050	Abrahamczik	London	(14 ac)
2 Jan 44	2300–0107	Bolten	London	
5 Jan 44	0130–0347	Abrahamczik	London	(15 ac)
5 Jan 44	0130–0320	Wachtler	London	2 x SD250
11 Jan 44	1233–1330	Bolten	Tagjagd	TO 1245hrs
11 Jan 44	1248–1448	Abrahamczik	Tagjagd	
13 Jan 44	1837–2035	Abrahamczik	London	
13 Jan 43	1843–2013	Bolten	London	
13 Jan 44	1843–2028	Wachtler	London	2 x SC250
14 Jan 44	1842–	Wachtler	London	Accident on take-off
14 Jan 43	1843–2026	Bolten	London	(4 ac)
21 Jan 44	2010–2215	Abrahamczik	London	Grossangriff. Hit by Flak
21 Jan 44	2014–2220	Bolten	London	Grossangriff. Hit by Flak
22 Jan 44	0355–0550	Abrahamczik	London	Heavy Flak
24 Jan 44	1330–1453	Bolten	Tagjagd	
28 Jan 44	2140–2330	Bolten	London	Beleuchter
28 Jan 44	2145–2320	Abrahamczik	London	Heavy Flak (16 ac)
29 Jan 44	2000–2150	Abrahamczik	London	
29 Jan 44	2000–2158	Bolten	London	Heavy Flak

Date	TO Times	Pilot	Target	Details
3 Feb 44	2005–2135	Abrahamczik	London	Heavy Flak (16 ac 12 SC500 30 SC250 4 SB70)
3 Feb 44	2006–2151	Bolten	London	Beleuchter
4 Feb 44	0430–0605	Abrahamczik	London	
4 Feb 44	2006–2125	Wachtler	London	2 x 250
6 Feb 44	0506–0605	Abrahamczik	London	Engine problems returned short of coast (14 ac 20 SC250)
6 Feb 44	0519–0649	Wachtler	London	2 x SC250
11 Feb 44	1913–1930	Wachtler	London	Returned early due to technical problems
11 Feb 44	1920–2047	Bolten	London	
12 Feb 44	2017–2137	Abrahamczik	London	Heavy Flak
12 Feb 44	2021–2144	Wachtler	London	MB1000
12 Feb 44	2031–2137	Bolten	London	(Störangriff 9 Fw 190s & 16 Me 410s; bombs dropped 2100–2106hrs
13 Feb 44	2010–2144	Wachtler	London	SB1000
13 Feb 44	2015–2230	Bolten	London	Grossangriff
19 Feb 44	0005–0212	Wachtler	London	SB1000
20 Feb 44	2007–2217	Bolten	London	Grossangriff
20 Feb 44	2115–2300	Wachtler	London	2 x SC250
22 Feb 44	0217–0317	Bolten	London	Störangriff; damaged in port engine by Mosquito of 96 Sqn
22 Feb 44	0220–0400	Abrahamczik	London	
22 Feb 44	2335–0143	Abrahamczik	London	Störangriff; 13 Fw 190 & 12 Me 410
23 Feb 44	2133–2205	Wachtler	London	Returned early
24 Feb 44	2105–2240	Wachtler	London	2 x SC250
29 Feb 44	2030–2222	Wachtler	London	2 x SC250 (Störangriff. 11 Fw 190s 14 Me 410. 3 Fw 190s attacked Brighton)
2 Mar 44	0259–0404	Wachtler	London	2 x SC250
15–16 Mar 44			London	7 Fw 190s and 8 Me 410 Störangriff. 5 ac bombed
16–17 Mar 44			London	15 Me 410 Störangriff. 6 Me 410 bombed

Date	TO Times	Pilot	Target	Details
22–23 Mar 44			London	9 Fw 190 10 Me 410 Störangriff
23–24 Mar 44			London	7 Fw 190 9 Me 410 Störangriff. Gresham Transformers, Hanwell hit
31 Mar 44	0344–0518	Bolten	Fernnachtjagd	Cambridge. RAF Thorpe Abbots 0440hrs
31 Mar 44	0344–0607	Wachtler	Fernnachtjagd	Cambridge
11 Apr 44	2351–0242	Wachtler	Fernnachtjagd	Lincoln damaged Beaufighter. 12 ac
12 Apr 44	2352–0247	Bolten	Fernnachtjagd	Lincoln
19 Apr 44	0044–0347	Wachtler	Nachtjagd	Lincoln. Halifax claimed by Uffz Albert Wolk (BF); Me 410 damaged in radiator. Little Snoring, Mepal 0202hrs
19–20 Apr 44			London	15 Me 410 Störangriff
21 Apr 44	0336–0526	Wachtler	Nachtjagd	Cambridge; crashed on landing (15 Me 410 attacked Seething 0345hrs, Horham 0435hrs, Lakenheath 0445hrs)
22 Apr 44				14 Me 410 Angriff auf RAF Flugplätze im Raum Cambridge (Rackheath).
26–27 Apr 44			Fernnachtjagd	11 Me 410s
27–28 Apr 44			Fernnachtjagd	10 Me 410 Feltwell 0340hrs [4 intruders active in Coltishall Sector following returning bombers with bombs dropped at Shipdham and a searchlight post near

Date	TO Times	Pilot	Target	Details
				Bury St Edmunds. At Feltwell, a returning aircraft from a Bullseye exercise was attacked while landing but was not hit
8 May 44	2151–2250	Bolten	Nachtjagd	Evreux

11/12 May 44 four Me 410 of II./KG 51 up 2315 to 2325 on harassing raid on ground organisation and intruder night fighting. Two of them operated in Cambridge area from 0005–0145, two broke off with technical trouble. Defence appreciated as slight searchlight activity in approximately Ipswich area.

12/13 May 44 eight Me 410s up 2325 to 2350 on intruder. Seven in areas south of the Wash and north of the Humber from 0010 to 0017hrs. One Me 410 attacked two aircraft at 0052 in approximately Kettering area and at 0108 in approximately Wyton area respectively. One Me 410 attacked an aircraft at 0052hrs in approximately Bury St Edmunds area and dropped 34 10kg bombs on unidentified target in same area. One Me 410 dropped similar load at 0048hrs in approximately north-east Norfolk area. One in Cambridge area at 0020hrs. Three Me 410 no sightings. One Me 410 broke off with technical trouble. Defence appreciated as strong light AA north of Humber and a little searchlight activity. At 0120hrs ship sighting about 10 miles off Lowestoft.

14–15 May 44			Bristol	15 Me 410 attacked airfields; pathfinding by six Me 410s of I./KG 51
22 May 44	0212–0427	Bolten	Fernnachtjagd	Lincoln

21/22 May 44 10 Me 410 (up 0001–0021hrs), intruder night fighting in areas Cambridge-Norwich-Ipswich. The following attacked: Nine Me 410, 0038–0200hrs. Claims: one Lancaster at 0048hrs in 5222/0045E; one at 0105hrs in 5302/0055E; one at 0112hrs in 5257/0025E. Observed in all cases that aircraft caught fire on crashing. Also eight four-engined aircraft effectively shot up. Further attacked: at 0117hrs in 5307/0045W, eight SD 70 dropped from 400m on illuminated airfield. No results observed owing to thick cloud. At 0141hrs in 5317/0025W, two AB 250 each filled with 17 x SD 10 dropped from 900m on airfield with aircraft landing. No results observed. One Me 410 broke off owing to compass damage. No losses.

Date	TO Times	Pilot	Target	Details
23 May 44	0157–0236	Bolten	Returned early technical	

22/23 May 44 Eight Me 410 up 2350–0001hrs for intruder ops in area Cambridge-Norwich-Ipswich. Seven attacked 0037–0143hrs. Four four-engined aircraft claimed shot up. Bombs dropped 0132hrs on airfield east of Cambridge; 0115hrs on lights near airfield, presumed huts of AA position between March and Littleport; 0117hrs on runway of airfield in same area; at 0122hrs on airfield runway area within 14 miles of Biggleswade. One convoy observed at 0143hrs north of Great Yarmouth. Fliegerkorps IX appreciated operation correct in time and place but hindered by bad visibility, low cloud base and local showers. Nevertheless, harassing effect achieved. Great Ashfield 0345hrs RAF Bourn 0320hrs [Latter airfield reported single aircraft fired five bursts of machine gun fire and dropped six 50kg bombs with no damage caused.]

24 May 44	0148–0407	Bolten	Fernnachtjagd	Lincoln (4 Me 410)
25 May 44	0326–0610	Mehls	Recce	Hastings to Worthing Tuddenham 0320hrs
29 May 44	0150–0440	Mehls	Fernnachtjagd	Wash to Cambridge (6 Me 410)

28/29 May 44: 12 Me 410s up 2339–2359hrs, two collided during take-off. Night intruder patrol in area Wash-Norwich-Ipswich-Cambridge. 10 Me 410s, of which one overdue, attacked 0025–0129hrs. Hangars in area 521730N/004500E and area 02230N/521500E fired on at 0049hrs, 0137hrs. At 0045hrs runway and parking places on illuminated airfield north of Cambridge and, at 0052hrs, illuminated hangars on airfield in 520730N/ 004500W bombed. At 0053hrs, light AA position in 530730N/ 004500W fired on. Deopham Green (USAAF) 0225hrs, Oakington 0253hrs and Tuddenham 0330hrs bombed

30/31 May 44 10 Me 410s up 0023–0032hrs. Intruding in area Norwich-Ipswich-Cambridge, of which six made no sighting, four attacked a searchlight in 5222N/0135E from 600m at 0110hrs; Norwich town from 1500m at 0112hrs and 0115hrs; settlement in Cambridge area from 500m at 0120 – all without observation of results. No losses.

1 Jun 44	0232–0410	Mehls	Fernnachtjagd	Raum C. Deopham Green attacked
2 Jun 44	0015–0235	Bolten	Nachtjagd	
6 Jun 44	0130–	Bolten		Shot down by Mosquito of 605 Sqn
6 Jun 44	2150–0056	Mehls	Invasion fleet	

Date	TO Times	Pilot	Target	Details
7 Jun 44	2306–0107	Mehls	Fernnachtjagd	Raum C. Framlingham 0011hrs and Tuddenham 0010hrs attacked
10–11 Jun 44			Fernnachtjagd	
13 Jun 44			Recce London	
13–14 Jun 44			Seine Bay	
14–15 Jun 44			Fernnachtjagd	Cambridge
15–16 Jun 44			Strassenjagd	
16–17 Jun 44			Fernnachtjagd	Beachhead
23 Jun 44	0158–0239	Wachtler	Nachtjagd	Cambridge
24–25 Jun 44			Strassenjagd	
28 Jun 44	0105–0327	Wachtler	Nachtjagd	Cambridge, shot down Lancaster 0231 hrs (LM164/V 90 Sqn (Flt Lt A H Burton) damaged and landed 0239hrs, Sgt W P Smith (RG) killed)
28 Jun 44	0114–0205	Mehls		Returned early with technical problems
3 Jul 44	2149–0145	Mehls	Frontflug	Engine failure near Lisieux
5 Jul 44	0106–0357	Wachtler	?	
6 Jul 44	0305–0440	Mehls	Beachhead	
6 Jul 44	2345–		Wachtler	Engine caught fire on landing
7 Jul 44	0026–0135	Mehls	Beachhead	Returned early due to weather
8 Jul 44	0333–0440	Mehls	London	8 x 50kg; attacked by nightfighter
9 Jul 44	0033–0240	Mehls	Beachhead	8 x 50kg near Bayeux
13 Jul 44	0016–0208	Mehls	Beachhead	8 x 50kg
15 Jul 44	0345–0536	Mehls	Beachhead	8 x 50kg
16 Jul 44	0355–0541	Mehls	Beachhead	8 x 50kg near Bayeux
17 Jul 44	2239–0034	Mehls	Beachhead	2 x AB250/SG 1
18 Jul 44	2237–0015	Mehls	Carpiquet	2 x AB250
19 Jul 44	2206–0003	Mehls	St Lo	SD10A
22 Jul 44	2202–2358	Mehls	N.Caen	2 x SD250/SD10A

Date	TO Times	Pilot	Target	Details
25 Jul 44			Fernnachtjagd	
26 Jul 44	2149–2342	Mehls	ENE St Lo	SD10A
27 Jul 44	2210–2340	Mehls	E.Caen	2 x AB250/SD10A
28 Jul 44	2204–2343	Mehls	NNE Touffreville	
7 Aug 44	2122–2331	Mehls	Beachhead	Badly damaged by Flak

Appendix XV

Messerschmitt Me 410 Claims, N.W. Europe, August 1943–August 1944

V./KG 2

Date	Time	Pilot	Unit	Claim	Identification
11 Aug 43	0425 hrs	Uffz Johann Trenke	16./KG 2	Stirling	Lancaster DS665/115 Sqn (Fg Off J F H Erwin) crashed Boughton Monchelsea, Kent
11 Aug 43	0436 hrs	Lt Hermann Walther	16./KG 2	Stirling	
18 Aug 43	0057 hrs	Unknown	V./KG 2	1-engined, 5 Ost/0226	
24 Aug 43	0408 hrs	Fw Heinz Graeber (BF)	15./KG 2	Lancaster, Cambridge	EE105/97 Sqn (Sgt C S Chatten) crashed Shouldham, Norfolk
4 Sep 43	0351 hrs	Lt Heinz-Günther Baack	14./KG 2	2-engined, Lincoln	
7 Sep 43		Unknown	V./KG 2		Stirling W7455/1657 CU (Sgt C J Gi kes). Shot down on training flight and crash-landed at Great Thurlow
23 Sep 43	0134 hrs	Maj Wolf-Dietrich Meister	14./KG 2	4-engined, Lincoln	Lancaster W4948/57 Sqn (Plt Off G A Duff) crashed Driby, Lincs 0043hrs
28 Sep 43	0112 hrs	Oblt Rudolf Abrahamczik	14./KG 2	4 -engined, Cambridge	Lancaster JA965/101 Sqn (Plt Off D W Skipper) crashed Wickenby 0120 hrs
9 Oct 43	1520 hrs	Maj Wolf-Dietrich Meister	14./KG 2	4 engined, Röm	
<u>Unconfirmed</u>					
27 Sep 43		Uffz Gottfried Wendler (BF)	15./KG 2	2 x 4-engined	Damaged near Great Yarmouth
3 Oct 43		Uffz Heinz Holzmann	14./KG 2	4 engined, Bedford	0235–0318hrs

3 Oct 43		Uffz Heinz Holzmann	14./KG 2	4 engined, Bedford	
3 Oct 43		Ofw Wilhelm Wessel	16./KG 2	2 x bomber	Damaged landing
14 Oct 43 PM		Maj Dietrich Meister	14./KG 2	4 engined Saarbrücken	
14 Oct 43 PM		Uffz Heinz Holzmann	14./KG 2	4 engined Bruchsal	
14 Oct 43 PM		Fw Hermann Bolten	Stab V./KG 2	4 engined Hagenau	1405–1546 hrs
11 Jan 44 PM		Fw Hermann Bolten	Stab V./KG 2	4 engined	HSS 1233–1330hrs

I & II./KG 51

31 Mar 44	0433hrs	Maj Wolf-Dietrich Meister	Stab./KG 51	Fortress E.Cambridge	Lancaster LM509 12 Sqn (Flt Sgt A F T L'Estrange) damaged near Norwich, 0425 hrs
31 Mar 43	0450hrs	Unknown	II./KG 51	Mosquito damaged	Mosquito XVII HK295/25 Sqn. RAF Coltishall Damaged in engines by gunfire taxing in from operations. Sub Lt J R Adams and Sub Lt H C Smith safe
12 Apr 44	0042hrs	Lt Wolfgang Wenning	Stab II./KG 51	Fortress N.Ipswich	B-17G 42–97556 413 BS/96 BG (Lt D M McGregor) crashed Great Glemham
12 Apr 44	0050hrs	Hptm Dietrich Puttfarken	5./KG 51	Spitfire 05Ost/1352	Spitfire BL581 64 Sqn (Flt Sgt G R Maunders) crashed Skeyton, Norfolk 0030hrs
12 Apr 44	0125hrs	Hptm Dietrich Puttfarken	5./KG 51	Halifax 05Ost/1482	Stirling LJ450/F 1654 CU (Flt Sgt J J G Nicholson) shot down over Bassingbourne bombing range
12 Apr 44		Uffz Franz Wachtler	4./KG 51	Beaufighter dam	Mosquito LR266/60 OTU. Lincoln Reported to have been damaged by an intruder. Flt Lt D A McFadyen/Fg Off J D Wight bailed out safely near Grantham

19 Apr 44	0225hrs	Hptm Dietrich Puttfarken	5./KG 51	Lancaster 05Ost/0330	Lancaster LL667/R 115 Sqn (Plt Off J Birnie) crashed Witchford, 0210hrs
19 Apr 44	0347hrs	Lt Wolfgang Wenning	Stab II./KG 51	Lancaster NW Hull	Lancaster ME734/Y 625 Sqn (Plt Off J P Cosgrove) crashed Swinhope Brats Binbrook 0230hrs
19 Apr 44	0348hrs	Oblt Klaus Bieber	5./KG 51	Lancaster Cambridge	Lancaster LL867/J 115 Sqn (Flt Lt C Eddy) crashed at Witchford 0348hrs
21 Apr 44	0510hrs	Fw Gustav Delp (BF)	6./KG 51	P-47 N.Cambridge	Master DL283 7 (P) AFU (Fg Off J Banister) crashed Walton Marholm, Peterborough 0515hrs
22 Apr 44		Hptm Dietrich Puttfarken	5./KG 51	Halifax unconfirmed	
22 Apr 44		Hptm Dietrich Puttfarken	5./KG 51	Halifax unconfirmed	
22 Apr 44	2204hrs	Fw Johann Trenke	6./KG 51	Fortress 05Ost/1384	
22 Apr 44	2205hrs	Lt Wolfgang Wenning	Stab II./KG 51	Halifax 05Ost/1368	
22 Apr 44	2210hrs	Uffz Eberhard Baier	6./KG 51	Halifax 05Ost/1384	
22 Apr 44	2210hrs	Fw Johann Trenke	6./KG 51	Halifax 05Ost/1384	
22 Apr 44	2214hrs	Hptm Werner Düro	4./KG 51	Unidentified 05Ost/1337	
22 Apr 44	2215hrs	Fw Gustav Delp (BF)	6./KG 51	Halifax S.Norwich	
22 Apr 44	2216hrs	Fw Johann Trenke	6./KG 51	Halifax 05Ost/1385	
22 Apr 44	2222hrs	Uffz Eberhard Baier	6./KG 51	Halifax 05Ost/1376	
22 Apr 44	2226hrs	Lt Uwe Laass	5./KG 51	Halifax 05Ost/1371	
22 Apr 44	2246hrs	Uffz Eberhard Baier	6./KG 51	Halifax W.Orfordness	

1. B-24J 42–109915 567thBS/389th BG (Lt F T Wilkerson). Crashed Cantley, 2217hrs
2. B-24H 42–94744 714thBS/448th BG (1/Lt M L Aspaugh). Crashed near Worlingham, 2225hrs (Baier)
3. B-24H 42–73497 715th BS/448th BG (Capt A D Skaggs). Landed in flames Seething Airfield (Laas)
4. B-24H 42–52608 715th BS/448th BG (Lt C C Pitts). Crashed off Hopton, 2207hrs (Trenke)
5. B-24H 41–28843 715th BS/448th BG (2/Lt E V Pulcipher). Crashed Kessingland, 2220hrs
6. B-24H 42–64490 735th BS/453rd BG (Lt J S Munsey). Attacked off coast and crashed Reydon Marsh, 2220hrs (Wenning)

7. B-24H 42–52353 754th BS/458th BG (Lt T G Harris) . Crashed Lakenham, 2210hrs
8. B-24H 42–42536 788th BS/467th BG (2/Lt J H Maxey). Crashed Mendham
9. B-24J 42–52445 791st BS/467th BG (1/Lt S C Reid). Crashed Barsham, 2222hrs (Delp)

23 Apr 44	0335hrs	Uffz Walter Brügel	4./KG 51	Halifax 05Oct/1228	Albermarle V1610 42 OTU (Sgt J E Hutchinson) crashed Holland Fen, 0400hrs
25 Apr 44	0358hrs	Uffz Eberhard Baier	6./KG 51	Halifax 05Ost/1357	Lancaster DV177/K2 626 Sqn (WO M L McPherson) crashed Colchester, 0410 hrs
25 Apr 44	0422hrs	Lt Wolfgang Wenning	Stab II./KG 51	Halifax 20km NE	Lancaster LK789/L 76 Sqn (Plt Off Cambridge D R Dibbins) crashed Welney 0420hrs
27 Apr 44	0425hrs	Fw Johann Trenke	6./KG 51	Unidentified 05Ost/0356	See below
27 Apr 44	0430hrs	Lt Wolfgang Wenning	Stab II./KG 51		Collided with Oxford LX196 18 (P) AFU (Plt Off C G W Moore) and crashed Frankton, Rugby 0430hrs
28 Apr 44	0415hrs	Uffz Artur Döhler	5./KG 51	Unidentified 15Ost/242	
7 May 44	0227hrs	Oblt Georg Csurusky	1./KG 51	Halifax SSW La Ferrière	Lancaster ND449/M 156 Sqn (Flt Lt H D Churchill) crashed Le Fidelaire
8 May 44	0302hrs	Oblt Georg Csurusky	1./KG 51	Halifax 25km NW Tours	Halifax LL280/O 138 Sqn (Wg Cdr W McF Russell) crashed St Denis d'Orgues
12 May 44	0238hrs	Uffz Walter Brügel	4./KG 51	4-engined Bredstedt	
22 May 44	0251hrs	Uffz Eberhard Baier	6./KG 51	B-24 05Ost/0356	Lancaster NN695/X 619 Sqn (Fg Off R H Redshaw) crashed East Wretham, 0255hrs
22 May 44	0256hrs	Uff Eberhard Baier	6./KG 51	B-24 05Ost/0367	
22 May 44	0305hrs	Fw Johann Trenke	6./KG 51	Lancaster 05Ost/0489	
22 May 44	0314hrs	Fw Johann Trenke	6./KG 51	Lancaster 05Ost/0317	
22 May 44	0322hrs	Fw Johann Trenke	6./KG 51	Lancaster 05Ost/0324	

[23 May 44-Lancaster JB417/R 582 Sqn (Sqn Ldr H W B Heney) attacked Little Staughton Beds 0310 hrs; Anson LT476 13 OTU Fg Off P A Davison) crashed Little Staughton, 0305hrs; 2 Mosquitoes of 105 Sqn damaged RAF Bourne 0320hrs]

29 May 44	0240hrs	Uffz Eberhard Baier	6./KG 51	Stirling 05Ost/EC2	Stirling R9298 1657 CU (Fg Off W A C Yates) crashed Stradishall 0239hrs into Stirlings LK506 & R9283
13 Jun 44	0125hrs	Uffz Josef Ottrin (BF)	6./KG 51	Unidentified	
13 Jun 44	0312hrs	Fw Severin Visintin	5./KG 51	Halifax 05Ost/0378	(Saffon Walden)
17 Jun 44	0200hrs	Uffz Josef Ottrin (BF)	6./KG 51	4-engined 05Ost/2225	(see 80km north of Ostend)
17 Jun 44	0215hrs	Fw Johann Trenke	6./KG 51	4-engined 05Ost/121	(south of Clacton)
28 Jun 44	0227hrs	Lt Anselm Markau	4./KG 51	4-engined 05Ost/0376	Lancaster NE145/D 90 Sqn (Plt Off C J Todd) crashed Icklingham 0226hrs
28 Jun 44	0230hrs	Lt Carl-Heinz Friedrich	5./KG 51	Stirling 15W/1223	B-24 42–95321 850th BS/801st BG (1/Lt W E Huenekens) Easton Socon, 0235hrs
28 Jun 44	0231hrs	Uffz Franz Wachtler	4./KG 51	Lancaster 05Ost/0378	Lancaster LM164/V 90 Sqn (Flt Lt A H Burton) damaged on landing at Tuddenham
3 Jul 44	0014hrs	Fw Johann Trenke	6./KG 51	Unidentified 05Ost/007	
6 Jul 44	0238hrs	Uffz Heinz Irmer (BF)	6./KG 51	2-engined 15W/UU (Caen)	

Appendix XVI

Messerschmitt Me 410 Combat Losses, N.W. Europe, June 1943–August 1944

Date	*Unit*	*Aircraft Details*	*Crew*	*Fate*
27 Jun 43	16./KG 2	Me 410A-1, 275, U5+IG	Fw Peter Hoff-F-+ Fw Walter Hillebrand-BF-+	Crashed at Avord following being damaged in combat.
14 Jul 43	16./KG 2	Me 410A-1, 238, U5+KG	Fw Franz Zwissler-F-+ Ofw Leo Raida-BF-+	Shot down by Flt Lt E N Bunting, 85 Sqn 5 miles off Felixstowe, 0010hrs
16 Jul 43	Stab V./KG 2	Me 410A-1, 237, U5+CJ	Hptm Friedrich-Wilhelm Methner-F-Gr Kdr-+ Uffz Hubert Grube-BF-+	Shot down by Plt Off B J Thwaites, 85 Sqn off Dunkirk 0100hrs
30 Jul 43	14./KG 2	Me 410A-1, 114, U5+BJ	Oblt Helmut Biermann-F-+ Uffz Willi Kröger-BF-+	Shot down by Wg Cdr G R, Park 256 Sqn 20 mile south of Beachy Head 0145hrs
12 Aug 43	14./KG 2	Me 410A-1, 226, U5+AE	Lt Günther Schnecke-F-+ Gefr Otto Kröger-BF-+	Crashed near Le Mans with engine failure due to running out of fuel returning from attack on Bournemouth
18 Aug 43	15./KG 2	Me 410A-1, 291, U5+GF	Oblt Helmut Niebler-F-Inj Uffz Alfons Umlauf-BF-inj	Crashed near Epinoy due to engine fire returning from attack on Lincoln
23 Aug 43	15./KG 2	Me 410A-1, 10120, U5+AF	Fw Walter Hartmann-F-+ Ogefr Michael Meurer-BF-POW	Shot down by Sqn Ldr G L Howitt, 85 Sqn, Chelmondiston, 0202hrs

Date	*Unit*	*Aircraft Details*	*Crew*	*Fate*
23 Aug 43	14./KG 2	Me 410A-1, 228, U5+EE	Uffz Hans-Johann Oertel-F-+ Fw Martin Küfner-BF-+	Shot down by Flt Lt C Kirkland, 29 Sqn 25 miles NE Foreness, 0230hrs
24 Aug 43	15./KG 2	Me 410A-1, 214, U5+CF	Hptm Wilhelm Schmitter-St Kap-uninj Ofw Heinz Graeber-BF-W	Shot down by Sqn Ldr P W Arbon, 29 Sqn, north of Knokke, 0337hrs
23–24 Aug 43	15./KG 2	Me 410A-1, 274, U5+DG	Lt Helmut Barzel-F-+ Uffz Heinz Hartmann-BF-+	Missing. Possibly shot down by Wg Cdr R E X Mack, 29 Sqn, 40 miles east of Manston, 2322hrs; Flt Lt G Goodman, 29 Sqn, near Dunkirk, 0225hrs; Lt J Rad, 85 Sqn off East Anglia, 02–0hrs
23–24 Aug 43	16./KG 2	Me 410A-1, 287, U5+EG	Fw Werner Benner-F-+ Uffz Hermann Reimers-BF-+	See above. Crew bailed out Pilot washed ashore at Veurnes
31 Aug 43	14./KG 2	Me 410A-1, 022, U5+BE	Lt Carl Jukel-F-+ Uffz Erich Pieper-BF-+	Missing from attack on Lincoln; pilot's body washed ashore Holland
4 Sep 43	16./KG 2	Me 410A-1, 10172, U5+NG	Oblt Günter Näder-F-St Kap-+ Ofw Lothar Küll-BF-+	Engine failure and crashed neat Zeist
16 Sep 43	15./KG 2	Me 410A-1, 10171, U5+AF	Ofw Horst Müller-F-+ Uffz Wolfgang Dose-BF-+	Missing from attack on Cambridge possibly shot down by Fg Off B C Jarvis, 29 Sqn off Brighton 0300hrs
23 Sep 43	15./KG 2	Me 410A-1, 10177, U5+FF	Uffz Hans-Willi Brogmus-F-uninj Uffz Helmut Lindemann-BF-uninj	Damaged by Flt Lt C G Houghton, 85 Sqn off Orfordness, 2350hrs which set starboard engine on fire and force-landed at Melsbroek, 0150hrs

Date	*Unit*	*Aircraft Details*	*Crew*	*Fate*
23 Sep 43	15./KG 2	Me 410A-1, 232		Force-landed Schiphol with engine fire
23 Sep 43	16./KG 2	Me 410A-1, 278		Force-landed Schiphol with engine fire
7 Oct 43	14./KG 2	Me 410A-1, 103, U5+QE	Fw Wilhelm Sohn-F-+ Uffz Günther Keiser-BF-+	Damaged by Fg Off B J Thwaites, 85 Sqn near Gravesend; crashed Sleydinge, Gent, Belgium 2320hrs
7 Oct 43	16./KG 2	Me 410A-1, 10185, U5+KG	Fw Georg Slodczyk-F-+ Uffz Fritz Westrich-BF-+	Shot down by Flt Lt W H Maguire, 85 Sqn, 10 miles S. Hastings, 2130hrs; Capt P Bugge, 85 Sqn, Gravesend, 2210hrs; Lt T Weisteen, 85 Sqn, off Dungeness 2223hrs; Flt Sgt W A Robertson, 157 Sqn, Shoeburyness, 2215hrs (damaged)
14 Oct 43	14./KG 2	Me 410A-1, 10262, U5+JE	- Uffz Walter Borlik-BF-inj	Force-landed Hagenau during Tagjagd
18 Oct 43	15./KG 2	Me 410A-1, 10176, U5+LF	Ofw Lothar Bleich-F-+ Uffz Ernst Greinecker-BF-+	Shot down by Sqn Ldr E N Bunting, 85 Sqn, Brentwood, 0220hrs
31 Oct 43-	15./KG 2	Me 410A-1, 10315, U5+FF	Uffz Hans-Willi Brogmus-F-+ Uffz Helmut Lindemann-BF-+	Missing from attack on 1 Nov 43 London
31 Oct 43	15./KG 2	Me 410A-1, 10245, U5+HF	Lt Rolf Proposch-F-+ Uffz Gottfried Wendler-BF-+	Shot down by Flak attacking London, crashed Frimley Green, 2250hrs
1Nov 43	16./KG 2	Me 410A-1, 10200		Landing accident, Juvinvourt
5 Nov 43	14./KG 2	Me 410A-1, 10301, U5+BE	Uffz Georg Baars-F-+ Ogefr Leopold Grün-BF-+	Shot down by fighters on daylight sortie; crashed 15km SW.Rheydt
5 Nov 43	14./KG 2	Me 410A-1, 10255, U5+FE	Lt Heinz-Günther Baack-F-uninj Uffz Georg Gillmann-BF-+	Shot down by fighters near München-Gladbach; believed crashed near Dinslaken
8 Nov 43	14./KG 2	Me 410A-1, 10262, U5+JE	Uffz Heinz Holzmann-F+ Uffz Wilfried Fischer-BF-+	Shot down by Fg Off R Stewart, 29 Sqn, S.Beachy Head, 2215hrs

Date	*Unit*	*Aircraft Details*	*Crew*	*Fate*
8 Nov 43	15../KG 2	Me 410A-1, 10244, U5+BF	Hptm Wilhelm Schmitter-F-St Kap-+ Uffz Felix Hainzinger-BF-+	Shot down by Sqn Ldr W H Maguire, 85 Sqn and crashed Eastbourne, 2243hrs
9 Nov 43	14./KG 2	Me 410A-1, 10311,U5+HE	Fw Tonie Knie-F-+ Uffz Ignaz Aberl-BF-+	Shot down by Fg Off G R Reed, 488 Sqn, 15 miles N.Manston, 0059hrs
20 Dec 43	14./KG 2	Me 410A-1, 420085, U5+HE	Lt Heinz Günther Baack-F-+ Uffz Michael Strasser-BF-POW	Shot down by Fg Off D N Robinson, 488 Sqn and crashed at Iden, 0240hrs
2 Jan 44	16./KG 2	Me 410A-1, 420005, U5+AJ	Fw Friedrich Hess-F-+ Maximilian von Poblotzki-BF-+	Shot down by Fg Off R D Uffz Bergemann, 488 Sqn off Dover, 2359hrs
3 Jan 44	14./KG 2	Me 410A-1, 420017, U5+AJ	Oblt Helmut Schultze-F-+ Gefr Heinz Berger-BF-+	Crashed at Marquise on return from attack on London. Possibly shot down by Wg Cdr J Cunningham, 85 Sqn, Pas De Calais, 2359hrs
11 Jan 44	14./KG 2	Me 410A-1, 420408, U5+FE	Hptm Rudolf Balzer-F-+ Uffz Erhard Grimme-BF-+	Crashed near Hesepe/ Osnabrück 1300hrs after being shot down by fighters during daylight intercept
11 Jan 44	16./KG 2	Me 410A-1, 420464, U5+CG	Oblt Hermann Walther-F-W	Shot down neat Fürstenau 1300hrs during daylight intercept
12 Jan 44	16./KG 2	Me 410A-1	Fw Hans Trenke-F-uninj Uffz Josef Ottrin-BF-uninj	Damaged by Fg Off R Densham, 29 Sqn near Fécamp 2115hrs and landed at Vitry
13 Jan 44	15./KG 2	Me 410A-1, 420402, U5+HF	Lt Matthias Emberger-F-+ Gefr Hans-Helmut Becker-BF-M	Missing from attack on London. An aircraft was reported to have been shot down by Flak and crashed near Cork Light Vessel off Harwich 1955hrs

Date	*Unit*	*Aircraft Details*	*Crew*	*Fate*
13 Jan 44	16./KG 2	Me 410A-1, 420464, U5+CG	Lt Hans-Heinrich Uecker-F-+ Uffz Emil Loppe-BF-+	See previous
22 Jan 44	Stab V./KG 2	Me 410A-1, 103313, U5+WJ	Hptm Kurt Heintz-F-Gr Kdr-+ Stfw Otto Runge-BF-+	Crashed for unknown causes Lydd 0515hrs
22 Feb 44	14./KG 2	Me 410A-1, U5+EE	Fw Helmut Bolten-F-ininj	Damaged by Flt Sgt T N Fw Wilhelm Lohf-BF-uninj Bryan, 96 Sqn and force-landed at Abbeville, 0317hrs
23 Feb 44	14./KG 2	Me 410A-1, 420463, U5+CE	Uffz Reinhard Eggers-F-+ Bednorz-BF-+	Shot down by Sqn Ldr P L Ogefr Stefan Caldwell, 96 Sqn and crashed at Framfield, 0030hrs
23 Feb 44	16./KG 2	Me 410A-1	Lt Felix Müller-F-+ Gefr Karl-Heinz Borowski-BF-+	Shot down by Flak and crashed at Radnage, 0045hrs
23 Feb 44	16./KG 2	Me 410A-1	Fw Karl Müller-F-+ Uffz Kurt Bein-BF-+	Believed shot down off Dungeness by either Fg Off E R Hedgecoe of 85 Sqn at 0032hrs or Flt Lt B Burbidge of 85 Sqn at 0045hrs

<u>BECOMES II./KG 51 1 MAR 44 (commencing 6 Feb 44)</u>

27/28 Mar 44	6./KG 51	Me 410A-1	Fw Hans-Erich Seemann-Funinj Uffz Karl-Heinz Steffen-BF-uninj	Returned on one engine and force-landed at Soesterberg
19 Apr 44	6./KG 51	Me 410A-1, 420414, 9K+GP	Fw Franz Dietrich-F-uninj Uffz Heinz Immler-BF-inj	Returned on one engine and force-landed Bergen 4km north of Alkmaar. Possibly damaged by Fg Off K V Panter, 25 Sqn 15–20 miles west of Ijmuiden, 0435hrs

Date	*Unit*	*Aircraft Details*	*Crew*	*Fate*
21 Apr 44	6./KG 51	Me 410A-1, 420289, 9K+BP	Hptm Dierk-Henning Vester-F-+ St Kap Ofw Paul Horn-BF-+	Crashed on take-off for operations, Soesterberg
21 Apr 43	4./KG 51	Me 410A-1, 420451, U5+DM	Uffz Franz Wachtler-F-inj Uffz Albert Wolf-F-uninj	Crashed on landing at Eindhoven, 0536 hrs
22 Apr 44	5./KG 51	Me 410A-1, 420314, 9K+MN	Hptm Dietrich Puttfarken-F-St Kap-+ Ofw Willi Lux-BF-+	Failed to return from intercepting B-24s returning from attacking Hamm
22 Apr 44	6./KG 51	Me 410A-1, 420458, 9K+HP	Oblt Klaus Krüger-F-+ Fw Michael Reichardt-BF-+ B-24 of 389th BG	Shot down by return fire from and crashed at Ashby St Mary, Norfolk, 2210hrs
27 Apr 44	Stab II./KG 51 9K+ZP	Me 410A-1/U2, 420446, Fw Gustav Delp-BF-+	Lt Wolfgang Wenning-F-TO-+ (P) AFU	Collided with Oxford of 18 and crashed at Frankton, 0430hrs
12 May 44	5./KG 51 9K+DN	Me 410A-1/U2, 420201,	Oblt Klaus Bieber-F-+ FhjFw Heinz Closhen-BF-+	Possibly shot down by Flt Lt H E White, 141 Sqn or Sqn Ldr R H Harrison, 151 Sqn, 50 miles E St Andre, 0150hrs and crashed 2km NE Beauvais, 0030hrs
29 May 44	5./KG 51 9K+AN	Me 410A-1/U2, 420431,	Oblt Helmut Niebler-F-St Fhr-+ Fw Otto Recknagel-BF-+	Collided with below on take-off from Gilze-Rijen
29 May 44	5./KG 51	Me 410A-1, 120008, 9K+EN	Uffz Arthur Döhler-F-inj Uffz Hans Obere-BF-inj	Collided with above
29 May 44	6./KG 51	Me 410A-1, 120006, 9K+KP	Fw Ernst Dietrich-F-+ Uffz Walter Schaknies-BF-+	Shot down by Wg Cdr C M Wight-Boycott, 25 Sqn off Cromer, 0336hrs
3 Jun 44	4./KG 51	Me 410A-1, 420448	Lt Martin Knies-F-W -	Damaged by nightfighter near Neuilly possibly Fg Off T L Wright of 239 Sqn,0130hrs

Date	*Unit*	*Aircraft Details*	*Crew*	*Fate*
6 Jun 44	4./KG 51	Me 410A-1/U2, 420428, 9K+AM	Ofw Hermann Bolten-F-W Fw Wilhelm Lohf-BF-+	Shot down landing at St Andre by Fg Off R E Lelong, 605 Sqn, 0148hrs. Crashed at Marcilly-la-Campagne
8 Jun 44	6./KG 51	Me 410A-1, 120018, 9K+DP	Fw Hans-Erich Seemann-F-+ Uffz Karl-Heinz Steffen-BF-+	Missing from operations in Raum C. Claims by Flt Lt D H Greaves, 25 Sqn
8 Jun 44	4./KG 51	Me 410A-1/U2, 420654, 9K+HM	Hptm Werner Düro-D-St Kap-+ Fw Walter Heinemann-BF-+	Happisburgh, 0020hrs and Plt Off D T Tull, 219 Sqn 10 miles east of Harwich
8 Jun 44	4./KG 51	Me 410A-1/U2, 420200, 9K+IM	FhjUffz Karl-Heinz Mono-F-+ Uffz Hugo Hagel-BF-+	0030hrs. Possible claim by Plt Off H McIntosh & Plt Off C B Sullivan 207 Sqn off Beachy Head 0233hrs. Possibly claimed by Sqn Ldr P Burke, 219 Sqn as Ju 188, off Harwich, 2359hrs
11/12 Jun 44	5./KG 51	Me 410A-1, 20005, 9K+MN	Fw Friedrich Fix-F-+ Uffz Hans-Peter Herrmann-BF-+	Crashed at Oudendijk/Noord-Holland.
13 Jun 44	6./KG 51	Me 410A-1, 420027, 9K+HP	Fw Siegfried Schönberger-F-+ Uffz Kurt Quatfasel-BF-+	Shot down by Flak and crashed Barking Marshes, 0400hrs
15 Jun 44	5./KG 51	Me 410A-1/U2, 420417, 9K+GN	Fw Heinrich Ramm-F-+ Uffz Karl Seeland-BF-+	Missing from Fernnachtjagd; believed shot down by Fg Off M J Gloster, 219 Sqn, Harwich, 0302hrs
18/19 Jun 44	6./KG 51	Me 410A-1	Uffz Eberhard Baier-F-uninj Uffz Heinrich Stübner-BF-uninj	Crash-landed Gilze Rijen after combat
25 Jun 44	5./KG 51	Me 410A-1/U2, 420419, 9K+CN	Ofhr Friedrich Jirmann-F-W Gefr Alwin Dreher-BF-+	Shot down over beachhead fgtby Flt Lt G E Jameson, 488 Sqn 20 miles SW Bayeux, 0407hrs. Crashed near Dangy. Strassenjagd

Date	Unit	Aircraft Details	Crew	Fate
6 Jul 44	6./KG 51	Me 410A-1, 420670, 9K+CP	Uffz Hans-Joachim Ziegler-F-+ Uffz Rudolf Mayer-BF-POW	Strassenjagd. Shot down by either Flt Lt C M Ramsay, 264 Sqn Falaise 0245hrs or WO J E Moore, 604 Sqn, 15 miles WSW Caen, 0235hrs Crashed Villers-Bocage
6 Jul 44	5./KG 51	Me 410A-1, 20009, 9K+EN	Lt Karl Denk-F-+ Ogefr Herbert Becker-BF-+	See above. Crashed La Neuve-Lyre SW Èvreux
7 Jul 44	4./KG 51	Me 410A-1/U2, 420656, 9K+DM	Uffz Franz Wachtler-F-inj Uffz Albert Wolk-BF-inj	Engine fire on operational flight and crashed 3km NE Cormeilles airfield
8 Jul 44	4./KG 51	Me 410A-1/U2, 420665, 9K+AM	Lt Anselm Markau-F-+ Uffz Hans Brose-BF-+	Missing from attack on Allied forward airfields. Possibly shot down by Sqn Ldr I A March, 410 Sqn SW outskirts of Paris, 0127hrs
13 Jul 44	5./KG 51	Me 410A-1/U2, 420460, 9K+DN	Uffz Johann Reisser-F-+ Uffz Ferdinand Böck-BF-+	Crashed at Resnescourt returning from attack on Allied forward airfields
15 Jul 44	4./KG 51	Me 410A-1/U2, 420671, 9K+FM	Oblt Heinz Pieper-F-+ Uffz Eugen Büchner-BF-+	Missing from attack on resupply lines
16/17 Jul 44	6./KG 51	Me 410A-1	Uffz Martin Golde-F-uninj Uffz Ernst Jorda-BF-uninj	Flak. Belly-landing Fl.Pl. Coulommiers
25 Jul 44	4./KG 51	Me 410A-1/U2, 470136, 9K+GM	Uffz Walter Brügel-M-+ Uffz Rudolf Sperlich-BF-+	Missing from Fernnachtjagd. Shot down by Sqn Ldr H B Martin, 515 Sqn, off Knokke, 0350hrs
25 Jul 44	4./KG 51	Me 410A-1, 150126, 9K+FM	FhjFw Heinz Ebeling-F-+ Uffz Kurt Keilholz-BF-+	Ground collision, Clastres taking off for operational flight
1 Aug 44	5./KG 51	Me 410A-1, 470139, 9K+LN	Lt Uwe Laass-F-+	Baled out during operational flight. Parachute failed to open and killed at Bargny, 13km SE Villers-Cotteretes

Date	*Unit*	*Aircraft Details*	*Crew*	*Fate*
1 Aug 44	5./KG 51	Me 410A-1, 470135, 9K+EN Ogefr Erwin Herbig-BF-inj	F-uninj	60% damage in crash-landing near Rosières
3 Aug 44	4./KG 51	Me 410A-1/U2, 420438, 9K+BM	Ofw Wilhelm Wessel-F-inj Fw Günter Reese-BF-inj	Engine failure on operational flight and crash-landed at Chauny
5 Aug 44	4./KG 51	Me 410A-1, 710374, 9K+AM	Ofhr Walter Fink-F-+ Uffz Otto Morcinek-BF-+	Missing from operational flight. Possibly shot down by Fg Off A L Shaw, 488 Sqn 10 miles NE St Lo 0055hrs. Crashed at
		<u>I./KG 51</u>		
14 Mar 44	1./KG 51	Me 410A-1, 420298, 9K+FH	Oblt Werner Pape-F-+ Uffz Georg Lösel-BF-inj	Crashed at St Andre taking off for operational flight
15 Mar 44	2./KG 51	Me 410A-1, 420420, 9K+KK	Lt Horst Eppendorf-F-+ Uffz Günter Zabrodsky-BF-+	Crashed at Beauvais taking off for an operational flight
22 Mar 44	2./KG 51	Me 410A-1, 420435, 9K+IK	Uffz Willi Krause-F-+	Damaged by Fg Off C K Uffz Günther Onderka-BF-W Nowell, 85 Sqn, 0040 hrs and crashed 4km W. Tancarville
24 Mar 44	2./KG 51	Me 410A-1, 10304, 9K+MK	FhjFw Joachim Hübner-F-+ Uffz Herman Bitzer-BF-+	Crashed at Chavigny taking off for an operational flight
12 Apr 44	1./KG 51	Me 410A-1, 120017, 9K+CH	Lt Helmut Siol-F-+ Fw Bernhard Liehr-BF-+	Missing attacking London. Bodies washed ashore, Liehr at Quend-Plage
14 Apr 44	3./KG 51	Me 410A-1, 420019, 9K+BL	Uffz Heinz Zehmisch-F-+ Uffz Heinz Kirstein-BF-+	Either shot down by Flt Lt D L Ward, 96 Sqn, off Dungeness 0100hrs 14 Apr or Sqn Ldr A Parker-Rees, 96 Sqn off Dungeness, 0138hrs 15 Apr 44

Date	*Unit*	*Aircraft Details*	*Crew*	*Fate*
14 Apr 44	3./KG 51	Me 410A-1, 420299, 9K+HL	Fw Karl-Heinz Bargstadt-F-+ Fw Joachim Lenhardt-BF-+	Crashed at Vitry-en-Artois on return from operational flight
14 Apr 44	2./KG 51	Me 410A-1, 20003, 9K+CK	Lt Wilhelm Batel-F-inj Uffz Johannes Ebert-BF-inj	Engine failure on operational flight and crashed at Epaignes
19 Apr 44	1./KG 51	Me 410A-1, 420293, 9K+KH	Oblt Richard Pahl-F-St Kap-+ Fw Wilhelm Schuberth-BF-+	Shot down by Wg Cdr E D Crew, 96 Sqn, Brighton, 0050hrs
19 Apr 44	1./KG 51	Me 410A-1, 120005, 9K+JH	Lt Reinhold Witt-F-+ Uffz Ernst Tesch-BF-+	Shot down by Flt Lt C L Brooks, 456 Sqn, Nuthurst, 2235hrs
15 May 44	2./KG 51	Me 410A-1, 10266, 9K+NK	Fw Fritz Hansch-F-inj Uffz Kunibert Heller-BF-uninj	Force-landed at Caen returning from Bristol short of fuel

Bibliography

Balke, Ulf, *Der Luftkrieg in Europa 1941–1945* (Bernard & Graefe Verlag, 1997)

Boiten, Theo, *Nachtjagd War Diaries Volumes 1 & 2* (Wing Leader, 2011)

Foreman, John, *RAF Fighter Command Victory Claims of World War 3. Part 2 1943–1945* (Red Kite, 2012)

Goss, Chris, *Dornier Do 17 The Flying Pencil in Luftwaffe Service* (Crécy, 2020)

Goss, Chris, and Streetley, Martin, *Junkers Ju 88 Day and Nightfighters* (Crécy, 2023)

Horn, Jan, *Das Flurschaden-Geschwader: Die Chronik des Kampfgeschwaders 51 „Edelweiss" zwischen dem 1. Januar 1944 bis Kriegsende* (Jan Horn, 2010)

Kaiser, Jochen, *Die Ritterkreuzträger der Kampfflieger Band 1 & Band 2* (Luftfahrtverlag-Start, 2010)

Mankau, Heinz, and Petrick, Peter, *Messerschmitt Bf 110-Me 210-Me 410* (Aviatic Verlag, 2001)

McLachlan, Ian, *Night of the Intruders* (PSL, 1994)

Obermaier, Ernst, *Die Ritterkreuzträger der Luftwaffe 1939–1945-Band I Jagdflieger* (Verlag Dieter Hoffmann, 1989)

Parker, Nigel, *Luftwaffe Crash Archive Volumes 9–12* (Wing Leader, 2016–2018)

Parry, Simon, *Intruders over Britain* (Air Research Publications, 1987)

Patzwall, Klaus, *Der Ehrenpokal für besondere Leistungen im Luftkrieg* (Verlag Patzwall, 2008)

Rökker, Heinz, *Chronik I. Gruppe Nachtjagdgeschwader 2* (VDM, 1997)

Scherzer, Veit, *Die Träger des Deutschen Kreuzes in Gold der Luftwaffe 1941–1945* (Scherzer Verlag, 1992)

Shores, Christopher, *Those Other Eagles* (Grub Street, 2004)

Shores, Christopher, and Williams, Clive, *Aces High* (Grub Street, 1994)

Index

PEOPLE

Aberl, Unteroffizier Ignaz, 94
Abrahamczik, Oberleutnant Rudolf, 86, 87, 90
Adams, Sub-Lieutenant James, 107
Alexander, Pilot Officer Charles, 44
Allen, Flying Officer Mike, 121
Allen, Squadron Leader Arthur, 12
Alt, Unteroffizier Vitus, 24
Ambery, Pilot Officer Len, 122
Arbon, Squadron Leader Paul, 81, 82
Arnold, Unteroffizier Helmut, 8
Ashcroft, Flying Officer Alfred, 81
Attenborough, Sergeant George, 15

Baack, Leutnant Heinz-Günther, 84, 92, 93, 94, 95, 96
Baars, Unteroffizier Georg, 93
Bähner, Unteroffizier Helmut, 22, 23
Baier, Unteroffizier Eberhard, 115, 119
Balcombe, Sergeant Fred, 96
Bamford, Flying Officer Norman, 103
Banister, Flying Officer James, 112
Bargstadt, Feldwebel Karl-Heinz, 109
Barzel, Leutnant Helmut, 81
Beare, Squadron Leader, 5
Becker, Leutnant Ludwig, 41
Beetz, Obergefreiter Wilhelm, 17
Beier, Oberfeldwebel Wilhelm, 6, 21, 27, 29, 32
Bein, Unteroffizier Kurt, 103
Bell, Sergeant Ralph, 15
Benner, Feldwebel Werner, 80, 81, 82
Bennett, Flight Lieutenant D.H., 85
Bennett, Sergeant Stanley, 17
Bent, Sergeant, 21, 23
Berschwinger, Unteroffizier Hans, 23, 24
Beul, Unteroffizier Heinrich, 25
Bieber, Oberleutnant Klaus, 107, 120
Biehne, Feldwebel Herbert, 14, 15
Biermann, Oberleutnant Helmut, 75
Birnie, Pilot Officer John, 106, 107
Bisang, Leutnant Dr Lothar, 28, 29
Blättler, Feldwebel Max, 60, 61
Bleich, Feldwebel Lothar, 92
Blum, Unteroffizier Gerhard, 7
Böhme, Leutnant Gerhard, 8
Bohn, Oberleutnant Paul, 5, 6, 25, 26, 29
Bolten, Oberfeldwebel Hermann, 55, 56, 64, 90, 97, 100, 122, 123
Bönsch, Oberleutnant Herbert, 1, 9, 20, 21
Born, Feldwebel Ludwig, 39
Bressieux, Sergeant Jérémie, 98
Bricker, Flying Officer Ralph, 95
Bridges, Pilot Officer Tom, 61, 62, 63
Britain, Pilot Officer Leslie, 23, 49
Brogmus, Unteroffizier Hans-Willi, 84, 85, 86, 90, 92
Brooks, Flight Lieutenant Clive, 111
Brotz, Gefreiter Franz, 17
Brown, Pilot Officer Ernest, 3
Brown, Pilot Officer Peter, 23
Brügel, Unteroffizier Walter, 114, 115, 119, 131
Bryan, Flight Sergeant Tom, 100
Büchner, Unteroffizier Eugen, 130
Bufton, Pilot Officer John, 42
Bunting, Flight Lieutenant Nigel, 70, 73, 74, 92
Burbridge, Flight Lieutenant Branse, 103
Burgess, Sergeant, 18
Burke, Squadron Leader Pat, 125
Burnard, Pilot Officer Fred, 28
Burton, Flight Lieutenant Alec, 129
Butterworth, Sergeant John, 8

Callahan, 2nd Lieutenant Robert, 128
Caldwell, Squadron Leader Peter, 102
Chattaway, Sergeant Bert, 8
Chatten, Sergeant Cliff, 81, 82
Chester, Sergeant Stanley, 5
Churchill, Flight Lieutenant Henry, 117
Clark, Flying Officer Terry, 94, 95
Clemo, Flying Officer Bill, 74
Clisby, Flying Officer Leslie, 54
Coleman, Sergeant Victor, 14
Collyer, Sergeant Walter, 21
Cosgrove, Pilot Officer J.P., 106
Costello, Sergeant Andrew G., 27
Coutts, Flying Officer Desmond, 8
Creagh, Flight Sergeant 'South', 60
Crew, Wing Commander Ed, 111
Crookes, Flying Officer Norman, 126, 127
Csurusky, Oberleutnant Georg, 117
Cunningham, Wing Commander John, 98
Czerny, Obergefreiter Eduard, 62

Danigel, Unteroffizier Heinz, 57
Davidson, Flying Officer Alexander, 76
Davidson, Flying Officer Paul, 120
Davies, Pilot Officer Anthony, 3, 4

Delp, Feldwebel Gustav, 112, 116
Denison, Flight Lieutenant Richard, 15
Denk, Leutnant Karl, 129, 130
Dias, Squadron Leader Oliver, 9
Dibbins. Pilot Officer Douglas, 115
Dietrich, Feldwebel Ernst, 121
Dietrich, Feldwebel Franz, 108
Döhler, Unteroffizier Artur, 117, 121
Dold, Leutnant Klaus, 109
Dreher, Gefreiter Alwin, 126, 127, 128
Duff, Pilot Officer Gordon, 86
Düro, Hauptmann Werner, 123, 125

Ebeling, Fahnenjunker-Feldwebel Heinz, 130, 131
Eddy, Flight Lieutenant Charlie, 107
Edwards, Corporal Sam, 32
Eggers, Unteroffizier Reinhard, 101
Elpers, Oberfeldwebel Karl, 93, 95
Engmann, Feldwebel Hans, 29
Eppendorf, Leutnant Horst, 102
Erwin, Flying Officer John, 76
Espley, Pilot Officer Bill, 39

Falck, Major Wolfgang, 1, 32, 40
Fellerer, Leutnant Leopold, 42
Feuerbaum, Leutnant Johannes, 20, 21, 43, 44, 45, 46
Fick, Unteroffizier Werner, 41
Filmer, Sergeant Francis, 32
Fink, Oberfähnrich Walter, 131
Fischer, Unteroffizier Wilfried, 93
Fix, Feldwebel Friedrich, 126
Forgatsch, Oberleutnant Heinz, 55
Floryanowicz, Squadron Leader Stefan, 8
Frach, Oberfeldwebel Hans, 111, 132
French, Pilot Officer Fred, 70
Friedrich, Leutnant Karl-Heinz, 128
Friis, Flight Sergeant Basil, 100

Gärtner, Feldwebel Hermann, 14
Gentzen, Major Johannes, 53
Gibson, Squadron Leadxer Guy, 15, 16, 17
Giessübel, Unteroffizier Vincenz, 30, 40, 46, 48
Gillmann, Unteroffizier Georg, 93
Glas, Feldwebel Otto, 16
Gloster, Flying Officer Mike, 125, 126
Goebbels, Josef, 96
Golde, Unteroffizier Martin, 130, 134
Goodman, Flight Lieutenant Geoff, 81
Göring, Reichsmarschall Hermann, 40, 90, 96, 97
Gosman, Flight Lieutenant Alexander, 20, 21
Götz, Unteroffizier Erich, 48
Graeber, Feldwebel Heinz, 81, 82, 83
Graf, Unteroffizier Reinhold, 61
Graham, Sergeant Tom, 32
Green, Pilot Officer John, 42
Greaves, Flight Lieutenant Douglas, 125
Gregory, Sergeant Rupert, 60
Griffin, Sergeant Peter, 26
Grundmann, Hauptmann Hans-Joachim, 83, 125

Haberland, Oberleutnant Ernst, 57
Häberlen, Hauptmann Klaus, 90
Hahn, Leutnant Hans, 3, 4, 5, 8, 12, 15, 18, 19, 29, 32, 34
Hainzinger, Unteroffizier Felix, 92, 93
Hanch, Feldwebel Fritz, 111
Hancock, Sergeant John, 26
Hanks, Flight Lieutenant Peter, 54
Hannah, Flight Sergeant Walter, 27, 42
Harrison, Squadron Leader Reg, 119, 120
Hartmann, Feldwebel Walter, 79, 81
Hassall, LAC Stanley, 28
Häuser, Oberleutnant Otto, 48
Havers, Flight Lieutenant Jimmy, 13
Hedgecoe, Flying Officer Edward, 103
Heintz, Hauptmann Kurt, 75, 77, 98, 99, 100
Heney, Squadron Leader Harold, 119
Herbig, Obergefreiter Erwin, 131
Herden, Unteroffizier Georg, 50
Herrick, Flying Officer Michael, 24
Herrmann, Oberleutnant Kurt, 3, 5, 8, 9, 10, 11
Hess, Feldwebel Fredrich, 97
Heyse, Major Karl-Heirich, 1, 5, 6, 39
Heyward, Sergeant Cliff, 2
Hewitson, Sergeant Frank, 16
Hillebrand, Feldwebel Walter, 70
Hissbach, Oberleutnant Heinz-Horst, 30
Hodges, Flight Sergeant A.C.G., 123
Hoff, Feldwebel Peter, 70
Hoffmann, Unteroffizier Richard, 21
Holzmann, Unteroffizier Heinz, 70, 90, 93
Hoos, Sergeant Ron, 9
Horrex, Flying Officer Reg, 119, 120
Houghton, Flight Lieutenant Cyril, 86
Howitt, Squadron Leader Geoff, 79
Hough, Flying Officer Alban, 2
Hübener, Feldwebel Joachim, 109
Huenekens, 1st Lieutenant Bill, 128
Hülshoff, Major Karl, 1, 3, 5, 6, 29, 31, 40
Hutchinson, Sergeant John, 115

Jameson, Flight Lieutenant George, 125, 126, 127
Jansen, Feldwebel Rudolf, 55, 63
Jarvis, Flying Officer Brian, 85
Jeschke, Oberfeldwebel Martin, 17
Jirmann, Oberfähnrich Friedrich, 125, 126, 127, 128
Johnston, Flight Lieutenant Tony, 59
Jones, Flying Officer Bill, 94
Jorda, Unteroffizier Ernst, 130
Jukel, Leutnant Carl, 83, 84
Jung, Hauptmann Rolf, 1, 8, 43
Jung, Major Rolf, 40, 43
Jung, Oberfeldwebel Hermann, 26

Kagelmacher, Feldwebel Ernst, 70
Kammhuber, Generalmajor Josef, 1, 32
Kästner, Major Martin, 66
Kee, Pilot Officer James, 40
Kelsey, Flight Sergeant P.D., 123

Kirkland, Flight Lieutenant Clive, 80,
Klee, Pilot Officer Bernard, 18
Kleine, Feldwebel Walter, 29
Knie, Feldwebel Toni, 94
Knies, Leutnant Martin, 119, 122
Körner, Gefreiter Hans, 13
Köster, Feldwebel Alfons, 32
Köster, Feldwebel Hans, 29
Krähler, Unteroffizier Otto, 8
Krause, Unteroffizier Willi, 109
Kröger, Gefreiter Otto, 14, 76
Krüger, Oberleutnant Klaus, 113, 114

Laas, Leutnant Uwe, 131
Ladiges, Obergefreiter Heinz, 28
Lamle, Oberleutnant Hans-Georg, 134
Landa, Pilot Officer Bohumil, 41
Lang, Unteroffizier Mathias, 5
Lardy. Leutnant Walter, 64
Laufs, Oberfeldwebel Peter, 13, 27, 29
Lee, Pilot Officer Terry, 4, 5
Lelong, Flying Officer Roy, 122, 123
Lettenmeier, Feldwebel Wilhelm, 48, 51
Lichtenfels, Hauptmann Karl-Egon Frhr von Dalwigk zu, 83, 84, 100
Licht, Oberfeldwebel Paul, 31
Lindemann, Unteroffizier Helmut, 84, 86, 90, 92
Lindholme, RAF, 14, 15, 90
Lindner, Unteroffizier Walter, 26
Lohf, Feldwebel Wilhelm, 56, 100, 123
Lucas, Pilot Officer Norman, 57
Ludescher, Gefreiter Kurt,7
Lux, Oberfeldwebel Willi, 115

MacFadyen, Flight Lieutenant Don, 108, 109
Mack, Wing Commander Bob, 81
Maclean, Sergeant Doug, 20
Maguire, Squadron Leader Bill, 74, 94
Main, Flying Officer George, 94
Makera, Unteroffizier Stefan, 54
Mandel, Gefreiter Hermann, 25
March, Squadron Leader Ian, 130
Markau, Leutnant Anselm, 128, 129, 130
Marland, Sergeant Rainford, 43
Martin, Squadron Leader Micky, 131
Matkin, Sergeant Sidney, 32
Mattey, Pilot Officer Gordon, 46
Matthews, Flying Officer Hugh, 13
Maunders, Flight Sergeant Gordon, 104, 105
Maurer, Oberleutnant Walter, 53, 54, 55, 56, 60, 61, 63, 64
Mawhood, Squadron Leader David, 82
Mayer, Oberfeldwebel Willi, 31
McLeod, Squadron Leader Don, 32
McGregor, Lieutenant Don, 103
McLaren, Flight Sergeant John, 122
McPherson, Warrant Officer Murray, 115
McVie, Sergeant Bill, 8
Mehls, Oberleutnant Werner, 123, 131,
Meissler, Unteroffizier Ernst-Wilhelm, 18, 19, 33
Meister, Major Wolf-Dietrich, 83, 85, 86, 90, 100, 103
Mellor, Squadron Leader Ken, 12, 13, 14
Menger, Leutnant Heinz, 59
Merzbach, Oberfeldwebel, 3
Methner, Hauptmann Friedrich-Wilhelm, 66, 68, 73, 74, 75, 77,
Meurer, Obergefreiter Michael, 81,
Meyer, Oberleutnant Ulrich, 6, 7
Mills, Sergeant Ken, 46
Moggs, Warrant Officer Bert, 108
Mono, Fahnenjunker-Unteroffizier Karl-Heinz, 125
Moore, Pilot Officer Gregor, 116
Moore, Warrant Officer Jeff, 130
Morcinek, Unteroffizier Otto, 131
Morton, Sergeant Douglas, 5
Mösges, Feldwebel Heinrich, 61, 62, 63, 64
Mould, Pilot Officer Peter, 54
Müller, Feldwebel Karl, 103
Müller, Leutnant Felix, 102
Müller, Oberfeldwebel Horst, 85
Mungo-Park, Squadron Leader John, 29
Munro, Pilot Officer Ian, 57
Munsey, Lieutenant Jim, 112
Murawski, Flying Officer Boleslaw, 8
Murfitt, Pilot Officer Tom, 4
Murlis-Green, Group Captain Gilbert, 16

Näder, Oberleutnant Günter, 68, 82, 83, 84
Nebelung, Oberleutnant Harald, 125
Nicholls, Sergeant Phillip, 48
Nicholson, Flight Sergeant Joe, 104
Nieber, Oberleutnant Helmut, 79, 121
Nowell, Flying Officer Chris, 109

Oakley, Sergeant Rupert, 5, 6
Oertel, Unteroffizier Hans-Johann, 80
Osterwind, Gefreiter Karl, 72

Page, Sergeant D.C.M., 123
Pahl, Oberleutnant Richard, 108, 109, 110, 111
Palm, Feldwebel Gerhard, 39
Palm, Feldwebel Werner, 3
Panter, Pilot Officer George, 2
Panter, Flying Officer Keith, 108
Pape, Oberleutnant Werner, 102
Park, Wing Commander Geoff, 75
Parker-Rees, Squadron Leader Alastair, 109
Parrott, Sergeant Reg, 18
Patston, Flight Lieutenant Arthur, 86
Peltz, Oberst Dietrich, 78, 79, 97
Perrin, Pilot Officer Des, 61, 62, 63
Pfeiffer, Leutnant Rudolf, 13, 29
Pieper, Leutnant Heinz, 130
Pitts, Lieutenant Cherry, 112
Pleasance, Squadron Leader Harold 'Flash', 21, 22, 23
Proposch, Leutnant Rolf, 90, 91, 92
Pryde, Flight Sergeant, 86
Puttfarken, Hauptmann Dietrich, 104, 106, 113, 115

Quatfasel, Unteroffizier Kurt, 125

Rad, Lieutenant Johan, 74, 81
Radusch, Hauptmann Günther, 39
Raida, Oberfeldwebel Leo, 70, 73
Ramm, Feldwebel Heinrich, 126
Ramsay, Flight Lieutenant Charles, 130
Ramsay, Sergeant Norman, 43
Raphael, Squadron Leader Gordon, 29, 30
Rawnsley, Flight Lieutenant Jimmy, 98
Redshaw, Flying Officer Bob, 119
Reed, Flying Officer Graeme, 94
Reese, Feldwebel Günter, 131
Reeves, Sergeant, 28
Reid, 1st Lieutenant Stalie, 112
Reid, Flight Lieutenant Douglas, 121
Reimers, Unteroffizier Hermann, 80
Ried, Unteroffizier Jakob, 22
Reinagel, Oberfeldwebel Heinz, 16
Rhodes, Pilot Officer Richard, 2
Richter, Oberleutnant Johannes, 109
Robinson, Pilot Officer Doug, 95
Röderer, Oberleutnant Hans, 53
Rogers, Sergeant Harry, 44
Rudolph, Unteroffizier Erich, 59
Runge, Stabsfeldwebel Otto, 98
Russell, Wing Commander Bill, 117

Sabine, Squadron Leader John, 8
Sanders, 2nd Lieutenant Robert, 128
Sartor, Oberleutnant Bernd, 83
Schaknies, Unteroffizier Walter, 121
Scheidt, Unteroffizier Helmut, 18, 19, 33
Schlicht, Feldwebel Kurt, 5, 6
Schmid, Oberfeldwebel Herbert, 48
Schmidt, Hauptmann Walter, 87
Schmitter, Hauptmann Wilhelm, 77, 78, 81, 82, 83, 92, 93, 94
Schönberger, Feldwebel Siegfried, 124, 125
Schneke, Leutnant Günther, 76, 79
Schramm, Feldwebel Gustav, 2
Schultze, Oberleutnant Helmut, 97, 98
Schulz, Feldwebel Heinz, 22
Schulz, Oberleutnant Albert, 8, 42, 43
Schürks, Unteroffizier Theo, 44
Schütze, Oberleutnant Hans-Georg, 26
Schwachenwald, Feldwebel Adolf, 100
Schwarz, Unteroffizier Hugo, 39
Shaw, Flying Officer Andy, 131
Seeland, Unteroffizier Karl, 126
Seemann, Feldwebel Hans-Erich, 125
Semrau, Oberleutnant Paul, 7, 8, 21, 27, 29
Sengschmitt, Oberleutnant Fritz, 78, 85
Simpson, Sergeant W., 102
Siol, Leutnant Helmut, 109
Skelton, Flying Officer Bill, 103
Skipper, Pilot Officer Desmond, 90
Slodczyk, Feldwebel Georg, 92
Smith, Flight Lieutenant C.B., 85
Smith, Flying Officer George, 85
Smith, Flying Officer John, 131
Smith, LAC Ralph, 28
Smith, Sergeant Walter, 129
Smith, Sub-Lieutenant Horace, 107
Sohn, Feldwebel Wilhelm, 92
Sommer, Oberfeldwebel Hermann, 3, 16, 21, 26, 40
Sperlich, Unteroffizier Rudolf, 131
Spurgin, Sergeant Arthur, 15
Stearns, Lieutenant Richard, 93
Stephen, Squadron Leader Harbourne, 29, 31
Stephenson, Sergeant Bill, 32
Sterling, Pilot Officer Robert, 2
Steward, Flying Officer Russell, 94
Stilson, 2nd Lieutenant Charles 'Red', 113, 115
Storp, Major Walter, 55, 60
Stradner, Leutnant Rudolf, 8, 28
Strasser, Unteroffizier Michael, 96
Strüning, Oberfeldwebel Heinz, 5, 9, 32

Thiemann, Oberleutnant Rudiger, 87
Thwaites, Flight Lieutenant Bernard, 74, 92
Thomas, Unteroffizier Herbert, 44, 50
Thompson, Pilot Officer, 22
Thompson, Pilot Officer David, 49
Thompson, Sergeant Bruce, 27, 42
Todd, Pilot Officer Cyril, 128
Trench, Flight Lieutenant Desmond, 9
Trenke, Unteroffizier Johann, 76, 112, 115, 119, 133, 134
Tull, Pilot Officer Desmond, 125

Unrau, Hauptmann Hans, 100

Vester, Hauptmann Dierk-Henning, 100, 112
Viel, Oberfeldwebel Erwin, 29, 30
Villers, Flying Officer William, 26
Völker, Leutnant Heinz, 14, 15, 27, 28, 41, 42

Wachtler, Unteroffizier Franz, 108, 109, 129, 130
Wall, Flying Officer Reg, 126
Walther, Oberleutnant Hermann, 75, 76, 97
Warren, Sergeant Ron, 13
Wendler, Unteroffizier Gottfried, 90
Wenning, Leutnant Wolfgang, 103, 106, 112, 115, 116, 117
Wessel, Oberfeldwebel Wilhelm, 90, 131
White-Boycott, Wing Commander Mike, 120, 121
White, Flight Lieutenant Harry, 121
Widdows, Wing Commander Charles, 13, 16
Wiese, Oberfeldwebel Otto, 2, 24
Wilkerson, Lieutenant F.T., 113
Williams, Pilot Officer Gerald, 8
Willins, Flight Sergeant Jock, 42
Willis, Pilot Officer Arthur, 76
Wilson, Sergeant Angus, 5
Winkel, Oberleutnant Eberhard, 100
Witt Leutnant Reinhold, 111
Wolk, Unteroffizier Albert, 70, 108, 130
Wright, Flying Officer James, 108
Wright, Flying Officer Tom, 122

Wright, Warrant Officer S.F.T., 123
Wyman, Flight Sergeant Len, 131
Wyrill, Flying Officer Hugh, 42

Zaprodsky, Unteroffizier Günter, 102
Zehmisch, Unteroffizier Heinz, 109
Zenkel, Oberfeldwebel Fritz, 2
Ziebarth, Feldwebel Ernst, 9
Ziesch, Unteroffizier Hans, 54
Zimmermann, Oberleutnant Paul, 5
Zwissler, Feldwebel Franz, 70

PLACES

Acklington, RAF, 61
Akeman Street, 28
Amiens, 16, 121
Ashbourne, 115
Ashwell, 27, 42
Augsburg, 64, 66
Avord, 70

Barking, 126
Barsham, 112
Bassingbourn, 27, 38, 48
Bassingham, 104
Bayeux, 126, 128
Beachy Head, 75, 85, 93
Beauvais, 64, 102, 120
Berlin, 15, 81, 84
Bergen, 108
Bircham Newton, 9, 16, 23
Bizerta, 54
Blyth, 61
Bondy, 28
Bournemouth, 76, 79
Boston, 9, 13
Bourn, 81, 119
Boxted, 115
Bradwell Bay, 82
Brentwood, 92
Bridlington, 18
Brighton, 75, 110, 111
Bristol, 111, 119
Brize Norton, 28
Burnham Westgate, 23
Bury St Edmunds, 119

Caen, 111, 130
Cantley, 113
Catfoss, 5
Cambridge, 70, 75, 80, 85, 119, 121
Cannock Chase, German Military Cemetery, 17, 33
Catterick, 8
Caxton Gibbett, 27, 32
Charleville, 26
Chatham, 60
Chauny, 131
Chauvency-le-Chateâu, 97
Chavigny, 109
Chelmsford, 75,
Chemondiston, 81
Chester, 2
Chilbolton, 111
Church Fenton, 33
Clacton, 29, 112
Clastres, 128, 131, 134
Colchester, 28, 79, 115
Coltishall 18, 19, 43, 44, 106, 107, 115, 121
Coulommiers, 126, 130
Cranwell, 9, 16, 32, 42

Darmstadt-Griesheim, 54
Deelen, 32
Deeping St James, 26
Deopham Green, 121
Dieppe, 60
Digby, 8, 19
Dishforth, 3, 38
Dongen, 17
Dordrecht, 56
Driffield, 14, 31, 32
Duisburg, 20, 119
Dungeness, 92, 103, 109
Dunkirk, 19, 74, 81
Duxford, 18, 19, 59

Eastbourne, 94
East Kirby 86
Eaton Socon, 128
East Wretham, 119
Eindhoven, 39
Elsham Wolds, 28
Ely, 107
Épinoy, 80
Évreux, 56, 60, 117, 122, 123, 130

Feltwell, 5, 8, 18, 19, 20, 32, 35, 76,
Felixstowe, 70, 75
Finningley, 14, 21
Flamborough Head, 8, 46
Ford, 84, 85, 86, 89
Foreness, 80
Framfield, 101, 102
Framlingham, 104, 123
Frankton, 116
Friedrichshafen, 51
Frimley Green, 91, 92
Fulbeck, 9

Gainsborough, 6
Gilze-Rijen, 2, 5, 7, 9, 10, 17, 19, 31, 38, 40, 47, 48, 49, 52, 121
Gloucester, 28

Grantham, 8, 18, 32, 33, 34
Gravesend, 92
Great Yarmouth, 2, 9, 19, 44, 60, 90
Great Ashfield, 119
Great Glemham, 104
Grimsby, 3

Haamstede, 1
Hannover, 44, 85, 90
Happisburgh, 8, 125
Hartlepool, 61
Harwich, 81, 125, 126
Hastings, 92
Hemswell, 3, 6, 17, 35
High Ercall, 109
High Wycombe, 102
Honington, 6, 32
Hopton, 112
Hörsching, 70, 80
Horsham St Faith, 113, 115
Hucknall, 16
Hull, 8

Icklingham, 128
Iden, 96
Ingleby, 3
Ipswich, 32, 75, 103, 115, 117, 119, 121
Ijsselmeer, 41, 108

Karlsruhe, 116
Kelstern, 107
Kettering, 119
Kings Lynn, 6, 7, 23
Kirton in Lindsey, 33
Knocke, 82, 131
Köln, 30

La Ferrière, 117
Lakenheath, 106
Landsberg, 55
Langham, 23, 44
Leamington Spa, 77
Lechfeld, 53
Leconfield, 18, 19, 33
Leeming, 38
Leicester, 28
Le Mans, 76, 79, 128
Lille-Vendeville, 70
Lincoln, 5, 6, 8, 9, 19, 79, 84, 86, 96, 103, 108, 121
Lindholme, 14, 15, 90
Linton on Ouse, 38
Little Staughton, 119, 120
London, 8, 75, 79, 90, 92, 93, 95, 96, 97, 100, 102, 103, 107, 109, 111, 125, 130
Louth, 7
Lowestoft, 2, 8, 112, 115
Ludford Magna,
Lünen, 3

Manby, 7, 35
Manchester, 16
Manea, 115
Manston, 81, 95, 122
Marquise, 97
Matlask, 57
Medlam Drain, 51
Melsbroek, 86
Memmingen, 70
Middleborough, 61
Mildenhall, 13, 115
Montigny, 72
München-Gladbach, 39, 93

Narborough, 44
Narford, 22
Newmarket, 19, 33, 75, 123, 128
New Marske, 62
Newton, 12, 14, 33
Norwich, 9, 10, 35, 103, 112, 119, 121
Nuthurst, 111

Oakham, 17
Oakington, 32, 121
Oosterwolde, 41
Ostende, 41
Oudendijk, 126

Paris, 96, 128, 130
Peterborough, 112, 139

Rackham, 113
Reading, 28
Rechlin, 55
Redcar, 61
Rheydt, 93
Rippon, 8
Rosières, 131
Rouen, 106, 130
Royal Aircraft Establishment Farnborough, 64
Rye, 95, 96

Saffron Walden, 129
Saint-André, 100, 102, 109, 120, 122, 123, 132
Sainte-Menehould, 54
Salisbury, 28
Scampton, 6, 8, 9, 41
Scheveningen, 5
Schiphol, 84, 93
Scunthorpe, 33
Selby, 6
Sherrington, 32
Shouldham, 81
Skegness, 42
Skerne decoy site, 31
Skeyton, 106
Sledgate, 63
Sleydinge, 92
Snetterton Heath, 103
Soesterberg, 57, 59, 60, 61, 64, 112, 123, 126
Southend, 9, 61
Southampton, 112

Southwold, 29, 32, 39, 99, 112
Spilsby, 6, 86
Spurn Head, 2
Stradishall, 29, 51
Swaffham, 9, 22, 44, 81

Tancarville, 109
Tangmere, 85
Terrington St Clement, 10
Texel, 26, 61
Thorney, 17, 38
Thorpe, 63
Tollerton, 16
Tours, 85, 117
Trappes, 122
Trowbridge, 28
Tuddenham, 107, 120, 121, 123, 128, 129

Upwood, 27

Veere, 31
Vendresse, 54
Villers-Bocage, 130
Villers-Cotterets, 131
Vitry-en-Artois, 109

Waddington, 3, 6, 8, 9, 19, 40
Wash, The, 5, 6, 7, 117, 121
Watton, 18
Wellingore, 8, 15
Wells next the Sea, 27
West Raynham, 6, 43
Weybourne, 43
Whitby, 20, 21, 46, 63
Wickenby, 90
Witchford, 106,
Withcall, 14
Wivenhoe, 28
Woburn, 28
Wyton, 41, 119

York, 8

Zeals, 126
Zeist, 84

UNITS

Luftwaffe units,
Luftflotte 2, 2
IX Fliegerkorps, 79
Nachtjagddivision 1, 1
KG 2, 78
I./KG 2, 39
1./KG 2, 85
IV./KG 2, 117
V./KG 2, 35, 64, 68, 72, 75, 79, 81, 83, 89, 90, 96, 98, 99, 100, 103, 134
3./KG 2, 103
5./KG 2, 68, 112
13./KG 2, 71, 72, 126
14./KG 2, 70, 76, 80, 83, 85, 86, 87, 90, 92, 93, 97, 101, 102
15./KG 2, 76, 77, 78, 79, 81, 84, 85, 86, 90, 91, 92, 121
16./KG 2, 76, 80, 81, 83, 84, 88, 92, 97, 102, 103
6./KG 5, 112
7./KG 6, 84
9./KG 6, 75
16./KG 6, 64, 70, 73
Z.St/KG 30, 1, 2, 7, 17
II./KG 40, 66, 77
4./KG 40, 77, 121
5./KG 40, 77
6./KG 40, 100
KG 51, 1, 83, 103, 125
I./KG 51, 70, 83, 90, 100, 103, 109, 111, 112, 117, 134
II./KG 51, 90, 100, 103, 106, 109, 112, 115, 116, 117, 119, 121, 122, 123, 125, 128, 129, 130, 131, 134
III./KG 51, 109
1./KG 51, 102, 111, 117
2./KG 51, 84, 102, 109, 111
3./KG 51, 109
4./KG 51, 108, 114, 119, 121, 123, 125, 128, 129, 131
5./KG 51, 80, 104, 107, 115, 117, 126, 127, 128, 129, 130, 131
6./KG 51, 83, 103, 108, 112, 115, 119, 121, 123, 124, 125, 126, 130, 131, 132, 133, 134
8./KG 51, 111
11./KG 51, 106
14./KG 51, 84
III./KG 54, 1, 7
7./KG 54, 1
8./KG 54, 5
9./KG 54, 5
2./KG 55, 1
II./KG 76, 39
III./KG 76, 39
I./KG 101, 85
III./KG 101, 75
10./KG 157, 1
I./NJG 1, 39
II./NJG 1, 2, 3, 39
1./NJG 1, 39
4./NJG 1, 2, 3, 13, 26, 41
5./NJG 1, 3, 40, 42
I./NJG 2, 3, 5, 9, 11, 13, 14, 17, 18, 19, 24, 27, 28, 29, 30, 31, 32, 34, 35, 36, 39, 52
II./NJG 2, 5
1./NJG 2, 5, 6, 7, 8, 9, 10, 13, 27, 28, 29, 30, 32, 47

2./NJG 2, 7, 16, 21, 26, 28, 30, 35, 40, 41, 42, 43, 47, 48, 49, 52
3./NJG 2, 3, 4, 5, 6, 7, 8, 14, 17, 21, 27, 29, 32, 42
4./NJG 2, 5, 6, 21, 22, 23, 24, 25, 26, 28, 29
ZG 101, 106
I./ZG 1, 1
9./ZG 1, 64
3./ZG 2, 53
ZG 26, 132
II./ZG 76, 105
2./ZG 76, 1
Erprobungsstaffel Me 210, 53, 55, 56, 57, 58

RAF/French units,
2 Central Flying School, 9, 16
22 Elementary Flying Training School, 27
2 Service Flying Training School, 9, 28
12 Service Flying Training School, 9, 32
11 OTU, 27, 42, 46
13 OTU, 120
17 OTU, 3
25 OTU, 21
42 OTU, 114, 115
51 OTU, 35
54 OTU, 15, 42
60 OTU, 108, 109
7 (Pilot) Advanced Flying Unit, 112
1654 Heavy Conversion Unit, 104
1 Squadron, 54, 61
9 Squadron, 2
10 Squadron, 8
21 Squadron, 8
25 Squadron, 17, 21, 22, 24, 49, 107, 108, 120, 121, 125
29 Squadron, 2, 13, 15, 80, 81, 82, 85, 94
37 Squadron, 2
44 Squadron, 9
49 Squadron, 8, 26, 41
51 Squadron, 26, 46
57 Squadron, 86
58 Squadron, 3, 39
61 Squadron, 5, 20
64 Squadron, 104
70 Squadron, 129
76 Squadron, 115
77 Squadron, 46
85 Squadron, 28, 29, 30, 70, 73, 74, 79, 81, 86, 92, 98, 103, 109
90 Squadron, 123, 129
96 Squadron, 100, 102, 109, 111
97 Squadron, 81
99 Squadron, 16, 26
101 Squadron, 90
102 Squadron, 3, 4, 8
103 Squadron, 12, 13, 14
105 Squadron, 118, 119
110 Squadron, 2
115 Squadron, 76, 106, 107
138 Squadron, 117
141 Squadron, 121
142 Squadron, 20
144 Squadron, 8
149 Squadron, 2, 13, 106
150 Squadron, 14
151 Squadron, 119, 120
155 Squadron, 44
156 Squadron, 117
192 Squadron, 76
206 Squadron, 9, 44
207 Squadron, 13
211 Squadron, 23
214 Squadron, 5
218 Squadron, 9
219 Squadron, 15, 125, 126
221 Squadron, 13
222 Squadron, 18, 43
234 Squadron, 29
239 Squadron, 122
255 Squadron, 43
256 Squadron, 75
257 Squadron, 18
264 Squadron, 130
266 Squadron, 57, 59
301 Squadron, 8
311 Squadron, 41
406 Squadron, 109
410 Squadron, 130
418 Squadron, 109
452 Squadron, 27
456 Squadron, 111
488 Squadron, 94, 95, 125, 126, 127, 131
501 Squadron, 98
515 Squadron, 131
582 Squadron, 119
604 Squadron, 130
605 Squadron, 122
610 Squadron, 60
617 Squadron, 15
619 Squadron, 119
625 Squadron, 106
626 Squadron, 115
582 Squadron, 14
Groupe de Chasse I/5, 98
USAAF units,
353rd Fighter Group, 93
79th Bomb Squadron, 112
350th Fighter Squadron, 93
389th Bomb Group, 113
448th Bomb Group, 112
453rd Bomb Group, 112
458th Bomb Group, 113, 115
467th Bomb Group, 112
567th Fighter Squadron, 113
715th Bomb Squadron, 112
735th Bomb Squadron, 112
754th Bomb Squadron, 113, 115
801st Bomb Group, 126
850th Fighter Squadron, 126

Dear Reader,

We hope you have enjoyed this book, but why not share your views on social media? You can also follow our pages to see more about our other products: facebook.com/penandswordbooks or follow us on X @penswordbooks

You can also view our products at www.pen-and-sword.co.uk (UK and ROW) or www.penandswordbooks.com (North America).

To keep up to date with our latest releases and online catalogues, please sign up to our newsletter at: www.pen-and-sword.co.uk/newsletter

If you would like a printed catalogue with our latest books, then please email: enquiries@pen-and-sword.co.uk or telephone: 01226 734555 (UK and ROW) or email: uspen-and-sword@casematepublishers.com or telephone: (610) 853-9131 (North America).

We respect your privacy and we will only use personal information to send you information about our products.

Thank you!